More Than Words®

A Parent's Guide to Building Interaction and Language Skills
for Children with Autism Spectrum Disorder or
Social Communication Difficulties

Fern Sussman

The
Hanen
Program®

A Hanen Centre Publication

illustrations by
Robin Baird Lewis

More Than Words®

By Fern Sussman

 The
Hanen
Program®

A Hanen Centre Publication

The Hanen Program®, The Parent-Child Logo and More Than Words® are trademarks owned by Hanen Early Language Program.

Library and Archives Canada Cataloging in Publication
Sussman, Fern, 2012
More Than Words®: A Parent's Guide to Building Interaction and Language Skills for Children with Autism Spectrum Disorder or Social Communication Difficulties

National Library of Canada
ISBN 978-0-921145-41-7

Copies of this book may be ordered from the publisher:

The Hanen Centre
1075 Bay Street, Suite 515
Toronto, Ontario M5S 2B1, Canada
Telephone: (416) 921-1073
Fax: (416) 921-1225
E-mail: info@hanen.org
Web: www.hanen.org

Parts of this book were adapted from *It Takes Two to Talk: A Practical Guide for Parents of Children with Language Delays* by Elaine Weitzman and Jan Pepper (2004) and *Learning Language and Loving It: A Guide to Promoting Children's Social and Language Development in Early Childhood Settings* by Elaine Weitzman and Janice Greenberg (2002), both Hanen Centre publications.

Illustrations: Robin Baird Lewis
Design: Counterpunch/Linda Gustafson, Sue Meggs-Becker, Peter Ross
General Editor: Matthew Sussman
Editors: Jennifer Glossop and Susan Goldberg

More Than Words® is a publication of The Hanen Centre. The book's first edition was supported by funding from the Ontario Ministry of Community and Social Services and the Autism Society of Ontario, Metro Toronto Chapter. All views expressed herein are those of The Hanen Centre and do not necessarily reflect the views of the Ontario Ministry of Community and Social Services or the Autism Society of Ontario.

Printed in Canada by Transcontinental Printing

Contents

Acknowledgements

Twelve years have passed since I wrote the first edition of this More Than Words® guidebook. I am grateful that many of the people who supported and inspired me at that time continue to do the same today. Elaine Weitzman, Executive Director of The Hanen Centre, helped me rework the book to include examples of language models that are in line with the current thinking on how to talk to children on the autism spectrum in the most natural way.

I am grateful to my professional colleagues, Lauren Chisholm, Cindy Conklin, Cindy Earle, Janice Greenberg, Catherine Hambly, Sue Honeyman and Barb Wylde whose desire to make sure that all Hanen materials reflect the most up-to-date information is reflected in the pages of this book.

A great big thank you to the following staff at The Hanen Centre: Ejona Balashi, Kelly Murray and Andrea Palmer, who all worked very hard to get this revised edition to print within a very short timeline, and to Tom Khan, who spreads the word about *More Than Words* on a daily basis. My thanks also go to Stacie Scherer, graphic designer, whose artistic eye and impeccable design skills are reflected in the changes to this book.

My family continues to be passionate about what I do. My husband, Jackie, my son Matthew, whose previous editing was meticulous and my daughter, Jillian, who now has her own son, Oliver, are still *More Than Words'* best cheerleaders.

The Ontario Ministry of Community and Social Services, Toronto Area Office and the Autism Society of Ontario provided generous grants to support the initial production of this book. Once again, I would like to thank their representatives for supporting The Hanen Centre in its efforts to help parents and professionals nurture the development of children with autism spectrum disorder all over the world.

A few words about a few words

About the term "autism spectrum disorder"

Autism spectrum disorder is a term that is currently being used by many professionals to describe children who have difficulties in social interaction, play and communication. In this book, I use this term in its abbreviated version – ASD. ASD is a convenient way of describing a large and diverse group of children who have similarities in the way they process information and understand the world. You may have heard the following terms associated with ASD: pervasive developmental disorder, autism, Asperger syndrome, hyperlexia and semantic pragmatic disorder. No matter what label has been given to your child, remember that first and foremost he or she is a unique individual with his or her own strengths and challenges.

Labels can be intimidating. But the label of ASD can help you access the information and services that are right for your child. Recognizing your child's special needs is the first step towards helping him or her develop and advance.

About the term "social communication difficulties"

Not all children who have trouble interacting and communicating with others have autism spectrum disorder. Some children know how to play with a variety of toys, but still have difficulties with social interaction and communication. These children may get a diagnosis of a social communication disorder.

Whether your child has a diagnosis of ASD, a social communication disorder or no diagnosis at all, you will find this book helpful if your child has difficulty:

- paying attention to you
- talking to you
- giving you eye contact
- understanding what you say

About the use of "he" and "she"

To reflect the prevalence of ASD in the population – three out of four children affected are boys – all chapters except for Chapters 3, 9 and 12 use "he" when referring to the child.

Some things to know before you get started

As a parent, you want to provide your child with every opportunity to develop and reach his or her potential. Professionals, such as speech pathologists, occupational therapists, psychologists and other educators will all be able to help you and your child in the journey ahead. But remember that:

- *You* know your child best.
- *You* care most about your child.
- *You* are the most constant and important person in your child's early years.

Communication is an essential part of life. Through communication we connect with others, make our wants known, share ideas and let other people know how we feel.

For children with autism spectrum disorder (ASD), communicating is just as important as it is for other children. However, they face special challenges because of their learning styles and sensory preferences, which often make interaction and communication difficult. Fortunately, there are some things that make all kinds of learning, including learning to communicate, easier for your child.

Your child will learn to communicate when he or she:

- pays attention to you
- finds enjoyment in two-way communication
- copies the things you do and say
- understands what others say
- interacts with other people
- has fun!
- practises what he or she learns often
- has structure, repetition and predictability in his or her life

The ideas in this book are based on More Than Words® – The Hanen Program® for Parents of Children with ASD (or related communication difficulties). This program teaches parents to help their children under six years of age learn to interact and communicate using opportunities that occur naturally throughout the day.

As our understanding about the nature of ASD has grown, new strategies have been developed to help the children it affects. In this book, we identify the difficulties that your child might have with communication, and we look at specific strategies you can use to help your child best. This guidebook is written so that you, the parent, can learn how to turn your child's everyday routines and activities into opportunities for communication learning.

How to use this book

Since each chapter draws upon the preceding one, it will be most helpful if you read the book from beginning to end. The first two chapters of this book look at what communication is and how it is so much "more than words."

In Chapter 1, "Get to Know More About Your Child's Communication," we look at some of the things that influence your child's communication. You'll use your knowledge about your child to identify his **stage of communication**. This will help you know what to expect from your child so you can give him the help that he needs. The colour coding for each stage will make it easier to find information about your child throughout the book.

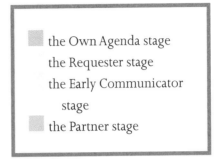

the Own Agenda stage
the Requester stage
the Early Communicator stage
the Partner stage

In Chapter 2, we start to "Set Goals by Using Your Knowledge about Your Child" according to your child's stage of communication. In the second part of this chapter, there are some practical ideas to get you started in achieving these goals.

The rest of the book offers ideas and suggestions for children at all stages of communication development. The first section of most chapters looks at how the information in the chapter applies to children at all stages. The second section outlines some additional information according to your child's stage. You may choose to read the general information at the beginning of the chapter and then find the section that gives specific information for your child. However, the descriptions under each stage are meant as guidelines only. Often some valuable suggestions for your child may be found in another child's stage. Each chapter concludes with a short summary of the important points covered.

Chapter 3, "Follow Your Child's Lead," gives you information on how interaction gets communication started and what to do to help your child progress during interactions.

In Chapter 4, "Take Turns Together," we look at how to keep your child interacting and playing with you in ways that promote back-and-forth turn-taking.

In Chapter 5, we "Make the Connection with People Games" and build structure and predictability into your child's activities. This chapter contains descriptions on how to choose and play turn-taking games with your child.

In Chapter 6, "Help Your Child Understand What You Say," we look at how you can adjust the way you talk to your child so that he can make sense of what you say.

Chapter 7, "Use Visual Helpers," outlines what you can do with objects, pictures and print to help your child understand situations, organize his life and express himself. You are welcome to reproduce the pictures used in Chapter 7 to make Visual Helpers for your child.

In Chapter 8, "R.O.C.K. in Your Routines," we look at how to use all the strategies from Chapters 1 through 7 to encourage interaction, understanding, independence and conversation during your child's everyday routines.

Chapter 9, "Make the Most of Music," taps into your child's love of music to improve interaction and communication.

In Chapter 10, we "Bring On the Books" and use them in a structured way to help your child understand more words and develop new thoughts and ways to communicate about them.

Chapter 11,"Take Out the Toys," describes the kinds of toys that will help your child develop play and communication skills.

Finally, in Chapter 12, "Let's Make Friends," there are practical suggestions on how to foster friendships in which your child continues to use his or her new communication skills.

A glossary at the end of the book provides an easy way for you to remind yourself about what some of the terms used throughout the book mean.

By using the strategies outlined in this book, you can provide your child with an environment that promotes learning and communication and allows your whole family to join in and have fun! With some patience and persistence, you can help your child reach his or her full potential in the early years of his or her life.

More Than Words® Program for parents

The approach in this guidebook is based on the content of **More Than Words® – The Hanen Program® for Parents of Children with Autism Spectrum Disorder**. This program is led by Hanen Certified Speech Language Pathologists, who guide parents in the application of *More Than Words* strategies. For more information on The Hanen Centre and its programs for parents, please visit www.hanen.org.

Get to Know More about Your Child's Communication

Benjamin is three years old and doesn't seem to like being with other people. He prefers to play alone, making his toy train go back and forth on the tracks. When he's not playing with his trains, Benjamin is always on the move, running from the living room to the kitchen and back again. Benjamin's parents are worried because Benjamin isn't talking and doesn't respond to his name.

Look at what your child likes and dislikes

Benjamin's parents don't know how to help him communicate. They don't even know if he hears them when they talk to him. But they *do* know many things about him. They know what food, toys and activities he likes. Though Benjamin's parents may not realize it, this is important information that they can use to help him.

When you know what your child likes you know what motivates him to communicate.

- What toy does your child like to play with best?
- What is your child's favourite food?
- What kinds of physical play does your child enjoy?
- Who does your child like to be with the most?

Some children give clear clues about their likes and dislikes. For example, your child may always play with the same toy or pull you towards the front door over and over again. In these situations, it's easy to figure out what he likes. But sometimes, you need to **observe** your child more closely to discover his preferences. You may then find that he likes to jump up and down, run back and forth or crawl under the furniture even more than you had thought.

The things your child likes may be hard to understand

The things your child dislikes may be hard to understand

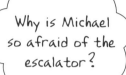

Your child may do other things that are hard to understand

Your child's actions show you how he senses the world – through movement, touch, sight, sound and smell

Many children with ASD, like the ones shown on the preceding pages, respond to the world around them in unusual ways. That's because they may not sense things the same way as you and I. Your child may be **over-sensitive** to certain sensations, which means that it only takes a small amount of the sensation to highly stimulate him. If your child is over-sensitive, he may become distressed and try to **avoid** the sensations that bother him. For example, Christopher, one of the children described earlier, is over-sensitive to the sound of the vacuum, so he covers his ears to block out the noise.

At the same time, your child may be **under-sensitive** to certain sensations and **seek** them out because it takes a lot of the sensation to stimulate him. Children who are under-sensitive to movement are especially active because they seek out the sensations they need by running back and forth, rocking or jumping. On the other hand, there are other children who are under-sensitive to sensations and yet are passive. They hardly react to the world around them because they aren't getting enough stimulation from it.

It's possible that your child has mixed reactions to sensations – he may be over-sensitive to some and under-sensitive to others. Many children with ASD are under-sensitive to speech and don't respond to it, even though other sounds bother them. If your child has trouble hearing speech sounds, it's going to be difficult for him to pay attention to what you say.

The behaviour of the children in the pictures on pages 3, 4 and 5, with the exception of Brent, can be explained by the sensations to which they are over-sensitive or under-sensitive.

Like many children with ASD, Brent, the little boy who doesn't know how to pedal his tricycle, has trouble with **motor planning**, which means that it is hard for him to plan and carry out movements.

If your child has motor planning difficulties, he may bump into things. Or he may play with his toys in a repetitive way, since he finds it easier to learn one set of actions rather than many. Talking is difficult for some children with ASD partly because speech requires a great deal of motor planning for the mouth, tongue and voice box.

Brent has trouble with motor planning. He isn't able to plan and carry out the actions he needs to ride the bike.

Link your child's preferences and actions to how he senses the world

These children are over-sensitive to some sensations and try to avoid them.

These children are under-sensitive to some sensations and seek them out.

Movement

Michael tries to avoid movement and is afraid of the escalator.

Ben seeks out movement by running around the house.

Touch

Justin is bothered by his father touching his head.

Lynsey likes the feeling of pressure on her body.

These children are over-sensitive to some sensations and try to avoid them.

These children are under-sensitive to some sensations and seek them out.

Sight

Jessica tries to avoid the light in her eyes.

Graham likes to watch his fingers moving quickly back and forth.

Sound

Some sounds seem very loud to Christopher.

At the same time, he doesn't seem to hear his father calling him.

Smell

Katie isn't eating her spaghetti because she doesn't like the smell of the spicy sauce.

Patrick enjoys the smell of his mother's hair.

Recognize your child's sensory preferences

The sights, sounds, smells, feelings and movements that your child enjoys or dislikes are called his **sensory preferences**. Recognizing these sensory preferences will make it easier for you to understand your child's behaviour.

It will also show you where to start in helping your child learn to communicate. When your child receives information through his preferred sense, he may be able to pay attention longer and learn more. By identifying your child's sensory preferences, you'll know what activities may be motivating and pleasurable for both of you. Fill in the sensory preference checklist on pages 10–13 to keep track of which sensations your child tries to seek out or avoid.

Benjamin's father turns Benjamin's love of motion into an interactive game.

My child's sensory preferences

Observe your child's sensory preferences. Then check the boxes that apply.

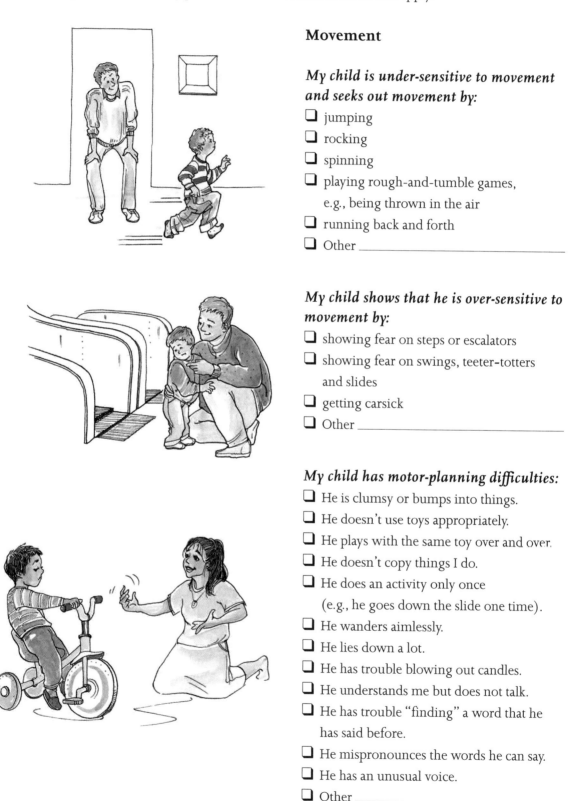

Movement

My child is under-sensitive to movement and seeks out movement by:
❑ jumping
❑ rocking
❑ spinning
❑ playing rough-and-tumble games,
   e.g., being thrown in the air
❑ running back and forth
❑ Other _____

My child shows that he is over-sensitive to movement by:
❑ showing fear on steps or escalators
❑ showing fear on swings, teeter-totters
   and slides
❑ getting carsick
❑ Other _____

My child has motor-planning difficulties:
❑ He is clumsy or bumps into things.
❑ He doesn't use toys appropriately.
❑ He plays with the same toy over and over.
❑ He doesn't copy things I do.
❑ He does an activity only once
   (e.g., he goes down the slide one time).
❑ He wanders aimlessly.
❑ He lies down a lot.
❑ He has trouble blowing out candles.
❑ He understands me but does not talk.
❑ He has trouble "finding" a word that he
   has said before.
❑ He mispronounces the words he can say.
❑ He has an unusual voice.
❑ Other _____

Touch

My child is under-sensitive to touch and seeks it out by:
- ❏ wanting long hugs
- ❏ wrapping himself in blankets
- ❏ squeezing himself into tight places
  (e.g., behind the couch)
- ❏ insisting on wearing tight-fitting clothes
- ❏ lying flat on the floor
- ❏ bumping into people
- ❏ clapping his hands
- ❏ holding objects
- ❏ putting objects in his mouth
- ❏ grinding his teeth
- ❏ rarely crying when he gets hurt
- ❏ Other _____

My child shows he is over-sensitive to touch:
- ❏ He doesn't like sticky things on his hands
  (e.g., playdough, mud and paint).
- ❏ He likes and dislikes certain clothing
  textures.
- ❏ He dislikes wearing hats and gloves.
- ❏ He dislikes getting his hair washed or cut.
- ❏ He dislikes crunchy, chewy foods.
- ❏ Other _____

Sound

My child is under-sensitive to sound:

❑ He doesn't appear to hear what people say.
❑ He likes music and certain sounds.
❑ He likes toys that make certain sounds.
❑ He likes it when I talk to him in an animated way.
❑ Other _____

My child is over-sensitive to sound and may avoid it:

❑ He covers his ears.
❑ He cries when I use appliances (e.g., dishwasher, vacuum, blow dryer).
❑ He likes it when I use a soft voice.
❑ He can hear the faintest sounds.
❑ Other _____

Sight

My child is under-sensitive to things he sees and seeks out visual sensations by:

❏ flicking the lights on and off
❏ watching repetitive movements
  (e.g., book pages turning, opening and
  closing doors, his fingers moving in front
  of his face)
❏ lining things up
❏ looking at things out of the corner of
  his eyes
❏ looking at things from unusual angles
❏ Other _____

My child is over-sensitive to things he sees and may avoid some visual sensations:

❏ He prefers the dark.
❏ He blinks often.
❏ He avoids the sun.
❏ Other _____

Smell and taste

My child is under-sensitive to some smells or tastes and seeks out these sensations:

❑ He explores things by licking and/or smelling them.

❑ He likes highly seasoned foods (e.g., very salty).

❑ Other _____

My child is over-sensitive to some smells or tastes and avoids these sensations:

❑ He likes bland foods.

❑ He is sensitive to certain smells (e.g., perfume).

❑ Other _____

Understand your child's learning style

Different types of learners

Learning styles are based on the way we acquire information. We can learn through seeing, touching and/or hearing. We also have different kinds of memories – some of us remember facts easier than others do. And some of us learn details, while others like to look at the big picture. Most people have a preferred learning style – the way they learn best. Your child has a preferred learning style too.

Rote learners

Many children with ASD, like Michelle, acquire information by memorizing things **by rote**. These children remember lots of information – like numbers and letters – when they are young, and many facts about a specific topic when they are older. While they can recite the information word for word, however, they often do not understand what they are saying.

Michelle can say the numbers from one to ten, but she doesn't understand the concept of numbers.

Nathan uses a memorized line from a song to tell his father he's sad. He may not understand the words, but he knows the sentence is about sadness.

Gestalt learners

Many children with ASD memorize sentences as whole chunks without comprehending the meaning of individual words. Children who process information in this way are said to have a **gestalt** learning style. For example, if you give your child a bath toy and say, "Put it in the water," he may do so. However, if you give him the bath toy and say, "Put it on the shelf," he may still put it in the water. Your child makes this mistake because he associates any sentence that includes the phrase "put it" with a specific action, regardless of what the other words in the sentence might be.

Unlike other children who learn to talk using single words and then gradually acquiring two-word phrases and short sentences, children who are gestalt learners start talking by repeating whole sentences. Children with this gestalt learning style tend to remember everything about a situation, but are often unable to sort out what is important from what is not.

In the picture on the previous page, for example, Nathan finds it difficult to make up his own sentence to tell his father how he is feeling. Instead, he repeats a line he has memorized from a song that he associates with being sad.

Christopher understands what he sees better than what he hears.

Visual learners

If your child enjoys looking at books or watching TV, he may be a visual learner. Most children with any language difficulties learn better by seeing things rather than by hearing them. Since sight is their strongest sense, many of these children are attracted to picture books and videos.

Hands-on learners

If your child loves to push buttons, swing doors back and forth and/or can figure out the most complicated toy, he is probably a hands-on-learner who learns best by touching things.

Auditory learners

If your child enjoys talking and listening to others talk, he may be an auditory learner who likes to get information through hearing. It is unusual for a child with ASD to rely primarily on auditory learning.

Put your observations to work

Your observations of your child's learning style give you additional information on how to help him

- If your child has a good rote memory, he will learn best from activities that are done the same way each time. These may include number and alphabet activities.
- If your child is a gestalt learner, he may learn to say a whole sentence before a single word. Your job is to help him understand the parts of the whole.
- If your child is a visual learner, present information through things he can see. For example, when saying a word show him the real thing or a picture. Give him opportunities to learn from picture books and videos.
- If your child is a hands-on learner, let him learn about the world by manipulating and touching things. Choose toys that he can operate with his hands.

Communication

Communication happens when one person sends a message to another person. You can send the message in a variety of ways, including facial expressions, gestures or words. And you can send the message for different reasons, such as to ask for help or to share an idea. The ways in which you communicate are sometimes referred to as the "**hows**" of communication, the reasons for which you communicate as the "**whys**."

Interaction

Interaction occurs whenever you and your child do things together and respond to one another. It is the basis of two-way communication. Every time you and your child interact, you make the connection that gets communication started.

Because of their learning style and sensory needs, all children with ASD have some degree of difficulty interacting with others.

It's hard for Carl's father to interact with him because Carl is more interested in watching the spinning wheels.

Even though Evan can talk, without interaction, he and his mother can't have a conversation.

To have successful interactions, your child needs to **respond** to others when they approach him and to start or **initiate** interactions on his own. Responding can be easier than initiating for your child. If he understands what you say, he can respond to your directions and simple questions. However, he may initiate only to get his needs met or ask you for something. It may take a long time before he starts an interaction simply to show you something or to be sociable.

Victor responds to his father's direction.

Andrea initiates an interaction to ask for help.

When Robin spins around, she starts an interaction with her mother just to be sociable. This is a big step forward!

Your child's ability to interact also depends on his personality, the people he's with and the things he does. By knowing how your child interacts, you can better plan how to help him participate in social interactions that he will find enjoyable.

Some children interact with only their parents and familiar adults in a few games and activities.

Some children are able to join in and play with their peers.

Get to know how and why your child communicates

He's telling me that he wants a cookie!

Although Kevin doesn't talk, he can let his father know what he wants without words.

Your child may not be saying any words, but communication is *more than words*. When your child takes you to the refrigerator, he is telling you that he would like a drink of juice. When he cries or stamps his foot, he's telling you that he is angry or frustrated. When he gives you a big smile, he's letting you know that you are special to him. Even when he flaps his hands, he's telling you something about how he's feeling.

Children communicate through actions, sounds or words. Looking at how your child communicates will help you to develop his strengths and to teach him other forms of communication, one small step at a time. For example, if your child isn't making any sounds, he may not be ready to talk. You'll need to start by showing him an easier way to communicate – perhaps through gestures.

An awareness of how your child communicates, however, is only one piece of the puzzle. You can't look at **how** he communicates without also knowing **why** he communicates. Once you know the purpose of his communication, whether it be to request, comment, or tell you how he feels, you can then help your child find more ways *and* reasons to communicate.

Look at how your child communicates

You child communicates with more than words!

There are many different ways to communicate, and some are more socially appropriate than others. Yet everything that your child does, even rocking, running back and forth or flicking his fingers in front of his face, communicates something about him.

Katie's facial expression and body language tell her mother exactly how she feels about eating her spaghetti.

Your child may communicate in some of the following ways:

- He may **cry** or **scream**.
- He may **move his body** next to people and things that he is interested in or turn his body away.
- He may use **gestures** or **facial expressions**.
- He may **reach** with an open hand to get the things he wants.
- He may **take your hand** to get you to do things for him.
- He may **look at things** he wants.
- He may **point** to things but not look at you.
- He may **look at or point to things that he wants and then look back at you.** Shifting his gaze between you and an object is called **Joint Attention**. It means your child can communitcate with you about his interests.
- He may communicate with **pictures**.
- He may make **sounds**.
- He may use **words**.
- He may use **sentences**.
- He may use **echolalia**.

Airplane!

First your child points to something without looking back at you . . .

Yes, it's an airplane!

. . . then he points and looks at you to make sure you're looking at the same thing.

Your child can tell you what he wants by pointing to a picture...

... or by giving you a picture of what he wants.

Echolalia

"Echolalia" is a term that describes the repetition of other people's words. It is a common feature in the speech of children with ASD.

At first, your child may repeat words he has heard without understanding what they mean. He may do this for a variety of reasons other than to communicate a message directly to you. In fact, you may not even be in the room. By repeating words and phrases, your child may be trying to calm himself, focus his attention on an activity or simply practise talking.

Echolalia is a good sign. It shows your child's communication is developing. Soon, he may begin to use these repeated words and phrases to communicate something to you. For example, after he repeats what you say, he may look at you or move closer to an object. Or he may remember the words you use to ask him if he wants a drink, and later use these memorized words to ask a question of his own. The words your child learns from echolalia open the door to meaningful communication.

When your child starts to talk, he may repeat what he hears other people say. This is called "echolalia," and it's often a sign that his communication is developing.

Do you want a drink of water?

You want a drink of water.

Christopher repeats some of his father's words to answer the question.

There are different kinds of echolalia:

- Your child may repeat words or phrases, usually the last part of what is said, immediately after he hears them. This is called **immediate echolalia**.

- Your child may memorize, or "lift" chunks of words or phrases he has heard and use them a day, a week, a month or even a year later. This is called **delayed echolalia**. Often, a child repeats something that he has heard in an emotional situation. For example, one little boy heard his mother shout, "Put it down!" when he picked up a pair of scissors, so he repeated the sentence "Put it down" whenever someone appeared to be angry with him. In this situation, the little boy understands *when* the words are used, but not what the words actually *mean*.

- Your child may change the echoes by saying them in a different tone or by changing some of the words in an effort to adapt them to different situations. This is called **mitigated echolalia**, and is a positive sign that your child understands how to use words meaningfully.

Look at why your child communicates

Your child's communication can be pre-intentional. Your child may do or say things without intending them to have an effect on those around him. For example, he may repeat words he knows when no one is even in the room, or he may reach for a favourite toy when no one is looking. These actions are called **pre-intentional communication**, because your child sends you a message without intending to. However, you can interpret his actions as if he were communicating directly to you.

Robbie's mother knows what he wants, even though he is not sending the message directly to her.

Your child may communicate pre-intentionally to:
- calm himself while he is doing something
- practise something
- focus or direct himself
- react to a pleasurable or upsetting experience
- reach for things he wants
- protest or refuse. The first protests your child makes are usually automatic responses to things that he doesn't like. When he cries, turns his head or pushes your hand away, he's avoiding you rather than trying to tell you how he feels.

Michelle is counting out loud to focus herself on the book. She isn't aware that her mother is asking her a question.

Your child's communication can be intentional. Communication will be easier when your child understands that what he does can have an effect on another person. Communicating with the purpose of sending a message is called **intentional communication**, and it represents a big step forward for your child.

Your child may communicate intentionally for different reasons

Protesting or refusing

Unintentional **protests** or **refusals** become intentional when your child sends the message directly to you. For example, instead of simply pushing your hand away he may look at you first. Or, instead of crying and turning away from you when you offer him something he doesn't want, he may shake his head "no." Intentional protests or refusals let you know that your child:
- doesn't want what you are offering
- doesn't want to start an activity
- wants to stop an activity

Benjamin must look at his father before pushing his hand away to make his protest intentional.

Sarah is letting her mother know that she wants something in the refrigerator.

Requesting

Your child may **request** to let you know that he wants:

- food or drink
- a toy, an object or an activity
- your help
- permission to do something

When your child begins to communicate for reasons other than getting his needs met, he is making progress towards becoming an effective communicator.

For example, your child may **request for social purposes**, such as to:

- ask you to continue physical games, called **People Games**, like Tickles or a ride on daddy's legs. He may do this by pulling your hand towards him or wriggling his body to show you that he wants another ride. (To find out more about "People Games," see Chapter 5.)
- get information
- let other children know he wants to play with them

He wants another ride!

Paul moves his body to ask his mother to keep the game going, a clear sign that he's starting to request for social purposes.

As your child becomes more sociable, he communicates for more reasons

Your child may communicate to **respond** to others by following their directions, making a choice or answering questions.

Your child may communicate to **greet** or **say good-bye.**

Your child may communicate to **get you to notice him**.

Your child may communicate to **show** you or **comment** on something.

Your child may communicate to **ask questions**.

Your child may communicate to **talk about the past and the future**.

Your child may communicate to **express feelings**, to tell you that he is happy, sad or afraid.

Your child may communicate to **pretend** and **imagine**.

Intentional communication continuum

It is helpful to view children as being on a continuum in terms of their intentional communication ability. At one end of the continuum are children who communicate mainly to get the things they want. At the other end are children who communicate for many reasons, such as to ask questions, comment on something or simply to be sociable.

This child communicates only to get things he wants, by pulling his father.

This child uses speech to be sociable.

Know your child's stage of communication

Your child's stage of communication depends on four things:

- His ability to interact with you
- How he communicates
- Why he communicates
- His understanding

It's important to identify your child's stage of communication so that you have a good idea of what he can and cannot do, as well as what you can expect him to do next. This knowledge will help you to set goals for him and give him the kind of support he needs.

The descriptions of the children at the four stages of communication may help you to identify your own child's communication stage. The four stages are:

> the Own Agenda stage
> the Requester stage
> the Early Communicator stage
> the Partner stage

Not all children pass through all these stages in order, but many children do start out at the Own Agenda stage, progress through the Requester and Early Communicator stages, and eventually reach the Partner stage as they get older. Other children may have characteristics from several stages. And, of course, children do different things depending on the people they're with, the situations they are in, and their own unique personalities.

Once you have read the descriptions of the children at all stages, observe your child closely over the next week. Then fill in the How and Why Checklist found in Chapter 2 on page 84 to identify your child's stage of communication.

The Own Agenda stage

Rebecca, who is two-and-a-half years old, is quite independent. She likes to do most things on her own, though she doesn't play with toys. Her favourite activity is playing at the park. Whenever she sees her mother getting ready to go out, Rebecca jumps up and down with excitement. Many times, Rebecca tries to open the door herself. But since she can't reach the doorknob, she often gets frustrated and cries. Her mother wonders why Rebecca never asks for help.

Rebecca never asks her mother for help opening the door. A child at the Own Agenda stage does not send any messages directly to you.

A child at the Own Agenda stage seems to want to play alone and appears uninterested in the people around him. He does not yet understand that he can affect other people by sending a message directly to them, so his communication is largely pre-intentional. You know how he is feeling through observing his body movements, gestures, screams and smiles. Many younger children are at the Own Agenda stage when they first receive a diagnosis of ASD.

Expect the child at the Own Agenda stage to do some of the following:

- interact with you very briefly and almost never with other children
- want to do things by himself
- look at or reach for what he wants
- not communicate intentionally to you
- play in unusual ways
- make sounds to calm himself
- cry or scream to protest
- smile
- laugh
- understand almost no words

Rebecca doesn't know how to play with her dolly yet.

The Requester stage

Kevin is a three-year-old child at the Requester stage, and communicates mainly by pulling or leading others to request things he wants. During bathtime, Kevin pulls his daddy's hand to ask for more tickles; when he wants to go outside, he leads his mother to the front door. Kevin also pulls when he wants one of his parents to get him a cookie from the kitchen cupboard. His parents are frustrated because it is difficult to get and keep his attention.

Kevin lets his father know that he wants more tickles by looking at him and pulling his father's hand onto his tummy.

The Requester is beginning to understand that he can ask you to do things by pulling or leading you.

Kevin asks to be taken to the park by pulling his mother to the door.

Kevin also asks for cookies by pulling his father to them.

A child at the Requester stage is just beginning to realize that his actions can have an effect on you. By pulling or leading you, he is able to ask you for things he needs or enjoys. He especially likes playing physical People Games like Tickles and Peek-a-Boo; when you pause during the game, he may look at you or move his body to get you to keep playing.

Expect the child at the Requester stage to do some of the following:
- interact with you briefly
- use sounds to calm or focus himself
- echo a few words to calm or focus himself
- reach for what he wants
- communicate mainly when he needs something by leading you or taking your hand
- request that you continue a physical People Game like Tickles or a game of Chase with eye contact and/or smiles and/or body movement and/or sounds
- occasionally follow familiar directions if he can see what he has to do
- understand the steps in familiar routines

The Early Communicator stage

Jake plays physical games like Chase and Tickles over and over again with his parents and his brother. Jake's mother holds him by his shoulders and says, "Ready, set . . ." and then waits for him to look at her and shout, "Go!" to let her know it's time to begin the chase. Mom usually gets tired of the game before Jake does! Sometimes, Jake will start the game with people other than his mother by saying, "Go!" Jake uses a few other words, too. Usually, he asks his mother to open the raisin box by making the "open" hand sign he learned at his preschool, but sometimes he says, "Open."

The Early Communicator can consistently use the same gesture, sound or word to ask for things he likes and to tell you that he wants to keep playing a game after it has started.

The Early Communicator has started to use specific gestures, sounds, pictures or words to ask for things in very motivating situations, like requesting favourite foods or toys.

Jake makes a hand sign and repeats the word "open" to ask for raisins.

Mark gives his father a picture of bubbles to ask for the real thing.

When your child is an Early Communicator, his social interactions last longer. His communication is more intentional, although he still communicates mainly to ask you to do things for him. But now he has figured out that he can use the same form of communication – **gestures, sounds, pictures** or **words** – consistently in certain situations. For example, he may always ask for juice or his favourite video by giving you a picture or saying the word. Yet he may continue to pull or lead you to ask for other things, like going outside.

An Early Communicator may start to "echo" many things that he hears, sometimes to communicate something to you. He will understand much of what you say to him if he has visual cues and you speak in simple, short sentences. When he finally starts interactions with you – by calling your name, pointing to something he wants to show you, and shifting his gaze between you and what he is interested in – two-way communication is on the way!

When the Early Communicator starts to share his interests with you by looking at something and then looking back at you, he has developed **joint attention**, a big step forward in learning to communicate.

Jake shares his interest in his toy pig with his father.

Expect the Early Communicator to do some of the following:

- interact with you and familiar people in familiar situations
- take more turns in People Games and play with you for a longer time
- request that you continue a few favourite physical People Games like Tickles or Chase, using the same actions, sounds or words each time you play
- sometimes request or respond by repeating what you say (use of immediate echolalia)
- purposefully make requests for motivating things (e.g., food, toys, physical People Games, help) using pictures, gestures or words
- begin to protest or refuse using the same action, sound or word
- occasionally use body movements, gestures, sounds or words to get your attention or to show you something
- understand simple, familiar sentences
- understand the names of familiar objects and people without visual cues
- say "hi" and "bye"
- answer Yes/No, choice and "What's that?" questions (see Chapter 4, pages 124–125)

The Partner stage

Jerry is a communication and play Partner. He enjoys interactions with other people and is able to have short conversations about his own interests. Yet his conversations often break down because he doesn't understand what the other person is saying or because he can't remember the words he needs to use. When that happens, he often relies on "echoing" what someone has just said.

Two-way communication between the Partner and another person can break down when the conversation gets too complicated for him.

The Partner is a more effective communicator than children at the other stages. Unless he has speech production difficulties, he is now talking and can carry on simple conversations. He can also talk about the past and future, such as what he did at school or what he wants for his birthday. Sometimes children at the Partner stage can't come up with their own words, but rely on memorized words or phrases. This happens most often in unfamiliar situations and when they don't understand all of what's being said.

When a child at the Partner stage communicates about his own interests, he doesn't have any difficulties. However, in unfamiliar situations, he often has trouble grasping the rules of conversation. For example, he may not consider whether what he says makes sense to his listener. He may start a conversation with, "I went there," not realizing that his listener has no idea where "there" is. Or, he may start a conversation with the same memorized sentence each time, such as "What colour is your car?" or a line from a favourite song.

A child at the Partner stage likes to play with you and with other children, but sometimes plays alone because he is unsure of what to do and say, especially in imaginary play. He does much better in physical play, like running or swinging, or in a structured game where he can learn the rules.

Expect the Partner to do some of the following:

- participate in longer interactions with you
- play with other children most successfully in familiar play routines
- use words or another method of communication to:
  - request
  - protest
  - greet
  - draw your attention to something
  - ask and answer questions
- *start* to use words or another method of communication to:
  - talk about the past and future
  - express feelings
  - pretend
- make up his own sentences
- have short conversations
- sometimes repair or fix what he says when someone doesn't understand him
- understand the meanings of many different words

Expect the Partner to still show difficulties in communication. He may:

- resist playing with other children when he doesn't know what to do, such as in imaginary play, which depends on language and pretending
- use echolalia when he doesn't understand what someone is saying or when he is unable to make up his own sentences
- have difficulty participating in conversations. He may:
  - respond to others rather than initiate conversations himself
  - try to keep the conversation on his favourite topics
  - make grammatical errors, especially with pronouns, such as "you," "me," "he" and "she"
  - get confused when conversations are complex and people are not talking directly to him
- have difficulty with the rules of conversation. He may:
  - not know how to start and end a conversation
  - not listen to what another person says
  - not stay on topic
  - not follow up on what has been said in an appropriate way
  (e.g., not ask others to clarify what they say when he doesn't understand them)
  - give too few details or too many details
- miss subtle social cues that another person is sending through facial expression and body language
- misunderstand sarcastic humour or plays on words because he takes what others say literally

A Partner often wants to play with other children but doesn't know how to ask them.

Look at how you affect your child's communication

Though the way you interact with your child depends on your personality and on your child's personality, there are some common roles that all parents tend to play. Let's take a look at these roles, when they are helpful to your child's learning, and when they are not.

The "Helper/Teacher" role

When your child doesn't seem to know how to do things or isn't able to communicate, it is natural to want to help him. But if you always do things for your child, he won't have the opportunity to show you that he can do more than you may have expected.

Your child may be able to do more than you think.

Many times, however, your child, especially if he is at the Own Agenda stage, may not understand what you expect him to do. In these times, he will need you to be his "Helper."

The Helper's Rule

The following "Helper's Rule" will help you identify when to be your child's Helper, and what you can do to give him the help that he needs: **Ask once and wait. Then ask again, adding help.**

Ask your child to do something and wait for him to respond. If he doesn't, ask again. At the same time, gently guide him to do what you asked. Take a look at how Eric's mother uses the "Helper's Rule" to help him put on his shirt.

Arms up!
Arms up, Eric! Eric, put your arms up!

Eric needs some help responding to his mother's request.

Arms up!

Eric's mother asks once and waits for him to respond. When he doesn't, she asks again, lifting his arms up above his head to help him put his shirt on.

At the end of one week, Eric's mother still needs to ask Eric to raise his arms once and then a second time, but she no longer needs to give as much help as before. Now, she simply needs to touch Eric's elbow to remind him to lift his arms above his head.

After one month, Eric is able to lift up his arms after the first time his mother asks him.

The "Do Not Disturb" role

If your child doesn't seem interested in interacting with you and rarely demands your attention, it is tempting to believe that this is his way of showing his independence. However, while all children do need time to themselves, it's important for your child to learn how to interact, something he can't do if he's by himself.

Persist in your attempts to join in on what your child is doing. For example, if he's watching television alone, sit right next to him on the couch. Or, if he's playing with a string, try pulling on it to get his attention. He may get angry and push you away, but this is still preferable to no interaction at all. After you begin interacting more with your child, he may eventually realize that play can be more fun if he includes you. (For more suggestions on how to join in, see Chapter 3).

Instead of letting your child "do his own thing" . . .

Put the cereal in.

. . . try doing things together.

The "Mover" role

Sometimes life feels like a race against the clock. Think of all the things that you have to do in the morning: get up, shower, dress yourself, dress your child, make breakfast, make the beds, walk the dog, etc. You probably find yourself rushing to stay on schedule. All those rushed moments are times when your child could be learning something. While it is not always possible to slow down, an extra five minutes at breakfast or when you're getting dressed *can* make a difference. Remember that your child needs extra time to understand what is happening around him and to think about what he can do or say. Your child will learn best when you *"get out of the race and slow down the pace!"*

Slow down the pace and give your child a chance to communicate with you.

The "Partner" role

Your child learns a lot when you are his partner in play.

You and your child probably play some games together like Tickles or Peek-a-Boo. Even when you are not teaching your child specific skills during these games, he is still learning a lot about communication by having you as his play "Partner."

As your child understands more and becomes a more able communicator, he will not need as much direction from you. In other words, when he is able to do and say more, you can do and say less! Too many of your questions and suggestions can prevent your child from initiating his own conversations. When you are in the role of the Partner, let your child lead and then respond to what he does.

The "Cheerleader" role

As a parent, you're often a good cheerleader.

All children can benefit from a hooray and a hug. When you reward your child's attempts to understand and communicate, you increase the likelihood that he will try to do these things again. But how you give your praise is also important. For example, when your child drinks all his milk, you may say to him, "Good job!" Even though your child will realize that you are happy, he may not know what the words "good job" mean. Give your child **descriptive praise** that tells him exactly why you are cheering for him. After he finishes his milk, say something like "Hooray! Your milk's all gone!" Then he can make the connection between your specific words and his own actions.

Be aware, however, that you can confuse your child with your praise. Imagine how you would feel if you were telling a friend something important and, in the middle of the conversation, she said, "Good talking!" You would probably find it odd that your friend interrupted you and you might forget what you were talking about. Your child may have the same feeling of confusion if you interrupt his attempts at communication with praise.

Instead of interrupting your child's communication with words that he may not understand . . .

. . . try rewarding him by responding directly to what he is trying to communicate.

Summary

In the first part of this chapter we looked at factors that affect your child's communication. What your child likes and dislikes, his sensory preferences and his unique learning style all affect his communication and give you insight into how you can begin helping him. In the second part of this chapter, you identified your child's stage of communication based on his ability to interact, how he communicates, why he communicates and his understanding. By knowing your child's stage of communication, you can give him the kind of help that suits him best. As a parent, you take on different roles with your child, depending on your own personality, your child's personality and the situation. By taking a closer look at your child and yourself, you are on your way to communicating together.

Set Goals by Using Your Knowledge about Your Child

In the previous chapter, we looked at your child's sensory preferences, learning style and communication stage, as well as your role in your child's communication. You are now ready to set some goals.

If your child isn't talking, you'll likely want to teach him to say some words. And, if your child is already talking, you're probably eager for him to carry on conversations. But both these goals – talking and conversation – can only be achieved in small steps.

The information in the first part of this chapter will help you set realistic expectations for your child. The second part of the chapter offers you suggestions on how to begin helping your child achieve his communication goals.

Set four goals

> **Your child will be a successful communicator if you help him achieve these four goals:**
> - to interact with you and other people
> - to communicate in new ways
> - to communicate for new reasons
> - to understand the connection between what you say and what's happening in his world

You can't work on all four goals at the same time. One day you might focus on how your child communicates, perhaps helping him progress from using a gesture to using a word. Another day, you might encourage him to communicate for reasons beyond simply asking you to get things. However, you *can* include the "interaction" and "understanding" goals in everything that you do with your child. Every day you need to help him understand the relationship between what you say and what is happening. And every day you need to try to make a two-way connection with him. Remember: "interaction gets communication started."

Goal 1: Interaction with you and other people

When you help your child with interaction, he:
- finds enjoyment in doing things with you and others
- understands that when he does something, it can have an effect on you and on others
- learns that communication is a two-way game

Up! Up! Up!

Encourage your child to interact with you in everything you do together.

Goal 2: Communicating in new ways

As you have seen in Chapter 1, learning to communicate is a progression. Although children with ASD don't develop their communication skills in the same way as most children, they do indeed follow a particular pattern of learning and growth.

Help your child progress from pulling or leading you to what he wants . . .

. . . to using pictures . . .

. . . or gestures.

Then, if he can, from using pictures or gestures . . .

... to using sounds with or without pictures or gestures ...

... to saying it all on his own.

Pick a way for your child to communicate

As you have read in Chapter 1, the first reason why your child initiates communication is to request things he wants by pulling and leading you towards them. The next step for you is to teach him a more effective, **symbolic** way to make these nonverbal requests.

You can teach your child to:

- use pictures,
- point to things, or
- use gestures or signs, or
- use words and sentences.

Using pictures

The **Picture Exchange Communication System**, developed by Lori Frost and Andrew Bondy of the Delaware Autistic Program, teaches your child to ask you for things he wants by giving you a picture of the thing in exchange for the actual object. Through Picture Exchange, your child develops **symbolic thought** – he learns that a picture, like a word, can stand for the real thing. Picture Exchange also has the advantage of forcing your child to interact with you.

In the initial stage of Picture Exchange, your child will need physical assistance to learn how to exchange a picture for something that he wants, like a cookie or a toy. Gradually, he will learn to exchange a few pictures without any help. In the early phases, your child doesn't need to recognize any pictures. The focus is on the exchange.

Your child may resist the exchange because he has difficulty holding the pictures in his hand. Or, he just might not be interested in pictures. Instead of using pictures, then, you may decide to teach your child to exchange objects for the things he wants. For example, he can give you a cup when he wants a drink. (Picture and Object Exchange are explained in more detail in Chapter 7, page 233.)

Aaron lets his mother know that he wants a drink by giving her his "special" cup.

Using pointing

Using his index finger to point to things is another way your child can learn to communicate with you. He can point to things to ask for them or just to bring your attention to something he finds interesting. It's a big step forward in his communication when he points to something and then looks back at you.

Using gestures and signs

One of the earliest ways your child can communicate is by using gestures. He can send you messages with his hands, arms or even his face. For example, he may lift his arms up to let you know he wants you to pick him up. He may shake his head, "no" or nod "yes." Sometimes, you might want to teach your child some specific signs for a few things that he wants often, such as the sign for "cookie" or "play."

After your child has mastered some of the nonverbal ways to communicate, he may start to use a few words and sentences, often beginning by repeating things he has heard you say.

Using a combination of methods

When your child is first starting to communicate, he may use a combination of pictures, gestures, signs and words. For example, in one situation, he may give you pictures to ask for some favourite foods or toys. In another, he may nod his head to let you know he wants to sing the song you suggest to him. Sometimes he might use a gesture and a word together. For example, he might lift his arms up and say "Up."

Goal 3: Communicating for new reasons

If your child is not yet communicating intentionally, you can try to turn what he *is* doing into intentional communication. For example, if your child is reaching for his toys all by himself, teach him to ask for your help in getting the toy. Once your child can make a few requests, encourage him to make more. For example, if he only asks for a cookie or to be picked up, set up situations where he can request a variety of other toys, foods or activities. (See pages 68–74 of this chapter for lots of suggestions on how to create situations that encourage your child to make requests.)

Then help him move forward by setting the stage for opportunities to communicate for reasons other than requesting, perhaps to answer a question or to say "Hi." As soon as he masters these new communication skills, create more situations in which he can practise them.

Help your child progress from pre-intentional communication...

...to intentional communication.

From requests...

...to social communication...

. . . to communicating about shared interests.

Goal 4: Understanding the connection between what you say and what's happening in your child's world

The only way to help your child understand what you say is to make what you say *meaningful* to him. He needs to be familiar with the people, objects and actions in a situation before he can make sense of your words. Words out of context don't mean anything. To understand, your child needs to actively participate in the situations in which the words are used and hear the words associated with them over and over.

Once he learns the meaning of a word in one situation, you can show him how the word can be used in different situations. For example, your child may understand that the orange liquid you pour into his cup is called "juice." However, he may not realize that there can be different kinds of juice. Or he may think that *all* drinks are called "juice." You can't assume that he understands things that you haven't explained to him.

Helping your child understand what you say often means taking the focus off getting him to talk. It's difficult for him to concentrate on making sense of what's happening when there are demands on him to do other things.

(See Chapter 6 for more about helping your child understand speech.)

For your child to understand the meaning of words, he needs to hear words that match the things that matter to him in his everyday life.

Use your child's preferences to achieve his goals

In Chapter 1, we looked at all the things that your child likes: the foods, toys, people, sights, sounds, smells, textures and movements. You may have filled in the preference checklists on pages 10–13 and now have a lot of information to help your child.

Benjamin's father knows Benjamin likes running . . .

. . . so he turns Benjamin's solitary running into a game for two!

When you know the things that your child likes, you know what words he needs to learn in order to request them.

This mother thinks "truck" will be her son's first word because he likes it more than his other toys.

Use your child's learning style to achieve his goals

In Chapter 1, we also looked at your child's learning style, which tells you how he acquires information. By knowing how your child learns best, you can adapt the way you give information so that it suits his needs.

Most children with ASD learn best when they use their **rote memories**. It is easiest for them to memorize things by rote when the things follow one another in a consistent, specific order. To help your child use his rote memory, plan his daily routines and play activities so that there is a predictable pattern. This way, your child can memorize the specific words and actions that go with these situations. As he becomes more familiar with what's happening, his understanding of what he's learned will improve. (Chapters 5 and 8–12 will help you add structure to your child's activities.)

Letters and numbers are easy for your child to memorize by rote, so make sure that you include these in your activities together. Count together or take turns naming the letters of the alphabet.

If your child is a **"gestalt" learner**, he will learn to talk by repeating whole chunks of what he hears. So, keep in mind that he will repeat what you say exactly as you say it. You can take advantage of this learning style by saying things "as he would if he could." (See Chapter 3, pages 95–101, for an explanation on how to give information to "gestalt" learners.)

If your child is a **visual learner**, give visual cues to help him understand the things that he hears. Point out the things that you are talking about. Exaggerate your facial expressions, and use videos to help your child make sense of his world. (For more on helping your child understand through visual cues, see Chapter 7.)

If your child learns by touching, use **hands-on learning** to teach him new words. For example, if your child likes to push the buttons on the car radio, use this as an opportunity to help him understand "off" and "on."

Lynsey likes to count, so her mother joins in and counts with her.

Base your goals for your child on his stage of communication

When you identified your child's stage of communication in Chapter 1, you found out whether your child is at the Own Agenda, Requester, Early Communicator or Partner stage.

Identifying your child's stage gives you information about how he interacts with you and others, how and why he is already communicating and his ability to understand what you say. You have information about what he can and can't do. With this knowledge, you can set goals especially for him, developing his communication skills one step at a time.

Goals for the child at the Own Agenda stage

Get your child hooked on joyful interactions with you in physical People Games

Interaction is the most important goal if your child is at the Own Agenda stage. You want him to find out how much fun he can have with you and how much influence he can have when he communicates directly to you. Help your child at the Own Agenda stage discover the joy of being with you by joining him in doing the things he likes.

Rebecca doesn't often interact with her parents. To get an interaction going with Rebecca, her parents must take advantage of something that she likes to do – like jumping up and down when she is excited.

Rebecca's mother helps her discover that it's more fun to jump with Mommy than it is to jump alone.

Set up situations for your child to communicate intentionally, starting with requests

Encourage your child to progress from pre-intentional communication to intentional communication. Let's look how Rebecca's mother does this for her.

At first, Rebecca has no idea that by sending a message to her parents she can get them to open the door. Rebecca tries to open the door all by herself...

... but when her mother gets face-to-face with her and extends her hand, Rebecca sees that it's easy to get some help.

Teach your child to take turns using body movement, eye contact, smiles and sounds in favourite physical and sensory play

The word "**turn**" describes whatever your child does – he may look at you, gesture, make a sound or say a word – to let you know he's participating in the interaction. Your child might take his first communication turns in rough-and-tumble games in which he uses his whole body and gets pleasurable sensations. His looks and smiles tell you he's having fun and wants to continue. The games won't last too long in the beginning. (In Chapter 5 we will look at the kinds of games you can play and how to play them.)

When Rebecca and her mother jump together, they don't take any turns at first. They just keep jumping until Rebecca's mother finally says, "Stop!" and does just that. Rebecca thinks this is funny; she laughs and looks at her mother before she starts jumping again. The laughter and eye contact are Rebecca's turns.

Increase your child's understanding of activities so that he can begin to respond to what you say

Your child doesn't understand any words yet, but if you keep doing things with him in the same way, he will start to predict what will happen. Then your words will start to have meaning for him.

When Rebecca starts jumping with her mother, she has no idea what to do when her mother says, "Stop!" Her mother has to show her. But, if they play Jump again tomorrow and the day after that, Rebecca will eventually understand how the activity works. Soon she'll figure out what the word "Stop" means, too.

Goals for the child at the Requester stage

Help your child use an action or sound to get you to continue a physical game, like Tickles or Chase

Interaction between you and your child at the Requester stage is usually best in physical People Games, like Tickles, Peek-a-Boo, Chase or Jumping. These games are often short because your child tends to lose interest quickly. Sometimes your child clearly asks you to continue the game with a gesture, sound or action, but sometimes he doesn't. Help him learn to take consistent turns and play longer in these games.

Remember Kevin, the little boy in Chapter 1, who likes getting tickles in the bath? Kevin lets his father know that he wants more by pulling his father's hand towards his tummy. Now Kevin needs to learn to add a sound to his action.

After Kevin has played the game often, he starts to use a sound when he pulls his dad's hand down for a tickle.

Help your child replace pulling and leading with gestures, pictures, sounds or word attemps

Kevin pulls his parents to let them know that he wants a cookie from the cupboard. Now, his parents need to show him how to ask for a cookie by giving them a picture of one.

Kevin's father helps Kevin go from pulling him to giving him a picture to ask for a cookie.

Increase the things for which your child makes requests

If your child only asks for one or two things, you'll need to experiment to find out what else he might want. Sometimes, you may find that he isn't asking for anything because in your role as "Helper" you anticipate his needs. In the second part of this chapter, there are many ideas that can encourage your child to make more requests.

Help your child understand several familiar words

Describe what your child does while he does it to help him understand the meanings of words. When your emphasis is on helping your child *understand* words, don't pressure him to talk.

Encourage your child to play the games that he plays with you with other familiar people, like siblings and grandparents

As soon as your child can play a couple of physical games with you, encourage him to play with other people so that he can **generalize** what he has learned. When your child generalizes his skills, he takes the things he has learned from playing with you and uses them when he plays with other people. Tell the new players how the game is played and what your child can do in the game.

Goals for the child at the Early Communicator stage

Interaction between you and your child is getting easier and lasting longer, especially in rough-and-tumble games and songs.

Teach your child to take turns consistently with you and other people in physical People Games

Remember Jake, the little boy in Chapter 1, who loves to get chased by his parents? Jake knows that he can start the game by saying, "Go!" after his parents say, "Ready, set...."

The game can only start after Jake takes his turn.

Encourage your child to initiate some physical games rather than waiting for you to do so

After Jake has played "Ready! Set! Go!" many times with his mother, the next step is for him to initiate the game with his older brother, Jesse. His mother helps by holding on to Jake while Jesse begins to run away. Wanting the game to begin, Jake says, "Ready, set, go!" and then begins the chase.

Encourage your Early Communicator to initiate his favourite games and play with other familiar people besides you.

Help your child increase his use of gestures, signs, pictures or words to make requests in new situations

Jake always asks his mother to open the raisin box by using the word "open" and a hand sign, just as he always asks for the game of Chase by saying, "Ready! Set! Go!" His parents want him to learn that the words "open" and "Ready, set, go!" can be used in other situations.

Help your child improve the way he communicates by:

- turning "echoes" into spontaneous speech
- turning gestures into signs, speech or picture communication
- turning picture communication into verbal communication
- turning single-word communication into short phrases

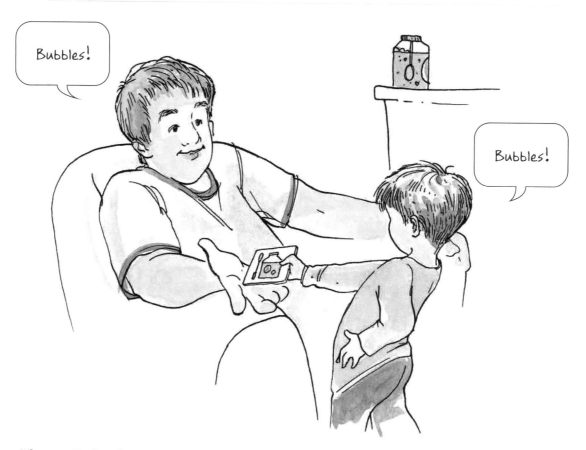

Whenever Mark exchanges a picture for bubbles, his father says, "Bubbles!" After hearing the word over and over again, Mark gives the picture and says the word too!

Help your child communicate for a variety of reasons, not just to get what he wants. Encourage him to:

- refuse and protest
- answer questions (Questions for the Early Communicator – choices, Yes/No questions and "What is this?" – are discussed in Chapter 4.)
- greet and say "bye" to people
- shift his gaze between you and something that he's interested in
- draw your attention to someone or something
- comment on unusual or favourite things

After Jake is able to ask consistently for a variety of foods and activities, his mother wants him to communicate for reasons other than requesting. So, she tries to set up a situation that will surprise Jake and encourage him to do something new. When his mother pulls a carrot out of the cookie box, Jake is certainly surprised. But it is his mother who is most surprised when Jake sees the carrot and says, "No!" for the first time.

Jake knows that carrots don't belong in the cookie box!

Help your child understand familiar words and phrases and follow simple directions

A child at the Early Communicator stage has learned to attach meaning to many words. To increase his comprehension, you need to make words stand out and connect them to real objects and people. (See Chapter 6: "Help Your Child Understand What You Say.")

Goals for the child at the Partner stage

Jerry is at the Partner stage. He's a friendly little boy who can carry on short conversations. He likes being with other children and is pleased when Jillian, the older girl he meets at the park, approaches him. As long as the conversation is simple, Jerry can participate. But as soon as Jillian speaks to him in longer sentences, the conversation breaks down. His father's goal is for Jerry to understand what Jillian is saying so that Jerry can answer her. Look at how Jerry's father helps him achieve that goal.

Jerry can't understand Jillian's question...

...so his father helps him by simplifying the question and pointing to what Jillian is talking about.

Help your child change the way he communicates

When Jerry's father helped him understand Jillian's question, he also helped Jerry use his own words instead of repeating Jillian's. At this stage, encourage your child to:

- replace "echolalia" with his own words (as your child's understanding increases, his use of echolalia will decrease)
- use correct words and sentences in conversation
- use a picture or computer system if he's unable to produce speech

Help your child communicate for a wide variety of reasons

Your child likely greets you, makes comments about things he sees, gets your attention by calling your name, asks and answers simple questions and tells you when he doesn't want things. Now the challenge is for him to do those things with other people and in many situations. He also needs to communicate about things beyond what's happening in the moment. Encourage him to:

- answer questions that begin with "What," "Who," and "Where," as well as **open-ended questions**, such as "Why are you sad?" or "How did you get hurt?" (see Chapter 4, pages 124–127)
- talk about the past, the future and feelings
- pretend

Help your child have conversations

Short, simple conversations about familiar things are easy. Conversations break down when your child, like Jerry, doesn't understand what's being said or can't think of what to say next. A child at the Partner stage needs to learn:

- how to start and end a conversation
- how to stay on topic
- that other people and other children don't always understand what he means, and that he may have to change what he says
- that he should ask for clarification when he doesn't understand something

Lisa's parents show her what she can say when she pretends to cook dinner.

Help your child improve his understanding

At the Partner stage, your child understands when you talk about things that he can see. However, he also must understand when you talk about things that he can't see or abstract concepts, such as:

- the past and the future
- feelings (e.g., happy, sad, angry)
- comparisons (e.g., bigger, hotter)
- how to behave or problem-solve
- other people's points of view
- questions that require thinking beyond the here-and-now (e.g., "Why are you doing that?" or, "How do you know he's sad?")

Help your child play and communicate successfully with other children

Your child may still prefer adults as playmates because he is unsure about what to do and say when he plays with other children. Children don't always take the time and effort to make it easy for your child to participate. He'll have the most success if he practises some specific games with you before he tries playing them with other children. (See Chapter 12 for more on playing with other children.)

Give your child a reason to communicate and then wait

It is tempting to put everything your child needs within his reach: his favourite toys on the lowest shelf or his favourite food on the edge of the kitchen counter. But if your child doesn't have any difficulty getting what he wants, he also doesn't have any reason to communicate with you. You must **engineer** situations to encourage communication.

The following suggestions* will help you set up situations that will tempt your child to interact and communicate for a variety of reasons – to request, refuse, greet, comment and make choices. These suggestions are suitable for children at all stages. In subsequent chapters in the book, many of them will be discussed in more detail.

Ways to help your child make requests

Place his favourite things within his view but out of reach

- Place your child's favourite food on a high shelf or countertop where he can see but not reach it.
- Place your child's favourite toy or video on a shelf that is out of his reach but within his view.

Randall's mother "engineers" his environment by putting his favourite video on the top shelf, hoping he'll ask for her help when he wants it.

* Adapted from A. Wetherby & B. Prizant (1989).

- Place a favourite object, like a candy or a little toy car, in a clear container that is hard to open or a plastic jar with a difficult screw-on top.

Rebecca can't open the jar to get her favourite candies...

...so she asks her mother for help.

Use People Toys

People Toys are hard-to-operate toys, like wind-ups, music boxes and bubbles, that encourage interaction: your child needs your help to make them work. Even if your child learns to operate a People Toy by himself, you need to show him that it is more fun to play with you than it is to play alone.

Kevin can't blow bubbles by himself yet. So he asks his father to blow some by pushing his hand to his mouth.

People Toys need two people to make them fun and are enjoyable for children at all stages.

The People Toys described below may interest your child. Let him spend some time figuring out how to use each toy and wait for him to get frustrated or ask for your help. Then, step in and make the toy work. Sometimes your child will discover how to use the toy on his own. When he does, celebrate his success with a hug or a hooray, and then find a different People Toy that he'll need you to help him with.

Wind-up and squeeze toys

A jumping mouse or a moving train may appeal to your child. Squeeze toys are also fun. These are toys that are activated when you squeeze a small hand-held air pump. Make the toy go. When it stops, hand it to your child and wait for him to request that you make it go again.

Bubbles

Open a jar of bubbles and blow a few. As soon as your child starts to watch or pop the bubbles, close the jar. Wait for him to ask you in some way to open it again. Or, blow bubbles to get your child's attention. Blow another bubble and then pause, holding the bubble wand at your mouth. Wait for him to ask you in some way for more bubbles.

Balloons

Blow up a balloon, and then let the air out. (Your child may like it if you let the balloon fly in the air.) Then put the balloon to your mouth and wait for your child to ask you, in some way, to blow it up again. Or, blow up a balloon partially. Then, with the balloon at your mouth, wait for your child to ask you in some way to blow it up more.

This little boy asks his mother to make the balloon bigger by showing her how to blow it up.

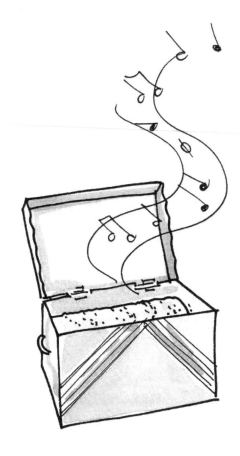

Music boxes

Wind up the music box and let the music play. Wait for your child to ask you to do it again.

Jack-in-the-box

Wind up the jack-in-the-box and let the character pop out. Wait for your child to ask for another surprise.

Spinning tops

Start spinning the top, and then wait for your child to ask for "more" when the top stops.

This father has turned himself into the toy!

Create your own People Toys!

Silly hat

Put a silly hat on your head and encourage your child to pull it off. After doing this a few times, put the hat on your head but make it difficult for your child to reach. Wait for him to ask you in some way for the hat. You can adapt this game using sunglasses or another appealing piece of clothing, like a soft, furry scarf.

Water taps

A tap or a water fountain can become a People Toy. Turn on the water and let your child play with it. Turn off the water and wait for your child to ask for more.

Mirrors

Many children, especially those who are strong visually, are fascinated by their reflection in the mirror. Take advantage of your child's interest in the mirror by playing Peek-a-Boo games. Hold your child away from the mirror, saying, "Where's Katie?" and then jump in front of the mirror, saying, "There's Katie!" After doing this a few times, hold your child away from the mirror for a longer time. Wait for him to let you know that he wants to see himself again before jumping back. Mirrors are also ideal for practising copycat games: touch Mommy's eyes, then your child's eyes; touch Daddy's nose, then your child's nose. You can play any game or sing any song in front of the mirror.

Offer things bit by bit

If you give your child everything he wants all at once, he won't need to ask you for anything. By giving your child small amounts, you provide more opportunities for him to communicate his needs to you.

Pour a small amount of juice into your child's cup and wait for him to ask for more.

Break potato chips and cookies into pieces and give your child one piece at a time so that he'll have a chance to ask for more over and over. Give one piece of a puzzle at a time.

Some toys are easy to give out bit by bit because they have multiple pieces. If you give your child puzzle pieces, blocks, Lego, stacking rings or train tracks one by one, he will have repeated opportunities to ask you for the things he needs to complete his constructions. If your child tries to grab the toy piece out of your hand, hide the object and then make it appear when he asks you for it. (Hint: Good hiding spots are up your sleeve or in your pocket.)

Give all but one

Give your child all but one of the things that he needs for an activity. Hold that one thing out of his reach but within his view, and wait for him to ask you for it. For example, give your child a piece of paper but hold on to the crayons, give him a pair of scissors but hold the paper, or give him the bubble wand but hold the bubble liquid.

Ways to help your child tell you "No," "Enough," "All done" or "Stop"

Picky eaters get a lot of practice refusing.

Offer the least favourite things

Offer your child a food, drink or toy that he doesn't like in order to give him an opportunity to say, "No!"

Let your child end the activity

Wait until your child gets bored with an activity, and then let him tell you, through facial expression, a sound or a word, that he has had enough. For example, continue to push him on the swing until he's tired of swinging, play a game over and over or let him play with a toy for a long time and then tempt him by showing him something else that he likes. (Warning: Sometimes he'll finish what he's doing very quickly, and other times you'll get bored and tired out before he does.)

Ways to help your child learn to greet and say "Good-bye"

Use puppets or stuffed animals

Hide a puppet or stuffed animal under the table and then call it by name (e.g., "Elmo!"). Make the toy appear, then wave to it, saying, "Hi!" Repeat this action several times and encourage your child to wave or say "Hi!" Finally, make the toy appear and wait for your child to wave or say "Hi" to it all on his own.

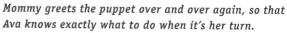

Mommy greets the puppet over and over again, so that Ava knows exactly what to do when it's her turn.

Use your window

Stand at the window, waving and saying "hi" to every person or car that passes by. Then, when another car comes, say and do nothing. Wait for your child to do the greeting on his own.

Ways to encourage your child to interact or make comments: Do the unexpected

Create routines that are predictable and then present a surprise

When your child is used to always doing something in the same way, you should do the unexpected! Changing the routine encourages your child to react to the surprise and maybe communicate about it.

Here are some ideas for everyday situations that are ideal for surprises:

Hide things in unexpected places

Put one of your child's favourite toys in his drawer and wait for him to discover the surprise.

Caitlin's mother hopes that her daughter will show her the photograph when she discovers it stuck inside her book.

Keep quiet

- Look through a few books. Point to and name the pictures. Then point to a picture and say nothing.
- Look out the window with your child and show excitement at what you see. Point, and say, "Look, a truck!" "Look, a pussy cat!" The next time you see something interesting, become animated but wait for your child to do the pointing or commenting.
- Let your child help you unpack the groceries. Show great interest each time you take something out of the bag, and name each item. When you come to your child's favourite food, wait for him to get excited or name it. You can try this at the grocery store too, by saying, "Here's the macaroni," "Here's the milk," "Here's the juice." Then, stand in front of your child's favourite food and wait for him to react. If you think that he can say the name of the food, start him off by saying, "Here's the . . ." and wait for him to complete the sentence.

Carl is surprised when his father gives him a Lego piece instead of a truck.

Offer something different

Play with toys that use multiple pieces, like Marbleworks (a toy where your child can send marbles down a ramp), puzzles, stacking cups or blocks. Give your child a few of the pieces, one at a time. Then give him something completely different, or a piece that will not fit, and wait for him to react.

Surprise with smell

Let your child smell something he likes but can't see. Get excited and comment. For example, put pizza in the oven, sniff the air in an exaggerated way and comment, "Yummy, pizza!" After doing this a few times, just sniff the air and then wait for your child to react in some way.

Surprise with touch

Place your child's hand in a cold, wet or sticky substance a few times until you've established a pattern. You can use pudding, goop or even water. Each time, get excited and describe the feeling (e.g., "sticky" or "wet"). Then put your child's hand in a different substance and wait to see if he reacts.

David guesses that his mother is making his favourite food.

Try a little "creative stupidity!"

Make mistakes "accidentally"

Children love it when their parents make mistakes. Do something silly and your child usually pays attention. When dressing your child, "accidentally" forget to put on an item of clothing. Or put something on the wrong way.

Your child may notice you when you "forget" how to put on his shoe.

Use the times when things go wrong

When things don't go as planned, use these situations to catch your child's attention. For example, if his dinner is too hot, don't just take it away to cool it off, but make a big deal by saying, "Uh oh! Too hot!" If you exaggerate your actions by blowing or waving to cool the pizza, your child may decide that this is an exciting situation that he wants to participate in or say something about.

When all is going smoothly, make something go wrong

When Raymond's mother "accidentally" drops her fork, Raymond lets her know.

Pretend you don't know where things are

If you act as though you don't know where things are, you and your child can search together. He may say or do something new in this unusual situation. For example, as you're about to leave the house, notice that you don't have his lunch, gloves or school bag. When your child asks for something, like a favourite toy, act as though the toy is lost. Exaggerate your distress and wait for your child's reaction.

Pretend something is broken when it isn't

Your child expects everything to work. How does he react when something doesn't work? Try putting your key in the door lock upside down so that it won't go into the keyhole. Say, "Uh oh. The key is broken." Wait for your child to let you know how he feels about the situation.

Pretend that you're broken

Set up situations where you act as though you are having difficulty doing things. For example, pretend that you can't see what your child sees or that you can't hear what he hears. You can stay "broken" as long as your child doesn't get too frustrated.

When Jerry's mother pretends that she doesn't hear the doorbell ringing, he has an opportunity to let her know what's going on.

Ways to help your child make choices

When you let your child make choices, you allow him to send a message to you and express how he feels. Imagine the sense of power for your child when he is able to tell you what he wants with gestures, pictures or words. Encourage your child to make choices based on what he likes and dislikes.

Sasha doesn't like his veggies, so it's easy for him to choose between his favourite treat and a piece of broccoli.

Start with easy choices

The easiest choice for your child to make is between two things that he can see: one thing he really likes and another that he dislikes. Hold the choices up in front of him.

At first, offer the favourite choice last

If your child is just learning to make choices, he often chooses the last object presented. He does this because it's the last item he *looks* at, just as, when he starts to develop echolalia, he repeats the last word he *hears*. Keeping this tendency in mind, offer the item you think he is most likely to take after you offer the less preferable one.

Later, offer the favourite choice first

When your child is experienced at making choices and repeating many of the things that he hears, offer the favourite choice first. You want to be sure that he's actually making a choice and not just repeating the last word he hears or choosing the last object he looks at.

Give visual cues

At first, your child may need visual cues to help him make choices. You can hold real objects in your hands, point to real objects or point to pictures of objects. (If you hold the objects, your child may find it easier to make his choice when you hold them one on top of the other rather than side by side.) Experiment with both objects and pictures to see what your child prefers.

Here are some choices to try:
- "Do you want your soap or your hat?" (before going outside)
- "Do you want milk or juice?" (when you know your child prefers juice)
- "Do you want a ball or video?" (when you know your child will choose the video)

Yes/No choices

If you want your child to practise answering "yes" and "no," you can offer something that you know he wants and something you know he doesn't want. Let your child see both items to help him understand that he has a choice between two things. For example, hold a doll (something he doesn't want) in one hand and a puzzle (something you know he does want) in the other hand. Hold the doll up and ask your child, "Do you want the doll?" Encourage him to answer, "No." If your child cannot answer, respond for him to show him what he could say. Then hold up the puzzle and ask, "Do you want the puzzle?" Encourage him to answer, "Yes."

Summary

It takes time for children to become communicators. In the first part of this chapter, we discussed four general goals that your child can attain one small step at a time: 1) to interact with you and other people, 2) to communicate in new ways, 3) to communicate for new reasons, and 4) to understand the connection between what you say and what is happening in his world. The specific goals you set depend on your child's present stage of communication. If your child isn't sending any messages directly to you, don't expect him to talk right away. However, expecting him to pay more attention to you *is* a realistic goal. By continually re-evaluating and setting new goals, you can help your child reach his full potential.

In the second part of the chapter, we looked at how you can do things to give your child a reason to communicate. When you make foods and toys less accessible, or act "creatively" stupid, you give your child countless opportunities to communicate. You are like an engineer, planning and manipulating your child's environment so that he can react and respond to what you do. Many of the strategies described will be mentioned again and again in this book to show you how to use them in daily routines, play activities, songs and books, and how to adapt them for your child and his communication stage.

The How and Why Communication Checklist

How Your Child Communicates

Why Your Child Communicates	Looks at you	Actions	Reaches/Points	Gives things	Sounds	Words/Echoes	Sentences
To calm or direct himself							
To protest or refuse							
To request: food/drinks							
objects/toys							
help							
to continue a People Game or song							
permission to do something							
information							
To respond to others: to follow directions							
to make choices							
to answer questions							
To greet: hello							
goodbye							
Draw attention/comment on: object							
person							
event							
self							
To talk about: past							
future							
feelings: happy							
sad							
angry							
afraid							
To pretend							

Follow Your
Child's Lead

3

Most of us pay attention to what interests us. For example, if you like tennis, you may watch a tennis game on television and easily remember the score and the names of the players. Yet, when you watch a sporting event that doesn't interest you much, say a football game, you probably won't remember much about it. Instead, you may lose interest and change the channel after only a few minutes.

A child with ASD, even more than other children, pays attention to what interests her. But because your child needs to be shown how to do things, you may spend a lot of time being her "teacher" or "helper" while she acts as the "follower." If you always tell or show your child what to do, she may not have a chance to do the things she really wants. And, she won't have an opportunity to start communication on her own.

In this chapter, we will look at when and how to follow your child's lead, as well as when it's not appropriate to follow. We'll see that if you learn to follow your child's lead, she can learn to communicate while you do things *together*.

The child who leads often gets what she needs

- A child pays more attention to things that she chooses than things that you choose.
- A child will often be more sociable and interactive when engaged in activities of her choice.
- It is easier for you and your child to focus on the same thing when she leads. When she can focus on the same thing as you, your child takes an important first step toward being able to relate to both you *and* her activity at the same time.
- A child who leads learns that she doesn't have to depend on you to know what to do or say in every situation. She can make choices for herself.
- A child who leads learns that she has the power to make things happen. Knowing that she can affect the people around her is an important step towards becoming a purposeful communicator.
- A child who leads doesn't have to shift her focus of attention, something that is difficult for children with ASD to do.

Use OWLing: Observing, Waiting and Listening

Following your child's lead begins with "Observing, Waiting and Listening" to your child.

O bserving

W aiting

L istening

Observing

Observing means watching your child closely in order to see the things that she is interested in. Then you can *include her interests* in what the two of you do together. Look at what Karen learns about her son Julian when she observes him closely during their back-and-forth ball game. She sees that Julian is more interested in holding the spoon in front of his eyes than in using it to hit the ball.

Karen's observation gives her some very important information about Julian. She now has a choice: she can continue to encourage Julian to hit the ball to her or she can pick up on his interest in the spoon and forget about the ball game. What do you think she should do? (We'll return to Karen and Julian later in this chapter.)

As you observe your child, **watch to see how and why she communicates and what she responds to.** After she "echoes" what you say, does she look at you or move closer to what you're talking about? Do you see a change in her facial expression when you bring out a certain toy? What your child does in those situations gives you information about where to start helping her learn to communicate.

Waiting

Waiting will give your child enough time to send messages in her own way. While you may think at times that your child is not communicating at all, maybe she is just not getting the chance to communicate.

Kelly's mother is worried because Kelly never asks her for anything. Then one day after lunch, when Kelly usually gets a cookie, her mother can't give it to her because she is on the telephone. Kelly stamps her foot and screams to let her mother know that she wants a cookie now. Then her mother realizes that Kelly can communicate if someone waits for her to do so.

If you don't rush in, your child will have a chance to do more than you may expect.

Waiting can also give your child a chance to take in and think about what you are saying. If you ask your child a question and she doesn't answer right away, you might assume that she doesn't understand the question and ask it again. However, your second question may distract her just as she is about to make sense of the first one. If she was about to recall a word, your second question might make her forget it.

All children take longer than adults to answer questions. It takes your child even longer. So wait at least fifteen to thirty seconds or more for your child to respond. To remind yourself to wait, count slowly to fifteen. But be careful! It is possible to wait too long and have your child lose interest. You have to fine-tune your waiting to your child's level of persistence. If your child gives up easily, your waiting time should be shorter. Your waiting will bring about the best results when your child, like Kelly, is motivated.

> Kelly's
> telling me
> something!

Kelly's mother discovers the importance of waiting.

Listening

When you listen carefully to your child's sounds, words or sentences, you learn about what she can already do and what you can build upon. For example, if your child produces a lot of sounds with her lips, like "pah" and "bah," you could emphasize motivating things that start with those sounds, like "park" and "ball."

When your child first starts to talk, she may not speak clearly. If she says "Ow" every time you get her coat from the closet, there is a strong possibility that she is trying to say "Out." If you listen carefully, you can respond to her "ow" by saying, "*Out.* Let's go *out.*" This will give her a **model** of the correct pronunciation of the word. Then you can listen for other times she says "ow" and respond by getting her coat, even if you haven't planned to go outside. Soon your child will figure out the power of her word.

You may hear your child use a word one day, and then not hear her say it again for days or even weeks. But if you listen and remember the word, you can do things that will encourage her to use it again sooner. For instance, if you hear your child say "no" once, you can increase her opportunities to use "no" again by offering her foods she doesn't like, singing songs with the word "no" in them, and looking at pictures of people shaking their heads and saying "no."

Listening is a valuable tool when your child is using echolalia (i.e., imitating or "parroting" the words or phrases that other people say). If you listen to the way your child repeats these words, her intonation will tell you a lot about why she is saying them. For example, if you ask your child "Do you want a cookie?" and she repeats your question *exactly* as you said it with the same questioning intonation, she may not have understood what you said. She may just be "echoing" because she feels stressed. However, if she repeats what you say and *changes* the intonation so it sounds more like a statement, it is likely that she has understood what you said and is telling you in the best way she can, "Yes, I want a cookie."

When your child uses **delayed echolalia,** "lifting" something that she hears from one context and using it in another, you need to be an especially good listener and observer to understand what she is trying to tell you. You will sometimes need to play detective to try to figure out what these "echoes" mean.

Stephanie likes to listen to an interactive story on her computer. Whenever it is time to "turn the page," the computer says, "Push option." When Stephanie wants her parents to turn on the TV, she also says, "Push option." While this makes perfect sense to her, it confuses her parents. But by listening to Stephanie and observing her at the computer, they come to realize that she associates the command "Push option" with getting something new to appear on both the computer screen and on the TV screen.

By observing and listening, Stephanie's parents realize that she thinks "Push option" means, "Make the screen (any screen) change!"

Since so many of your child's words, phrases and sentences may be borrowed from other situations, make sure that those words will be useful for your child to learn. After Stephanie's parents listened to what she was saying and realized why she was saying it, they tried to find new computer programs that gave instructions (e.g., "Push the button" or "Next") that Stephanie could use in other situations.

When You OWL, the best place to be is face-to-face

Sujit's mother can't see what he's interested in when she is behind him.

When Mom is face-to-face with Sujit, she sees that he is playing with a string and now she can follow his lead by joining in on what he is doing.

If you position yourself face-to-face with your child, you will be able to see what she is interested in. By placing yourself at your child's level, you become part of her world.

Since it may be difficult for your child to make eye contact, make it easier for her. For example, sit her on your knee so that she's facing you; lie on your stomach or side if she is playing on the floor; crouch in front of her if she is standing.

Our faces convey important social information that can be difficult for your child to understand. Even when your child can carry on a conversation, she may miss the frowns, smiles and eye movements that say as much as words. So get down to your child's physical level and give her every opportunity to see your face "talk."

Your child will do best when she knows what to expect. If you play face-to-face with her frequently, she will come to expect and anticipate your presence. If one day you aren't there, she may just go and get you to come and play with her as you usually do.

Use the Four "I" way to follow your child's lead

> **The Four "I"s:**
> 1. Include your child's interests
> 2. Interpret
> 3. Imitate
> 4. Intrude

The Four "I" strategies help your child improve her interaction and communication skills. You can use the Four "I"s with your child at any stage of her communication development: at the Own Agenda, Requester, Early Communicator or Partner stages. Three of the Four "I"s – include your child's interests, imitate and intrude – will help you to encourage your child to participate in activities and interact with you. The "interpret" strategy helps you to give your child information once the two of you are already interacting.

The first "I": Include your child's interest

Notice what your child is doing and then join in

That's what Sujit's mother did when she saw Sujit playing with the string. Think back to Karen and Julian at the beginning of this chapter. While playing, "Hit the ball with the spoon," Karen noticed that Julian was more interested in putting the spoon in front of his eyes than in using it to hit the ball. Although she wanted Julian to play a game that involved taking turns, she felt that if she pushed him to keep playing with the ball, he would get up and leave. So she decided to put the ball aside.

Instead, Karen moved closer to her son and, a few moments later, when he put down the spoon, said, "Peek-a-boo!" Julian laughed and put the spoon in front of his eyes again. Soon, he started to say "Peek-a-boo" after Karen. Julian hid behind the spoon eight times before he tired of the game, and maintained eye contact with his mother the whole time. By looking at his mother, Julian kept her engaged so that he could continue playing.

Notice that after Sujit's mother and Karen realized what interested their sons, they joined in the play as "partners." Joining in means that you become a "kid" and do whatever your child is doing.

Sometimes your child may have limited interests and will rely on you to introduce her to new activities. Present her with an enticing object or activity, wait for her to discover it and then follow her lead by joining in.

Once Karen realizes that Julian does not want to play with the ball, she follows his lead by joining in on what he is doing and turning his interest in the spoon into a game of Peek-a-Boo.

Bring what your child looks at into your shared space

Including your child's interest means that when your child is interested in something, you show an interest in it too. You can do this by bringing the toy or object that she is interested in closer to both of you. For example, if a brightly coloured rock catches her eye, pick it up and look at it together (even if may seem strange to you that she is more interested in a rock or a string than in a brand new toy).

You can also share in your child's interest by noticing what she's looking at and then pointing to the person, thing or action and commenting on it. A **comment** can be one word ("ball") or a sentence ("That's a big ball") that gives your child information about her interests. For example, if your child notices a bird, you can point to it and say, "Look! A birdie!" You must be close to your child and close to what you're pointing to for her to see what you are doing. If possible, place her hand on the object so that she knows exactly what you're talking about. Later, your child may discover that *you* also have exciting things to show her. Perhaps she will be interested in things that you notice before she does.

Christopher's father points at and names the "birdie" for his son.

The second "I": Interpret

Treat whatever your child does as if she were intentionally sending you a message

When you treat whatever your child does as if she were intentionally sending you a message, you help her realize that she can have an effect on what you do. This kind of interpreting works especially well with children at the **Own Agenda** and **Requester** stages, who do not consistently communicate directly to you but often let you know what they want through their actions.

For example, if your child picks up your car keys, you can say, "Keys. Let's go!" Even though she isn't communicating directly to you, you're responding as if she were. If you do this over and over again, your child may connect the keys with riding in the car, and eventually *give you* the keys the next time she feels like a ride.

Eduardo's mother acts as though he is asking her to go for a ride in the car.

Then one day, he really does ask her by handing her the keys.

You can also interpret and respond to your child's *words* by treating whatever she says as if she were talking to you. For example, if you hear your child saying "mama" while she plays in another room, you can respond as if she is actually calling you by going to her and saying, "Here's mama."

Say or do things "as she would if she could"

If your child shows an interest in something or tries to send you a message, you need to "interpret" her communication attempts by saying or doing it "as she would if she could." When you say or do it "as she would if she could," you use the words and actions that you would like your child to use in the future, giving her a **model** that she can eventually copy. A **physical model** demonstrates what your child can do. A **verbal model** demonstrates what she can say. For example, if your child shows an interest in a bird, point to it (a physical model) and say "Look! There's a bird." (a verbal model). Draw attention to your models by slowing down before you say or do them and emphasizing or exaggerating your words and actions. When you make a model stand out, your child takes notice and is more likely to copy it.

Interpret for the Own Agenda and Requester stages

Your child may just be starting to communicate to ask you for things by pulling your hand or giving you an object or picture in exchange for what she wants. Those are important times to give her the words that she "would use if she could." **Label** the object, person or activity that she is asking for by saying its name. Avoid using pronouns like "it" and "them" because these words aren't as specific as "cookie" or "books."

Since your labels also help your child understand the meanings of words, use them often to comment on her interests.

When interpreting for Carl, his mother keeps what she says "short and sweet" so Carl can eventually ask for pizza himself.

Sometimes, the first words that your child may say are silly, nonsense words that are easy to pronounce and fun to say, like "Uh oh" or "Yucky!" You can use these **FUN words** when you interpret. (See Chapter 6, page 201 for a list of FUN words.)

Make your models stand out by exaggerating them, and be consistent with the inflections and stress patterns that you use to emphasize the models. Your child's growing association of intonation with specific words or phrases will help her remember them.

Before your child repeats what you say, she is likely to repeat *how* you say it, imitating your intonation but not actually saying the words. Don't be surprised that when she does start to talk, she may use your words *and* your intonation pattern. If your child is interested in music, you may even want to sing certain words to her!

"Uh oh!" is a "FUN word" that is easier and more fun for Raymond to say than "The fork fell!"

Christopher learns to say hello in the same sing-song way as his father.

Interpret for the child at the Early Communicator stage

If your child has not yet started to talk, but sends intentional messages with gestures or pictures, your verbal model should be a single word that you say right after she gestures or gives you the picture.

If, however, your child, like so many children at this stage, starts to talk by echoing phrases and sentences, it's important that your verbal models contain words she can "lift" and use later. By modelling words for your child, you give her a **script** to memorize and use in the future. Once she learns what to say in one situation, she may be able to apply it in another. When eventually she becomes a more able communicator, she will rely less on the script and more on her own ideas of what to say.

At first, Andrew learns what to say by rote when he repeats what his father says.

Then Andrew shows that he understands the words by using them in a similar situation.

Your child will tend to remember and repeat the last thing she hears. So you can emphasize important words by placing them at the end of what you say. For example, if you want your child to learn the word "open," say "The door's open" rather than "Open the door."

Say it her way!

If your child is going to use your exact words to express herself, it is important to provide a verbal model from her point of view. If you say, "Do you want a drink of water?" your child may understand exactly what you are asking, even if she doesn't understand what each word means. Because of her tendency to echo, she may repeat your question instead of giving a proper answer. If you want your child to learn to say things in a more appropriate way, you should say it "as she would if she could!" Instead of asking the question in the usual way, take your child's perspective and say, "I want water." To show your child who "I" refers to, help her touch her chest with her hand.

You may find it strange to talk to your child this way, but it is important to take advantage of her ability to imitate what you say so that she can start using her words meaningfully. While you can't say everything "her way," try to do so every time she is motivated to talk, *especially when she wants something from you but doesn't have the words to ask.*

Remember to draw your child's attention to the model by slowing down before you say it and saying it with emphasis. Your child is more likely to repeat what you say when you make it stand out.

If your child imitates readily, all you need to do is emphasize the model, look expectant and perhaps touch her chest or point to her to let her know it's her turn to speak. One of the best ways to help your child learn how to use pronouns, such as "I" and "you," correctly is to provide many opportunities for her to hear other people using them (see Chapter 4, pages 116–117).

To tell his father that he wants a drink of water, Christopher repeats his father's question exactly as he hears it.

Later, he asks his dad for a drink by using this memorized sentence.

When his father says it "as Christopher would if he could," Christopher has a more appropriate model to copy.

Use **Carrier Phrases** in your verbal models so that your child learns some key phrases that can be useful in a variety of situations.

What are Carrier Phrases?

Carrier Phrases consist of words that often go together and are used as a unit.

Examples of carrier phrases appropriate for all children are:

"I want . . . ," "I like . . . ," "I have . . . ," "I see . . . ," "I am going . . . ," "Give me . . . ,"
"Let's . . . ," "What's that?"

From one word to two words to three

Not all children at the Early Communicator stage learn to talk by repeating whole chunks of what they hear. Some first acquire a vocabulary of single words, usually for names of things such as favourite foods and toys. Then they progress to combining these labels with other kinds of words. They may combine these labels with people words (e.g., "Mommy," sister's name), action words (e.g., "drink," "jump"), location words (e.g., "in," "on," "there") or descriptive words (e.g., "big," "dirty") to form short phrases and sentences. For instance, a child might first say "Juice" to ask for a drink and later say, "I want juice." When you interpret for a child who uses single words, help her progress from saying one word to saying more. Do this by giving her a slightly longer model, using the word she has just said and saying it "as she would if she could." For example, if she brings you a video and says, "Video" to ask you to play it for her, you could say, "Play the video." If a child says two words, use those two words when you interpret and expand on them a little bit. So, if the child points to her new shoes and says, "New shoes," you can say, "I like those new shoes!"

Child says...	You could say...
"Baby"	"Baby's eyes." (point to eyes)
"Duck"	"A mama duck."
"Ball"	"It's a big ball."
"Baby nose"	"Let's kiss the baby's nose."
"Dog woof!"	"A dog goes 'woof, woof'!"

Interpret for the Partner

You will need to use the "interpret" strategy less with a child who is at the Partner stage of communication because she is starting to make up her own sentences. Yet, it's still important to model words and phrases that you'd like your child to learn. You can also say it "as she would if she could" to give her the information she needs to correct any errors she might make. If you hear your child make a mistake, immediately present the correct verbal model, and exaggerate the correction so that she notices the change.

Julie can correct her mistake if her mother interprets for her.

> She funny!

> Yes, HE's funny.

How you can model pronouns

Early Communicators and Partners who rely on lifting and re-using what they hear can benefit not only from your models of pronouns, but also from those of others. Watching and listening to family members talking to each other and using "I," "me" and "you" in their conversations gives your child verbal models of these words that she can eventually copy.

Early Communicators and Partners *understand* pronouns better than you might think. They often realize to whom the word "you" refers, even though they may not be able to use "you" correctly in a sentence. These children need two kinds of pronoun models: one that models how they would use pronouns if they could, and another that demonstrates how pronouns are used naturally in conversation. (See Chapter 6, page 206 for more on how to help your child understand and use pronouns.)

> I want cake.

> Do you want cake?

Jerry's parents model how Jerry can use pronouns at the dinner table.

The third "I": Imitate

Follow your child's lead by copying her actions and sounds

Imitation can help your child get involved in two-way interactions, with chances for each of you to copy one another.

Your child may pay attention to you if you bang a block after she bangs a block, if you jump after she jumps, or if you make the same sounds right after she makes them. You can even try copying some of her sensory behaviours, such as spinning or flapping her hands. She may feel pretty powerful when she realizes that she's leading and you're following. If you imitate your child's actions and sounds, she may start to imitate you back. Then you can add something new for her to duplicate. **It will be easier for your child to imitate you if you use a toy that is the same as, or very similar to, hers.** This game of copycat is very important – your child can learn a lot by watching what you do.

At lunchtime, Sean bangs the table with his spoon. Sean's father follows his lead by banging his own spoon on the table just like Sean. This gets Sean's attention! After banging his spoon again, Sean looks at his father, as if to say, "It's your turn, Daddy."

Oliver's father imitates him with a spoon that is just like the one Oliver is banging. And Dad adds something new to the game – words.

If your child does not show an interest in playing "copycat" games, you may want to *teach* her to imitate you. Begin by showing your child an action and then, if she can't copy you, physically help her to do so. When she successfully completes the action, reward her with praise, hugs or a favourite treat. Start by having her copy actions with toys, such as pushing a car along the table top. Then progress to having her copy actions without toys (e.g., "touch your nose"), and then to copying some sounds, like animal sounds.

The fourth "I": Intrude

Insist on joining in on what she is doing, even if she doesn't welcome you at first

It's not always easy to join in with a child who is reluctant to interact with you or who likes to do repetitive things on her own. But remember that she's not doing these things because she doesn't want to include you. She simply doesn't know *how* to include you. Instead of getting discouraged, look for opportunities to work yourself into what she's doing. This might mean sitting next to her when she doesn't seem to want you close by or blocking her path when she's running away. Get down right beside your child and play with similar toys! Don't worry if she doesn't seem happy about it at first. Eventually, she'll learn that it's more fun to play with you than to play alone.

Remember that your child still needs to hear models of words she can say. When you intrude with your child, you also need to interpret.

Ali likes to run back and forth. His father tries following his lead by running beside him, but Ali doesn't seem to notice. Then his father blocks Ali's way and says, "Stop!" Ali is not pleased and tries to avoid his dad by going around him, but his dad moves too. Ali is forced to push him out of the way. Moving aside, his father says, "Go!" allowing Ali to resume his running. After this happens a number of times, Ali starts to expect the "roadblock" and laughs when his father gets in front of him. Three weeks later, when Ali is running around the living room, he looks for his dad. As soon as his father jumps in front of him, Ali, for the first time, says, "Go!" to get his father to move out of his way.

By creating a "roadblock," Ali's father turns Ali's running into an interactive game and gives his son the chance to learn a new word.

There is often more than one way to intrude on what your child is doing. You may have to try a few different things before you and your child make the connection.

Like Ali, who runs back and forth over and over again, your child may do things that don't appear to be productive. It is likely that these actions fulfill a sensory need. For example, your child may like to drop things on the floor and watch them as they fall. Or, she may line up objects, like toy cars or books, because she likes the way the lines look.

Here are some ideas for intruding on those repetitive and solitary activities to turn them into positive two-way interactions between you and your child.

The "keeper" strategy

- **If your child likes to drop things, like blocks, on the floor, treat the dropping as if she were intentionally starting a game.** Place a basket or box on the floor to catch the objects, and say, "In the box. Blocks. In the box." Then, make yourself a part of the block-dropping game by becoming the "keeper" of the blocks. Gather up the blocks as soon as your child has dropped them and offer one back to her. Interpret at your child's level: if she is at the Own Agenda or Requester stage of communication, say, "block." If she is an Early Communicator, and is able to repeat what you say, say, "I want a block." A child at the Partner stage will probably find her own way to tell you that she wants a block. Give your child a block. After she drops it, give her another one, along with the appropriate verbal model. Once you establish a pattern, wait a few seconds before returning the block. This will give your child time to reach out, make a sound, repeat your model or use her own words to ask you for it.

Remember that your child may not be too happy about any of your intrusions, but with some playful persistence on your part, solitary activities can be turned into interactive games.

When she insists on catching the blocks in a basket, this mother turns her daughter's repetitive throwing of blocks into an interactive game.

- If your child likes to line up objects, you can use the same "keeper" strategy as you would with a child who likes to drop things. Gather all the objects that your child lines up (e.g., toy cars, alphabet letters or blocks) and hand her the objects one by one until she learns that you are part of the play. When you are the "keeper" of the objects that your child wants, she has to include you in what she is doing.

Carl's father holds the last car that Carl needs to finish his line, so that Carl has to interact with him to get it.

- Help your child to make the line by putting an object in the line yourself. Just slip it in very naturally and say something like, "Here's another car."

  After your child allows you to participate, introduce a variation, like adding a different toy to the line or putting the same toy in the line but in an unusual way (e.g., upside down or on its side). She may not like the change, but when she screams or cries, remember, that's communication! If you persist in a gentle, playful manner, her new play routine may soon include you.

Carl makes his feelings clear when his father tries to put a piece of Lego into the truck line-up.

Hiding and searching

- Take one of the objects out of the line and hide it up your sleeve, in your pocket or under your shirt. This almost guarantees that your child will interact with you (although she may enjoy the "hiding" game so much that she starts searching everyone's shirtsleeves and pockets!).

- Hide the objects that your child likes to line up and then help her search for them. To help make her search successful, make sure that the objects are partly visible, whether they are under the couch, behind the door or on top of a table.

   When you search, use words and phrases that are appropriate for your child's communication stage: a simple word if your child is at the Own Agenda or Requester stage (e.g., "Car!"); one or two words or a sentence containing a carrier phrase for an Early Communicator (e.g., "*I see* a car!"); or a sentence including a new word or concept (such as, "Let's look *under* the chair!) for a Partner.

Carl's father hides Carl's cars so that when he wants to line them up,
he has to go searching for them with his father first.

Get in the way

- **Get in the way so that your child has to do or say something to ask you to move.** That's exactly what Ali's father does when he blocks Ali's path, making it impossible for his son *not* to interact with him if he wants to keep on running.

  Find other opportunities to block your child's way. If she reaches up to get a favourite toy, try standing in front of the shelf. Interpret for her when she pushes you out of the way, saying something like, "Move!" or "Go!" Stand in front of doors, the steps, the ladder leading to the top of the slide and even the TV set. If you're blocking your child from something she wants, she's going to let you know about it.

If Ali wants to pass, he has to tell his father to move.

Join in the play

- **When your child is playing alone with a toy, find a similar toy and insist on joining in on the play.** For example, crash your toy car into her toy car, and say something like "Crash!" or "Oh no!" Make your dinosaur eat her dinosaur, creating excitement by growling and saying, "Got you!" for the Own Agenda, Requester or Early Communicator, or "Argh! I'm eating triceratops" for the Partner who knows her dinosaurs' names.

Liam likes to play with his dinosaurs all by himself until his mother insists on being a part of the game. Then he discovers a new game that's fun only when two people play it.

Lynsey likes to sit alone on the couch, until her mother intrudes with the "squishing" game.

- **If your child always wants to sit alone, try sitting very close to her and playfully "squishing" her.** For the child at the Own Agenda, Requester or Early Communicator stages, say something like, "Squish," "Push" or "Uh oh! Mommy on Lynsey." For the child at the Partner stage, say something like, "Let's play squish." If she turns her back on you or moves away when you approach her, it's easy to assume that this means "Do Not Disturb!" But if you back off, you won't make a connection. So persist (always playfully!) in sharing her space with her.

Intrude to carry on conversations
- **If your child is at the Partner stage of communication, intruding may mean more than just getting involved in what she is doing.** You may not need to intrude as often to make a connection with your child or to get her to notice you. Instead, you may use the "intrude" technique to help your child carry on conversations.

If your child asks the same question over and over, or insists on keeping the conversation on her own topic, following her lead isn't always the best idea. If you let her continue talking about only the things she wants, she won't learn how to carry on a conversation.

Joey loves to list all the bus stops that he knows. Sometimes, his father follows his lead and tries to include Joey's interest in their conversations. However, his father wants Joey to talk about other things besides buses. Look at how his father intrudes to help Joey move away from his favourite topic.

Joey's father helps him change the topic of the conversation by introducing a new one.

How to intrude when your child goes off-topic or insists on his topic:

- Re-introduce the first topic or introduce a new one. Warn your child that there's going to be a change in the conversation (e.g., "One more thing about . . . then let's talk about . . .").
- Retell what had already been said before your child changed the topic.
- Lead your child back on topic by partially retelling what has been said and then letting her complete the rest (e.g., "We're talking about school. First, you painted. Then you played with . . .").
- Make sure your child understands you. If your child has switched to a familiar subject because the conversation confuses her, try to simplify what you've said. Turn a difficult question into a statement. Then ask an easier question.

Times not to follow your child's lead

It is not always appropriate or helpful to your child to follow her lead. She still needs to learn many things from you, and one of those things is how to behave. The decision about when to follow and when not to follow your child's lead is often based on your common sense.

It has been suggested that you try to turn repetitive unproductive behaviour into interactive play. But if your child's actions are a result of frustration or anger, you need to show her other ways to deal with these feelings. For example, if she is throwing blocks in anger or to let you know that she is not interested in playing with them, don't reinforce this behaviour by trying to turn it into a game. Instead, let your child know that you won't accept what she is doing by telling her "no throwing" or "stop" firmly and clearly to prevent her from throwing any longer. Once the throwing stops, guide your child to pick up the toys that she has thrown, saying something like, "Pick up! Pick up!"

Some children's sensory needs are so strong that they can be difficult to satisfy. For example, an interactive game of chase may not be enough for the child who craves movement. For this child, you must find other ways to give her the sensations she needs, such as a mini-trampoline or a swing. An occupational therapist who is knowledgeable in the area of sensory issues can help you decide what sensory input your child needs and how you can give it to her.

Summary

When you **OWL** – observe, wait and listen to what your child does and says – you find out exactly what her interests are. Then you can follow your child's lead by joining in and **including those interests** in your interactions together. Sometimes she may be resistant to you joining in. Then, you must gently **intrude** into her world. Another way to get the interaction going is to **imitate** your child by copying her actions or sounds. Any time you feel that your child would communicate "if she could," give her the information she needs by **interpreting**, saying the words from her point of view.

Take Turns Together

If you follow your child's lead, as suggested in Chapter 3, you may notice that you and your child respond to each other in many ways. When you tickle your child, for example, he may look at you to let you know that he's having fun. If you stop tickling for a moment, then your child may pull your hand towards him to get you to continue. In this situation and others like it, you and your child take **turns**. The word "turn" describes whatever two people do – look at each other, gesture, make sounds or say words – to let one another know that they're participating in the interaction.

In this chapter, you will discover how to extend interactions with your child by using **cues** that signal to your child that it's his turn to do or say something. As your exchanges with your child get longer, they start to resemble **conversation**.

Conversation is two-way communication in which each person takes a turn at the right time, sending messages back and forth. You can have a conversation with words, but there are other kinds of conversations, too. For instance, in a game of Peek-a-Boo, you take the first turn when you cover your child with a blanket. When he pulls the blanket away, he takes his turn. Then you say, "Boo!" (your turn) and your child laughs (his turn). You and your child alternate taking turns, just as two people alternate speaking in a conversation. Now the challenge is to make the game last as long as possible by keeping the turns going!

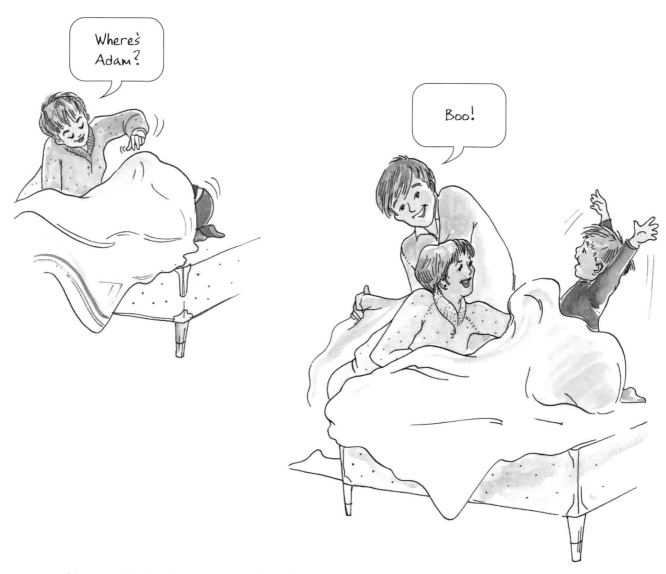

This game of Peek-a-Boo is a conversation without many words.

Rules of conversation

To engage in a simple conversation without words, such as a game of Peek-a-Boo, your child has to understand some of the rules of conversation. In verbal conversations, it becomes even more important to follow the rules.

Help your child learn to follow these rules of conversation:
- Pay attention to the person you're interacting with.
- Start conversations.
- Respond when others start conversations.
- Take a turn at the right time.
- Give the other person a chance to take a turn.
- Continue taking turns, staying on topic.
- Consider the other person's words, body language and point of view.
- Clarify or "say it another way" when your listener doesn't understand.
- Ask the other person for clarification when needed.
- Change the topic when suitable.
- End the conversation appropriately.

There are a lot of rules and even adults have trouble following them all. Just imagine how difficult it is for your child to learn them! He is going to need your guidance and support to learn how to have conversations that are rewarding for both of you.

Joey needs help changing the topic of his conversation.

Cue your child to help him take a turn

Your child may have trouble knowing when and how to take his conversational "turn." The best way you can help him is by using **cues**, prompts that signal to your child when to take his turn and sometimes show him how to take it. There are two categories of cues:

- **Explicit cues** show your child what he should do and leave little room for him to do something incorrectly. When you give explicit cues, you take either all or part of your child's turn for him. For example, in a game of Pat-a-cake, your child may not know what actions he should do. When you guide his hands into a clap for him, you use an explicit cue called **physical help**. In addition to physical help, explicit cues in which you take all of your child's turn for him include **physical** and **verbal models** and **speaking instructions**. Cues in which you take only part of your child's turn for him, such as **partial models,** are the least explicit of the explicit cues.

- **Natural cues** do *not* show your child what to do. They simply *hint* at what he should do. For instance, as your child becomes more familiar with how to clap in a Pat-a-cake game, you can **slow down**, **pause** and **look expectant** to indicate when he should clap his hands. Natural cues also include **visual cues, questions, hints, instructions** on what to do and **comments.**

You are the best judge of what types of cues are most appropriate for your child. You will probably start by using the most explicit cues and gradually move to the more natural ones. Ultimately, the most natural cues don't ever need to be eliminated. We use them "naturally" in our conversations all the time.

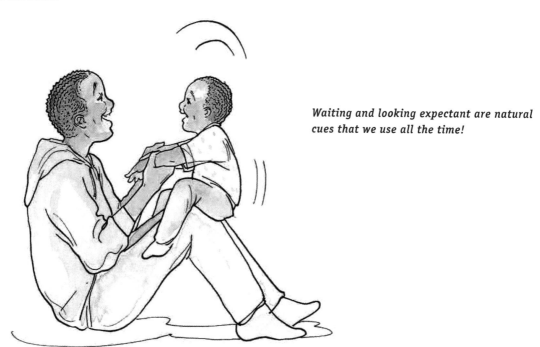

Waiting and looking expectant are natural cues that we use all the time!

Use explicit cues

Physical help

Your child may need some gentle physical assistance when learning how to perform actions in games or songs or how to take his turns in activities. If he doesn't know what to do on his own, try to show him exactly what to do by physically guiding him through the movements. Physical help can assist your child in performing specific gestures or actions and is useful because it shows your child exactly how to do things without allowing him to make any mistakes. He learns the right way to do something the first time he tries. However, you should be careful not to overuse physical help because your child may become accustomed to always having your guidance.

The parents in the following pictures are giving their children physical help so that their children can take a turn and participate in the action.

Kevin's mother physically guides his hands into a clap so that he can take a turn in the song.

Use physical help to teach your child to give you a picture in exchange for something he wants.

You can also use a **physical cue** to get your child's attention. Touching your child's back, chest, arm, shoulder or face while saying his name is a good way to get him to notice something, including you!

Ali wanders away from the slide after one turn, so his father physically guides him back to the ladder.

Daddy tries to get Rebecca's attention by tapping her shoulder.

Physical and verbal models

When you give your child a model, you cue him to copy your words or actions and show him what you expect him to be able to do or say himself. You take his turn for him until he knows what to do on his own. Models can be physical or verbal.

A **physical model** shows your child an action. Whenever you demonstrate actions in songs or turn a page in a book, you give your child a model to copy and learn from. At the same time as you show your child what to do, describe what you're doing in simple, short sentences.

A **verbal model** lets your child hear words, phrases or sentences that he can repeat after you or say on his own later on. Your child benefits not only from your verbal models, but from other people's too. For example, if your child has difficulty with pronouns like "I," "me" and "you," watching and listening to other people use these words is one of the best ways that he can learn how to use them himself. Adapt your model to your child's stage of communication. (For more on verbal models, see Chapter 3, pages 95–101.)

Remember that a model will cue your child to do or say something only if he is paying attention. Draw attention to your models by slowing down before you give them and then emphasizing them. To encourage your child to take his turns on his own, try to fade out your models or replace them with less explicit cues (e.g., fill-in-the blanks) as soon as possible.

Jerry learns those tricky pronouns by watching and listening to other people use them.

Speaking instructions

In addition to verbal models, you might include a **speaking instruction**, such as, "Say . . ." or "Tell me, ..." This cue is occasionally useful, particularly in social situations where you instruct your child about exactly what to say to another adult or child. For example, if your child doesn't know how to start a conversation with a friend, you can give him the exact words he needs to use.

To help Justin start to play with Kayla, his mother tells him exactly what to say.

However, there are problems with giving speaking instructions frequently. First, the instructions interrupt the natural flow of conversation. In addition, many children who are **echolalic** tend to repeat everything they hear, including the instructions. If your child cannot understand where the instructions end and the model begins, try to avoid using speaking instructions at all. Instead, continue to model what you want your child to say and then wait for him to copy you.

If your child doesn't understand your instructions, he'll probably repeat them.

Instead of giving your child speaking instructions, model what you want him to say.

If you are already accustomed to using speaking instructions, here are two suggestions to prevent your child from repeating the instructions along with the model. Try saying "Say" or "Tell me" in a monotone, and then emphasize and animate the model that you would like him to repeat. You can also try whispering the instructions in your child's ear and then touching his shoulder and giving him the model of what he is supposed to say in your regular speaking voice.

Partial models

When you use a partial model, *you* start doing or saying something for your child, and then let *him* finish the model himself. In partial models you take *part* of your child's turn for him and then wait expectantly for him to do the rest.

Use a partial model to cue your child to perform an action:

• **Start doing an action and wait for your child to complete it on you or on himself.**

Before Christopher's mother sings the last word, she brings her finger part-way to her nose and waits for Christopher to finish touching her nose for her.

Use a partial model, called **fill-in-the-blanks**, to cue your child to say something:

• **Say the first part of a word, phrase or sentence and wait for your child to complete it.**
  Fill-in-the-blanks can be a transition stage that your child goes through before learning how to answer questions. Before your child can come up with answers to questions all on his own, he'll need you to help him get started.

This mother says the first part of a word and then waits for her child to say more.

Christopher's father says the first part of a sentence and then waits for Christopher to fill in the blank.

If your child answers questions easily, you will use use fewer partial models to help him to take his turn. However, when your child can't answer a question, try making the question easier by using fill-in-the-blanks. That's exactly what Carl's mother does.

When Carl can't answer his mother's question . . .

. . . she helps him by turning the question into a fill-in-the-blanks.

Fill-in-the-blanks is a useful cue to help your child turn "echoes" into spontaneous speech. Start by giving your child the entire verbal model (e.g., "I want juice."). Then say, "I want . . . ," and let him fill in the blank with the word "juice." Then just say one word, "I . . . ," and wait for him to complete the sentence with "want juice." Finally, use only natural cues, like waiting expectantly, to signal your child's turn.

Use natural cues

Visual cues

Visual cues can be extremely useful for children who have trouble understanding what they hear. Not only do they help children learn to make sense out of the world, but they also act as constant reminders about the things children can do or say in different situations.

Your child's world is filled with visual cues — like people, furniture, objects and pictures — that you can draw his attention to. By holding something up, tapping it or pointing to it, you can remind your child to communicate.

Do you want broccoli or raisins?

It's easy for Sasha to make a choice when he sees what's available.

Even the seating arrangement at the dining room table can suggest to your child what to do and say.

The empty chair reminds Jerry that his father isn't home yet and helps him start a conversation.

Your child's world is also full of visual cues in the form of signs and logos that encourage him to communicate.

Michelle knows what she wants when she sees the sign.

Pictures are also helpful visual cues because they remind children what to do or say. If you put one or two pictures of your child's favourite foods on the refrigerator door, they might cue him to ask you for something.

Pictures remind your child to tell you what he needs.

You can use pictures to create **Visual Helpers**, such as special boards that show your child pictures of toys, foods and activities that he can choose from. Pictures can also cue your child to talk about things that happen when you're not with him. For example, if his preschool teacher sends your child home with a picture of a child or a toy he played with at school, he can show or tell you what he did that day. (See Chapter 7, "Use Visual Helpers," to learn more about using pictures as cues.)

Carl's teacher sends him home with a picture that helps him tell his mother what he did at school.

Questions

Asking your child questions will keep him involved in the conversation. But your child will not be able to answer a question if he can't understand it. Because children at the Own Agenda and Requester stages understand very few words, you will have to both ask *and* answer your own questions, providing verbal models that they can eventually copy.

In Chapter 2, we looked at choice questions and Yes/No questions. Let's review them briefly.

Choice questions

It is easier for your child to answer a choice question that asks him to choose between things mentioned right in the question than it is to answer a more **open-ended** question. For example, "Do you want cereal or toast?" is easier to respond to than "What do you want to eat?"

Yes/No questions

It is slightly more difficult for your child to answer Yes/No questions than to answer choice questions. Teach "no" before "yes" because your child needs a way to protest or refuse things other than by crying or having a tantrum. Begin by offering your child things that he will likely refuse. Then provide a verbal and physical model to show your child how to refuse – shaking your head and saying "no." Gradually, wait for your child to answer on his own. Introduce "yes" questions after he has practice answering no. Offer your child a few things that you know he doesn't want and then something that he does want. (See Chapter 2, pages 82–83 for more on using choice and Yes/No questions.)

Do you want more juice?

Rebecca's mother makes sure that her child has a lot of practice answering "yes" by offering her juice, bit by bit.

"Wh" and "how" questions

These questions ask "what," "who," "where," "when," "how" and "why." Your child will probably understand how to answer "what" questions first, then questions that begin with "who" or "where." Questions that ask "when," "how" and "why" are more difficult; some children continue to have difficulty with these questions into their school years.

"What?" questions

The simplest **"what"** question is "What is that?" Your child can learn to answer this question if you provide verbal models of possible answers. The next most common "what" question is "What do you want?" When a child is ready to answer this question, he is usually at the Early Communicator stage.

At first, questions need to be given with other cues to help your child understand them. Ask a question and then indicate the answer by looking at, pointing to or holding up real objects or pictures.

"Who?" "Where?" and "When?" questions

Answers to **"who,"** **"where"** and **"when"** questions may start to appear in the language of children at the Partner stage of communication. Understanding begins as you model these questions and their answers over and over in routines, songs and games. To make sure your child gets practice answering questions that begin with "who," "where" and "when," work them into your conversation as often as you can. For example, point to the people sitting at the dinner table or look at photo albums, asking "Who is that?" You can be "creatively stupid": "accidentally" drop your napkin under the table and ask, "Where's the napkin?" Then playfully put the napkin on your child's head and say, "Now, where's the napkin?"

"Who," "where" and "when" questions can be confusing. Often your child will require extra help learning how to ask and answer them. (See Chapter 7, page 251 for how to teach these questions with Visual Helpers.)

Eric's mother helps him answer "where" questions by playing a hiding game.

Cara's mother uses book time to give Cara practice answering "wh" questions.

"How?" and "Why?" questions

"How" and "why" are the trickiest questions to answer because they are open-ended, and require your child to think about things that he can't see. Even a child at the Partner stage of communication can continue to have problems with these questions for a long time.

When your child is just starting to learn to answer "how" and "why" questions, you can help him by asking one of these questions and then rephrasing it to make it simpler. Turn a "how" or "why" question into a description that tells your child what he is doing. Then ask a simple Yes/No question that is easier to answer. For example, ask "Why are you screaming?" and then change it to "You're screaming. Are you mad?" Once your child understands "how" and "why" questions, you no longer need to rephrase them, but he may still have trouble coming up with the answers. Model the answers until your child can respond on his own.

Beware of too many or too difficult questions!

If your child is good at answering questions, it is easy to fall into a pattern where *you* ask question after question and your child gives all the answers. This puts your child into the role of the "responder" – where he depends on you to initiate all the interactions. Though it is tempting to ask your child many questions as a way to keep him in the conversation, he must also have opportunities to initiate communication.

Questions that are too difficult can also be overly demanding for an Early Communicator or Partner who can't come up with the answers. In his frustration, your child may use one of his sensory calming strategies, like flapping his hands, tapping the table or jumping up and down. Another way he may let you know that your questions are too difficult for him is by increasing his use of echolalia, as if to say, "I don't understand the question, but I know I should answer. So I'll take my turn the best way I can – by repeating what you say."

Asking too many questions poses a third problem for a child whose main way of carrying on a conversation is to lift and re-use what he hears others say. If he hears question after question, he will later repeat this model and ask question after question as his main method of keeping a conversation going.

When your child shows you that your questions aren't helping him, try the following:

- Ask fewer questions and provide more comments and verbal models. Asking fewer questions often results in an increase in your child's spontaneous speech.
- Ask an easier question.
- Ask the same question again, start to answer it and wait for him to fill in the blanks. After your child fills in the blanks, you can try re-asking the question.

Instead of bombarding your child with questions...

... make comments that will help your child stay in the conversation.

Instructions

All parents tell their children what to do to some extent: "Wave bye-bye," "Bring me the book," "Put this in the garbage." Simple, clear instructions can help your child understand what to do, as long as you don't give him too many.

You can prepare children at the Partner stage of communication for future social situations by giving them instructions about what to do and say. For example, to help your child become a better listener, you can give him an instruction that tells him what to do: "When someone else talks, try to listen." Guidelines on what to do can be presented visually, which is discussed in Chapter 7.

If your child is at a very advanced Partner stage, you can give him instructions that will help him carry on conversations. Below are some examples of instructions that you can give to your child:

- "Here are some ways to start a conversation: You can smile and say, 'Hi. How are you?'; You can say something nice to the other person; You can show the person your photo album." (Give one instruction at a time.)

- "Here are some ways to stay in a conversation: You need to listen to what the other person says. Then, say something about what the other person just said. You can say, 'I think so too,' or 'I don't think so.'"

- "Here is one way to end a converstation: You can say, 'I have to go now. Bye.'"

Justin's mother gives him instructions on what to do and say to start an interaction with Kayla.

Hints

We all use hints to give other people ideas of what we'd like them to do. For example, when you make a point of admiring something in a store in front of your spouse the week before your birthday, you may be hinting at what you'd like for a birthday present. Your child can also benefit from several types of hints.

Nonverbal hints

Slowing down, pausing, leaning towards your child and **looking expectantly** are effective cues (especially when combined with verbal hints). These cues signal to your child that it is his turn. They are some of the most natural cues and you will use them often when playing with your child.

Zachary's mother looks at him expectantly, waiting for him to let her know that he wants another ride on her knees.

He responds to her cues by wriggling his body to tell her to keep the fun going!

Verbal hints

Verbal hints only work if your child understands what you say. If your child has a good comprehension of words, you can use verbal hints in subtle ways to remind him to do things. For example, to prompt your child to ask you for his favourite toy, try saying, "Time to play!" Or to remind your child to say something about an unusual situation, try saying, "Oh no! Look at that!" You can also pair verbal hints with visual cues, something teachers do all the time at school when they say "Tidy up time!" and flick the lights on and off. After you say "Time to play!" try pointing to your child's favourite toy, which should be placed out of reach on a nearby shelf. This may cue your child to ask you to get the toy.

Verbal reminders can also help a child who insists on keeping a conversation on his own topic. For example, if your child gets stuck talking about trains, you can say something like, "One more thing about the train and then we'll talk about school." If he doesn't answer a question, remind him to answer by saying something like, "Daddy asked you a question."

Comments

Comments are brief remarks that you make in response to your child's interests or to share your thoughts with him. By saying something about a certain topic, you can give your child a new idea. Unlike models, your child is not expected to repeat your comments word for word, but sometimes he might. When you want your child to take a turn in a conversation, try commenting and then waiting expectantly. For example, you could say, "Mommy cut her hair," and then wait for your child to say something. Combining a comment with a question, like the father does in the picture below, makes it even easier for your child to respond.

It's easier for Melissa to answer her father's questions if she hears his comment first.

Combined cues

Often you will give your child two or three kinds of cues at the same time.

Carl's mother gives her son a visual cue (the pizza) and then waits expectantly for him to fill in the blanks.

In addition to all of the cues that you have just read about, refer back to the suggestions given in the second part of Chapter 2 on how to create situations that give your child a reason to communicate. Many of those ideas on how to engineer your child's environment, such as giving him his food bit by bit or doing something silly, also cue him to take a turn.

Conversational turns are different from turns during play

In order to socialize with other children, your child needs to learn how to take turns during play. He needs to learn that he has to wait for others to go down the slide before he can go, and that he is not the only one who wants a turn to paint at the easel. However, turn-taking during play differs from conversational turn-taking. Though learning how to take turns during play leads to better relationships with other children, it doesn't necessarily lead to two-way communication. Your child will gradually learn how to take turns during play as he plays with you and then other children. We will look at this kind of turn-taking in Chapters 11 and 12.

Waiting for his turn is a necessary skill that your child needs to get along with other children, but it doesn't teach him much about having conversations.

Turn-taking at your child's stage of communication

The following section outlines the kinds of turns you can expect your child to learn at his stage of communication. It also suggests activities that will promote turn-taking and recommends the cues you can use to signal him to take his turn.

The Own Agenda stage

If your child is at the beginning of the Own Agenda stage, he does not communicate directly to you or take turns. Instead, he smiles, cries, looks and makes sounds regardless of whether you're with him. Before he can be engaged in two-way interactions, you've got to get his attention. Once you do, you can help him interact.

What turns you can expect

The turns you can expect the Own Agenda child to learn to take are:

- looking at you
- smiling at you
- reaching
- refusing by crying, turning away from you or pushing your hand away
- giving you an object
- performing a couple of actions directed to you (e.g., moving your hand to make you continue tickling him)
- making sounds directed to you

Where you can expect the turns

Your child will find it easiest to learn to take turns:

- during physical games (i.e., People Games) with pleasurable sensations like rocking or hugging
- when singing songs
- when he really wants something, like a cookie or his bottle

What you can do

Types of cues that will help your child take his turns:

- physical cues to get his attention (e.g., tapping his shoulder)
- physical help to guide him through actions
- physical models to show him how to perform actions
- verbal models to show him what he can say
- visual cues (showing him real objects at this stage)
- waiting expectantly before his turn in highly motivating activities
- situations engineered to give him a reason to communicate

The Requester stage

If your child is at the Requester stage, he communicates mainly by leading you by the hand and reaching when offered a choice. He may also take a few turns in physical games by looking at you, smiling at you, performing actions or making sounds directed to you.

What turns you can expect

The turns you can expect the child at the Requester stage to learn to take are:

- looking at you more often
- performing more actions directed to you
- smiling at you
- making sounds directed to you
- initiating Object or Picture Exchange to request one or two favourite foods or toys, or to ask for help
- refusing things he doesn't want by crying, turning away or pushing you away

Where you can expect the turns

Your child will find it easiest to learn to take turns:

- during highly motivating daily routines when he wants something
- during physical activities (People Games)
- during exchange games, like catch
- while singing songs
- while playing with interactive books with flaps, sounds and smells
- while playing with People Toys that interest him and are hard to operate

What you can do

Types of cues that will help your child take his turns:

- physical help to guide him
- verbal and physical models to demonstrate what he can do and say
- partial models (for actions in People Games)
- visual cues (tapping, pointing, showing objects)
- choice questions (between two things that he can see)
- questions with answers that you model
- nonverbal hints: slowing down, waiting, leaning forward, looking expectantly
- situations that have been engineered by:
  - placing things within sight but out of reach
  - offering things bit by bit
  - doing the unexpected

The Early Communicator stage

If your child is at the Early Communicator stage, he takes turns to communicate intentionally using gestures, sounds, pictures, words, echoes, looks and smiles. He still communicates mainly to request things that he wants.

What you can expect

The turns you can expect the child at the Early Communicator stage to learn to take are:

- using gestures/sounds/pictures/words more often for a variety of reasons:
  - to make requests for a variety of things
  - to make choices
  - to comment
  - to respond to Yes/No and "What's that?" questions
  - to respond to a comment (usually by imitating what you say)

Where you can expect the turns

He will find it easiest to learn to take turns:

- while playing People Games like Chase
- during exchange games like catch
- during daily routines, especially at mealtime and snacktime when he wants something
- while singing songs
- while looking at books (especially predictable books)
- while engaged in structured **collaborative** routines, such as making jello with another person (For more on collaborative routines, see Chapter 8, page 283.)
- while playing with People Toys or hard-to-operate toys
- during very familiar toy play in which your child knows the "script"
- when greeting in familiar situations (e.g., saying "bye" to a parent in the morning)

What you can do

Types of cues that will help him to take his turns:

- physical help to teach him what to do (he'll need less than a child at the Own Agenda and Requester stages)
- physical and verbal models of the things he can do and say. Models of words, phrases and short sentences from his point of view are especially important if he is starting to repeat what he hears.
- visual cues to remind him what to do and say as well as how to answer some questions
- fill-in-the-blanks
- questions that present choices, Yes/No questions and questions that start with "What" and possibly "Who"

- speaking instructions such as "Say" or "Tell me" followed by the exact words that he can say (Only use speaking instructions to help your child in social situations or if he understands the difference between the instructions and the model that follows them.)
- hints such as slowing down, leaning forward, pausing and/or looking expectantly, which let your child know that you expect him to repeat your model or to complete a fill-in-the-blanks
- comments paired with visual cues
- situations that have been engineered by:
  – placing things within sight but out of reach
  – offering things bit by bit
  – doing the unexpected

The Partner stage

If your child is at the Partner stage and does not have problems with speech production, he is already taking verbal turns in conversations: you say something and he responds. The length of his conversations depends on his communication ability. If your Partner is able to have conversations that last a while, the conversation may still break down because he does not understand all the rules of a conversation. (See the beginning of this chapter for a list of those rules.)

What turns you can expect

The turns you can expect the child at the Partner stage to learn to take are:

- commenting and asking questions
- answering questions that start with "What," "Who," "Where," and later, "Why" and "How"
- starting a conversation appropriately
- listening to what the other person says, then saying something on the same topic
- clarifying what he says when his listener doesn't understand him
- introducing a new topic appropriately
- ending a conversation appropriately

Where you can expect the turns

He will find it easiest to learn to take these turns:

- during familiar routines with familiar people
- while playing games with rules (made-up games or store-bought games, like Lotto or Bingo)
- during scripted pretend play (like pretending to go to the store, cooking a pretend dinner or eating in a pretend restaurant)
- during structured **collaborative** activities (like making apple sauce or playdough) and daily routines (like mealtime or bathtime) (For more on collaborative activities, see Chapter 8, pages 283 and 295.)
- while singing songs
- while looking at books

What you can do

Types of cues that will help him to take his turns:

- visual cues (e.g., pictures and print)
- physical help to guide him towards other children
- models of words and sentences he finds difficult, such as those that include "I," "you" and "me"
- questions (What? Who? Where? Why? How?) plus comments or models of the answers
- fill-in-the-blanks
- nonverbal and verbal hints
- instructions on the rules of conversation
- situations that have been engineered to give him a reason to communicate

   (See Chapter 3, pages 108 and 109 for more ideas on how to help your Partner carry on conversations.)

Summary

As soon as you succeed in getting your child involved in two-way interactions, the challenge is to keep him there. You can give him a variety of cues to let him know that he needs to take a turn. Your child may at first need a great deal of support, and you can use explicit cues to help him. Provide a model to cue him to take his turn by copying what you say or do, or give him physical help to perform certain actions. It's important to fade out these kinds of cues quickly so that your child can take turns without your help. The most natural cues, such as pausing and looking expectantly, are the ones that you hope will work best. All children can benefit from visual cues – the ones that occur naturally in your child's world and the ones that you can create using pictures. Questions are also useful cues, but too many questions can cause your child to become dependent on you or distressed by their difficulty. Create situations in which your child's time is balanced between being the "initiator" and the "responder."

Make the Connection with People Games

Kelsi doesn't play with many toys, but she loves to make music on her toy piano. Her father tries to join in with her but as soon as he touches the keyboard, Kelsi pushes his hand away. When her father persists on playing, Kelsi gets up and takes her piano to her bedroom.

Her father follows her, but instead of trying to play the piano again, he picks Kelsi up and throws her into the air. Kelsi loves to be tossed, so she laughs and looks right into his eyes. After a few more tosses, Kelsi is having such a good time that she forgets all about her piano.

I guess Kelsi doesn't want me to play.

Kelsi doesn't know how to include her father in her play with toys . . .

Whee!

. . . but she thinks her dad is the best toy she's ever played with when he throws her up in the air.

People Games: What are they?

Think about what makes it possible for you and your child to "make the connection" and have fun together. If your child, like Kelsi, has trouble including you when he plays with toys, then your most interactive times may be during games that you play together *without* toys. Almost all children love physical activities – to be chased, tickled or thrown in the air. When you and your child have fun together without toys, interaction becomes easier and there are more opportunities for communication.

In this chapter, we will see how you can turn the physical activities you play with your child into structured and predictable games, called **People Games**. People Games teach your child about communication because you and your child both need to take turns to play. Let's look at how Kelsi's father creates a People Game for her.

Kelsi's father sees that his daughter loves to be tossed in the air, so he decides to make a game out of it. After tossing Kelsi a few times, he stops and waits to see what she will do. Kelsi extends her arms to ask for another toss – taking her first turn. Then her father takes a turn of his own by tossing Kelsi in the air. Now Kelsi and her father both know exactly what they must do to keep the play going: Kelsi asks for more, and her father continues the game. What was once just a fun activity has become a structured game in which both players have predictable turns.

Everything your child needs to know about communication can be learned in a People Game.

By playing People Games, your child learns to:
- pay attention to you and copy what you do
- take a turn
- give you a chance to take a turn
- continue taking turns
- start the game
- end the game
- start a new game

It's easy for your child to take turns in People Games because:
- they are structured and predictable
- they have repetitive actions, sounds and words
- your child knows what his turn is and when to take it
- they include sensations that your child likes
- they are fun and exciting for your child, motivating him to keep the game going

By waiting, Kelsi's father gives her a chance to take a turn.

Though you can start a People Game for your child on your own, usually the best way to create a People Game is to observe your child and then join in on what he's doing. That's exactly what Benjamin's and Lynsey's parents did and the results were better than if they had spent hours thinking up games for their children.

Benjamin likes to run back and forth...

... so his dad turns his love of movement into a game of Chase.

Lynsey likes to hide behind the couch...

... so her mother turns her hiding into a game of Hide and Seek.

R.O.C.K. when you play People Games

Playing People Games is a little like dancing to Rock and Roll. You need a partner for both activities – and each partner must take his or her turn at just the right time! Both People Games and dancing are fun, but they require a lot of practice before each partner masters his or her turn.

Use the four letters of the word **R.O.C.K.** to help remember the most important things you must do when you play People Games with your child.

R.O.C.K.

 Repeat what you say and do.

 Offer opportunities for your child to take his turn.

 Cue your child to take his turn.

 Keep it fun! Keep it going!

Repeat what you say and do

- When you start the game
- When you play the game
- When you end the game
- Repeat the game often and with different people

Each time they play, Kevin's mother starts the Tickle game by saying the name of the game and making tickling movements with her hands. Kevin is excited by her actions – every time he sees them he knows exactly what to expect next.

Repeat what you say and do when you start the game

Every People Game needs an identifiable **beginning** – specific words and actions that your child associates with the game. If you begin a game the same way every time, you let your child know what is going to happen and give him a model to copy so that he can eventually ask for the game himself. But, if you change what you say (e.g., "Gonna get you" one time and "Let's play Chase" the next), you make it hard for your child to understand which group of words starts the game. You can call your child by name to get his attention but make sure that you wait several seconds before you ask him to come and play. This will prevent a "gestalt" learner from thinking that his name is part of the instruction.

If your child is using pictures to communicate, make one to represent his favourite game. Your child can ask for the game when he wants to play by giving you the picture.

Kevin has watched his mom start the Tickle game so many times that he finally starts the game all by himself!

Repeat what you say and do when you play the game

Counting "One, two, three" is part of every People Game that Lynsey plays with her mother.

If you say and do exactly the same things every time you play, your child will learn the "script," just as an actor learns his part by rehearsing it over and over until he can do it from memory. With practice, your child will anticipate what his turn is and when to take it, as well as how to let you know that it's your turn. For example, every time you want to cue your child to take his turn in a game, you can say, "One, two, three . . . " and let your child fill in the blank with something like "up" or "go." You can also try other repetitive phrases (e.g., "Ready, set – go!") or make up your own phrases, like "Now (*your child's name*) goes up, up – up!" You will find examples of scripts for People Games in the part of this chapter called "Some People Games to Play with Your Child."

Once your child is an experienced People Game player, taking and giving turns consistently, you can vary the game so that he learns something new. But in the beginning try to keep things as predictable as possible.

Repeat what you say and do when you end the game

As well as an identifiable beginning, every game needs a specific **ending**. Without an ending, your child will probably abruptly leave the game when he gets bored, or he'll cry to show you he does-n't want to play. But if you have specific actions and words that end the game the same way each time, your child learns that there is another way, besides crying or screaming, to let people know that he has had enough.

Always do and say the same things at the end of a game. For example, raise your arms and shout "Hooray" and then say "All done" or "Finished." ("All done" is easier to say for children just beginning to speak.) You can use any gesture you want to indicate that the game is over, as long as you are consistent. You may want to consider using a special gesture, called a **hand sign**, for "finished" or "all done," like the one Kevin's mother is using in the picture. If your child is in preschool, his teachers will probably know one of the two ways to sign "finished."

Kevin's mother ends every game by saying, "All done!" and making the "finished" sign, hoping that one day Kevin will do the same.

You may also want to use **pictures** to end your games. For example, you might put a picture of the completed game into a "finished" envelope. (For more information on pictures see Chapter 7.)

Repeat the game often and with different people

Besides repeating the same words and actions every time you play, repeat the game many times during the day, every day and with different people. You want your child to **generalize**, or transfer what he learns from playing with you to his play with other people in similar situations.

Kevin plays the Tickle game several times every day, sometimes with his father and sometimes with his mother.

Offer opportunities for your child to take a turn

- Plan when you will offer your child a turn
- Plan what turns your child can take
- Offer new opportunities for turns as your child progresses

Plan when you will offer your child a turn

When you start playing People Games together, you and your child will have a lot of fun. And because you're enjoying yourself, you may be tempted to continue playing the game in the same way. But if you keep on tossing your child in the air or tickling his tummy without giving him an opportunity to do more than have a good time, he isn't going to learn anything. You need to pause at specific times to let your child communicate with you by taking his turn.

Bumpity, bumpity, bump! Bumpity, bumpity, bump!

This is fun, but Zachary doesn't have a chance to take a turn.

He's asking me for another ride.

When his mother waits, Zachary wriggles his body to let her know he wants another ride.

For example, Zachary is having a great time riding on his mother's legs, but there is no opportunity for him to take a turn: his mother continues to give him a ride even though he never asks for it. However, if she stops after a few bounces and then waits, she lets him know that he is expected to do something. She isn't sure what kind of turn he'll take, but she knows *when* he will take it. If given a chance, Zachary will ask for another ride by moving his body up and down or making a sound.

To help your child take his turn, you need to offer him a chance to take the **same turn** at the **same place** every time you play together until he can consistently take his turn. For example, if Zachary's mother doesn't wait after giving him a ride the next time she plays with him, he won't have a chance to practise his turn.

Plan what turns your child will take

The kinds of turns that your child can take depend on his stage of communication. Sometimes identifying them requires some detective work on your part.

If your child is at the **Own Agenda** stage, he may do a number of different things when you wait for him to take his turn. He may look, wiggle or make a sound. Whatever he does, treat it as if he meant it to be his turn. If your child doesn't do anything, show him what he can do by modelling his turn for him.

In the previous example, Zachary's mother didn't know how Zachary would ask her for another ride, but when she observed and waited she soon discovered that he took his turn by wriggling his body. In the same game, a child at the **Requester** stage may make a sound in addition to wriggling his body. A child at the **Early Communicator** stage may make the same movements and say a word that you have modelled. By the time a child is at the **Partner** stage, he can ask for another ride in many different ways, as well as suggest changes to the game.

Offer new opportunities for turns as your child progresses

As you play a game over and over again, your child will find it easier to take his turn, and the kind of turn he takes will change as he advances in his communication development. For example, your child may progress from looking at you or moving his body to saying a word. To help him move forward, add new elements to the game that will change both why and how your child takes his turn. Eventually, provide an opportunity for your child to begin the game on his own, taking on the role of the initiator. You'll find that the way you and your child play the game the first time and the way you play it three months later can be very different!

Cue your child to take his turn

- Give explicit cues when your child doesn't know how to take his turn
- Give natural cues once your child is familiar with the game

Give explicit cues when your child doesn't know how to take his turn

All the cues that you read about in Chapter 4 can help your child take turns in People Games. In the beginning, when your child doesn't know how to participate in the game, your cues must contain a lot of information. You need to give him **models**, demonstrations of what he should eventually do. Slow down before you give these models and then exaggerate them so that they stand out. In addition to models, your child may also need **physical help** to learn the game's actions.

Give natural cues once your child is familiar with the game

Pausing, leaning forward and looking expectantly
cue your child to take a turn.

As soon as your child knows the game, give natural cues to signal when it is his turn – pause, lean forward and look expectant. These cues let your child know that he should do or say something.

Once your child is familiar with the game, it will become easier for him to "fill in the blanks," especially if he has already seen or heard your model. For example, if you count "One, two, three" aloud and on your fingers before you give him tickles or a ride on your knees, the counting serves as a cue. The next time you hold up your finger for "one," he may copy you or hold up two fingers and say "two."

If you give your child a reason to communicate using the ways suggesting in Chapter 2, such as doing the unexpected or offering choices within the game, you give him additional cues that help him take new turns.

Keep it fun! Keep it going!

- Be lively and animated
- Make the interaction last as long as possible

If your child is having a good time, he will want to keep the game going. And the longer he plays, the more opportunities he has to learn. You can make sure that your child has fun by choosing a game that he will like. Most children like games that involve some kind of physical play. Think of your child's sensory preferences. They will tell you which games will be fun for him and which will encourage him to pay attention to you.

If your child likes movement try:
- running games, like Chase and Horsey Ride
- up-and-down games
- swinging games
- jumping games, like Pillow Mountain
- rocking games

If your child likes the feeling of pressure on his body or hands try:
- hiding games, like Peek-a-Boo, using pillows and heavy blankets
- squeeze games, like hugs
- touch games, like Tickles
- hand-holding games, like hand squeezes, High Fives, Tug of War and Pat-a-Cake
- Horsey Ride, if he lies tummy down on your back

Running and jumping into pillows is fun for children who like to move.

It feels good for some children to ride the "horsey" tummy-down.

Adapt People Games to your child's stage of communication

How you R.O.C.K. depends on your child's communication stage. When you play a People Game with a child at the **Own Agenda** stage, your focus is on wooing him into the game. When you play the same game with a child at the **Requester** stage, you're trying to "keep it going" a little bit longer. With an **Early Communicator,** it's important to offer opportunities for him to use his emerging communication skills. And when you play with a child at the **Partner** stage, the focus is on verbal turns and conversation. The following section elaborates on how you should play People Games with children at each of the communication stages.

People Games at the Own Agenda stage

A child at the Own Agenda stage is not an experienced player so he doesn't know that playing with you can be more fun than playing alone. In the beginning, your games won't last long – your child may take one turn and then forget all about you.

At this stage, your child's goals are to:
- enjoy playing the game
- communicate intentionally to you

As you play, you can expect your child to look or smile at you and move his body.

What you can do
- **Get your child hooked on playing the game.** Woo him into the game by making it seem fun and exciting.
  - Perform an action that grabs his attention, such as acting out large tickling movements in the air or getting down on your knees for his "horsey" ride.
  - Act excited when you join in on something that he's already doing, like jumping or running.
  - Call him with an animated voice and announce the name of the game.

- To get him to communicate intentionally, **repeat the game the same way over and over,** gradually introducing pauses before the places where your child can take a turn.

- **Give your child explicit cues to encourage him to take a turn.** At first, you must do all the work, giving physical help when needed and modelling your child's turn for him. Make the model stand out by slowing down, pausing before you give it and then exaggerating it.

- **Treat any reaction from your child as his turn.** He may move his body, glance at you or make a sound. Even if he doesn't intend these actions to be his turn, act as if they are. When your child realizes that these specific actions keep the game going, he's likely to repeat them the next time he plays.

- Gradually, **give more natural cues** – slowing down, waiting, leaning forward and looking expectantly – before he is supposed to take his turn.

- **Follow your child's lead.** Sometimes, you may have a plan for a game while your child has a different idea. When this happens, you need to forget about your plan and follow your child's lead, making up a new game that **includes his interests**. For example, you may start out "rowing your boat" back and forth and find that your child prefers to row side to side. If you do what he does, you and your child have a new game.

Sometimes your child leads you to new ways of playing the game.

People Games at the Requester stage

At this stage, your child is intentionally communicating to you during People Games to ask you to continue. He may look at you, move his body, perform an action, pull your hand or make a sound. Even though he knows how much fun it is to play the game, he can get distracted or tire of the game quickly.

At this stage, your child's goals are to:

- play for a longer time
- take turns consistently
- increase the requests he makes to keep the game going
- change the way he makes requests in familiar games (e.g., from pulling your hand to making a sound)
- use the turns he already knows ("learned requests") in new games
- communicate for another reason besides asking to keep the game going
- start to play People Games with other familiar people

What you can do

- **Increase your child's opportunities to request by changing the game once he knows it.** Use some of the suggestions offered in Chapter 2 to change the game. For example, doing the unexpected can give your child a new reason to request. Think of what might happen if you were playing Row Row Your Boat with your child, and instead of holding your hands out for him to keep on rowing, you put them under your legs. Zachary's mother tries this strategy and look what Zachary does.

Do the unexpected and maybe your child will do something unexpected too!

- **Change the way your child requests in familiar games.** Once your child is consistently taking his turn in the game, change what he has to do to request by giving him a new model. For example, add a count of "One, two, three" to the beginning of your game. If your child has been pulling your hand as his turn, now he must count on your fingers or on his own to keep the game going. When you first introduce a new turn into the game, such as counting, exaggerate this new model and slow down before you give it.

To keep the game going, Lynsey used to count on her mother's fingers . . .

. . . but now she can count on her own.

After she copies her mother's model, they jump up and down together.

- **Help your child communicate for a new reason (other than requesting) in very familiar games.**

  – Set the stage for choices. After you have expanded a game by creating a new turn, you can eventually offer your child a choice between the new turn and an old one. For example, after your child can consistently ask for "up" and "down" in a game of Up-and-Down, add something new. Instead of always lifting your child, try spinning him around. Later on, you can offer him a choice between going "up" or for a "spin."

  – Be ready to follow your child's lead. Nothing ever goes as planned. If your child has another idea, be prepared to include it in the game. That's what Zachary's mother did (on page 152) when she followed Zachary's side to side "rowing."

  – Some children are resistant to changing their old familiar games. Don't give up too easily, but if you find that your child is really unhappy about playing differently, simply find another game to play.

- **Help your child use the turns he already knows ("learned requests") in new games, songs, books, routines and other activities.** When your child transfers something he learns in one situation to another situation, it's called **generalization**. Help your child generalize by giving him opportunities to take the same turns in different games. For example, if he lifts his arms up in order to be thrown in the air in a game of Up-and-Down, give him other chances to use his "up" turn, such as in Ring-Around-a-Rosy. You can even try waiting for him to extend his arms to ask you to go "up" the stairs. Generalization is important because your child learns to use his new communication skills in many places.

Kelsi's father waits for Kelsi to look at him to let him know she wants to go "up."

Later, he slows down and waits for her to take the same turn before he reads "up" in her book.

People Games at the Early Communicator stage

Your child is more experienced in playing People Games at this stage. He is developing more consistent ways of communicating and sometimes he is the one who starts the game. In addition to performing actions on his own, he often copies your verbal models.

At this stage, your child's goals are to:

- consistently make requests for you to continue the game
- change the way he makes requests in established games (e.g., from repeating what you say to filling in the blanks)
- communicate for reasons other than requesting, such as to make choices, comment or answer simple questions (e.g., Yes/No questions)
- exchange roles with you
- start the game on his own
- use the turns he already knows in new games
- play the games with other familiar people

What you can do

- **Repeat People Games often to help your child consistently take turns.** The more often you play a People Game together, the more likely your child is to take turns that he knows will keep the game going.

- **Change the way your child requests by providing models for his turns.** Include useful phrases in your models so that your child can transfer meaningful words from the game to other situations (e.g., "Give me," "Stop," "Go" and "I want more"). As your child progresses, use fewer models and more natural cues, like fill-in-the blanks and waiting expectantly, to encourage him to use more words spontaneously.

- **Expand the reasons for which your child is communicating.**
  – Offer your child choices within the game. For example, ask your child what kind of tickles he wants ("big or little"), where he wants his tickles ("on tummy" or "under arms") or where to search for Mommy ("in the closet" or "behind the door").
  – Include Yes/No questions in your People Games (e.g., "Do you want to stop?").
  – Change the game to give your child a reason to comment. Add something new to the game, do the unexpected and use some creative stupidity to create more opportunities for verbal turns like requests, responses and comments.

Benjamin and his father play the "chasing" game the same way for a long time.

For example, Benjamin's father adds something new – a box – to their chasing game. When Benjamin notices the box, his father points to it and says, "Look! A box." After playing this way for a few weeks, Benjamin's father just says, "Look!" and waits for Benjamin to fill in the blank.

- **Encourage your child to change roles with you** so that he can experience something from another person's point of view. For example, if you usually chase your child, change the game so that your child is chasing you! If your child has been getting all the tickles, it's time for him to be the "tickler" himself.

When Benjamin's father places a box on the floor, Benjamin has something new to say and do in the game.

- **Engineer the situation so that your child can initiate the game.** If you have consistently given your child a model of words and actions to start the game, he may have learned how to ask you to play. Help him ask by giving some hints on how to start the game. For example, you could get into a position associated with one of the games or go to the room that you usually play in. Putting up a picture of the game where your child can see it will also remind him to ask you to play. To get him started, you may have to make the suggestion, "I want to play," and then wait for your child to say or do something to let you know that he wants to play too.

- **Have your child play with other people besides you.** People Games are the ideal place for brothers and sisters to start having longer, interactive play with their siblings. As well, bring in Grandma and Grandpa, aunts and uncles, cousins or your friends' children. If your child goes to preschool, let his teacher know about his games so he can play them at school with a few of the other children.

Your Early Communicator can learn to do and say more in People Games when he switches roles and plays with other people.

At first, Jake gets chased by his mother.   *Then, he becomes the Chaser!*

People Games at the Partner stage

Your child can play many People Games with you and others. He talks spontaneously, but the majority of his language may still come from repeating your words. At this stage, many children aren't limited to making requests, but can also ask you questions and suggest changes in the game. Games for the child at the Partner stage are starting to become more complex and less scripted than games for children at the other stages.

At this stage, you child's goals are to:
- play games in which he can communicate for a variety of reasons, especially to share his thoughts spontaneously
- play more complex games with new turns
- practise new vocabulary and grammar (e.g., asking and answering questions that begin with "What," "Who" and "Where")
- add some pretend play to the games
- play with other children

What you can do

- **Change the way your child communicates.** Since most children at the Partner stage use some echolalia, you should continue to provide models of comments and questions that your child can copy.

- **Help your child communicate for a variety of reasons in People Games.** One of the best ways to expand your child's communication beyond the game's script is to introduce novelty.

  Try some **"creative stupidity."** Now that your child is an experienced People Game player, anything unusual that you do will probably get his attention and encourage him to comment. Simply pretending not to know how to play the game may compel your child to explain the rules to you!

  Look what Jerry's father does in a family game of Ring-Around-a-Rosy, and the effect this has on Jerry's communication.

When Jerry's dad pretends he doesn't know what to do, Jerry has a chance to tell him how to play.

Daddy, fall down!

- **Help your child in the art of conversation.** Try talking about what's going on as you play the game together. For example, give him a compliment on how he's playing (everyone loves compliments!). In a game of Chase, for instance, you can say to your child, "You're a fast runner. I'm a slow runner," and wait for him to comment. Keep him on topic with an easy question, such as, "Do you run at school?" or suggest another room to run in and ask him where he wants to go. Think of as many ways as you can to keep the conversation going. However, remember not to bombard your child with too many questions – that almost guarantees an end to the conversation.

- **Help your child play games that are more complex by creating new turns in the game.** For example, add different obstacles to a game of Chase to make the game more interesting. A chair that has to be climbed over or a bed that has to be jumped on make the game much more exciting for your child, and give him opportunities to do and say new things.

- **Help your child work on his developing vocabulary and grammar skills.** Because People Games are repetitive, they give your child an opportunity to practise his developing vocabulary and grammar skills over and over again. For example, if your child needs help with questions that begin with "Where," play a game like Hide-and-Go-Seek, in which the question "Where is *(name of person)*?" is used repeatedly. You can target any vocabulary word or grammatical form that your child needs to work on in People Games. A speech language pathologist can help you decide which targets to choose.

- **Introduce imaginary play into the games.** Introduce pretending into all of your People Games. For example, in a game of Chase, you can become the Big Bad Wolf and your child can be one of the little pigs. If he doesn't run away fast enough, that little pig is going to get eaten for dinner! Or, maybe your child would enjoy getting tickles from the "tickle monster" or playing Hide-and-Go-Seek with his favourite stuffed animal. Then you can pretend that the animal gets sad or surprised when someone finds him. When you pretend, become the monster or the Big Bad Wolf – and stay in character! This will be more fun for both you and your child. And, by modelling what these characters say and do, you give your child something to copy when it's his turn to play your part. (See Chapter 11 for more on pretend play.)

People Games are even more fun when you add make-believe!

- **Help your child play with other children.** After your child has had a lot of practice playing with you and family members, he is ready to play with another child. Coach your child's new playmate on the rules of the game so that he or she plays the game the same way your child knows.

Some People Games to play with your child

Most of the games in this section are appropriate, with adaptations, for children at all stages of communication development. Choose games that give your child the sensations he needs and avoid ones that may overstimulate him. Some suggestions for the kinds of games that your child might enjoy are given at the beginning of this chapter (page 149).

In this section, you will find a detailed description of how to play Peek-a-Boo, Hide and Go Seek, Tickles, Chase, Horsey Ride and Up-and-Down for children at each of the four stages of communication. To adapt any other games for your child, refer to the section "Adapt People Games to Your Child's Stage of Communication" in the preceding section of this chapter.

Peek-a-Boo

Peek-a-Boo is one of the first People Games that children learn. Put a blanket over your child and ask, "Where's (*your child's name*)?" Then pull the blanket away to "discover" him. Plan what turns your child can take to keep the game going and when he can take them – both when the blanket is over his head and after you've pulled the blanket away. The kinds and number of turns depend on your child's stage of communication.

Variations on Peek-a-Boo:

- Put the blanket over yourself instead of your child. Now your child's turn is to pull the blanket off of you. If possible, have another person involved in the play who can keep your child interested in the game while you're busy hiding under the blanket. If your child is at the Own Agenda or Requester stage, he or she can also guide your child's hand to the blanket if he needs physical help.

- If your child enjoys the feeling of deep pressure on his body, hide him under a few pillows. If he likes the feeling of softness against his skin, you could use a blanket made of a soft fabric, like velour or flannel.

Adam likes to hide under a soft blanket when he plays Peek-a-Boo.

Peek-a-Boo at the Own Agenda stage

What you can expect

The turns your child takes will change as he plays the game over and over. Initially, he may not do anything when it is his turn, but later you can expect him to do some of the following:

- wriggle under the blanket
- look briefly at you when the blanket comes off
- make a sound before the blanket comes off
- push the blanket away
- smile or laugh

What you can do

- **Create excitement right at the start** by holding up the blanket and exaggerating what you are about to do. When your child is under the blanket, say in an excited voice, "Where's (*your child's name*)?" After a few seconds, pull the blanket away and say, "Peek-a-boo!" or "It's (*your child's name*)!"

- **Repeat the game** until your child no longer runs away after the blanket comes off. Then, the next time you cover him up, don't immediately pull the blanket away. Wait for your child to push the blanket himself. He may do something else altogether – such as wiggle under the blanket or make a sound. At this stage, treat whatever he does as his turn and then pull the blanket off, saying, "It's (*your child's name*)!"

- Gradually, **wait a longer time** before you put the blanket over your child and before you pull the blanket away. Tempt your child to ask you to cover him by holding the blanket above his head and looking expectantly. He may then take a turn by pulling your hands down so he can get under the blanket and continue the game.

Lynsey likes the feeling of pressure on her body, so her mother hides her under some pillows.

Peek-a-Boo at the Requester stage

What you can expect

At this stage your child will play longer and let you know that he wants to continue playing by using a specific sound or action. If you provide the opportunities, he can take new turns.

When it's your child's turn you can expect him to learn to do some of the following:
- ask you with a look, action or sound to put the blanket over his head or take the blanket off
- copy your finger counting
- take the blanket off of himself or you to keep the game going
- ask you to put the blanket over his head by pulling your hand
- wave "hi"

What you can do

- **Begin the game** by holding up the blanket when your child is looking at you. Say something like, "Hide Adam." Then hide your child under the blanket. Say, "Where is Adam?" After a few seconds of waiting, expect your child to push the blanket away. Then say something like, "Here's Adam!" or "Hi!" and wave "hi" to your child. Wait for your child to use either a sound, an action or both to let you know that he wants you to cover him again.

- **Play the game** this way until your child consistently takes a turn both before and after you cover him with the blanket.

- **Add new turns to the established game.** For example, add counting ("one, two, three") to the beginning of the game and wave "hi" to a puppet when the blanket comes off. Your child may copy these actions. If he doesn't copy your model of waving "hi" you can help him by physically guiding his hand into a wave. Later, just tap his elbow to prompt him to say "hi."

- **Change the game** after your child has mastered the turns of the original game. Put the blanket over your head instead of your child's.

- **Use the turns he learns in Peek-a-boo in another game**. For example, play a hiding game behind the door or curtain. Make sure you keep the script the same. If your child's turn has been to push the blanket off his head, he can now push the door open or the curtain away to take his turn.

At first, Adam waits for his mother to pull the blanket away.

Then Adam comes out from under the blanket all by himself!

Adam's Mother shows him how to take a new turn – waving "hi" to Daddy.

Peek-a-Boo at the Early Communicator stage

What you can expect

At this stage, your child is playing longer and taking his turns with words or actions. He may even make a comment about the game all on his own.

When it's your child's turn you can expect him to learn to do some of the following:

- push away the blanket
- say "Hi" or "Here I am" when the blanket comes off and wave "hi"
- look at you and use a gesture, word or phrase to ask you to continue the game
- complete fill-in-the-blanks, such as "Where's (*name of the person under the blanket*)?"
- respond to simple questions, often by repeating the last word that you say (e.g., choice questions, such as "Blanket on Mommy or Adam?")
- respond to Yes/No questions with a head shake or word
- start the game by giving you a picture or throwing the blanket on you or himself and saying, "Where's (*name of the person under the blanket*)?"
- make one or two comments
- use the turns he learns in this game in other activities
- play Peek-a-boo with other familiar people

What you can do

- **Play the game several times:** in the morning, at bedtime and at a minimum of one other time during the day.

- If you expect your child to wave and say something like "Here I am" or "Hi" when the blanket comes away, **make your models of these words and actions stand out** by slowing down before you say and do them. As your child learns the models, gradually give less explicit cues, such as starting a sentence with "Here . . . " and waiting expectantly for him to fill in the blanks.

- Once your child is familiar with the game, you can **offer choices within the game,** such as a choice between objects that your child would like to hide behind: "Pillow or blanket?" Once you have a repertoire of a few games, have your child make a choice between the games he would like to play. You can put pictures of the game choices on a board. (See Chapter 7 for more on Choice Boards.) Involve other people in the play and then let your child choose who will get hidden under the blanket: "Daddy or Adam?"

- **Change the game by doing something unexpected,** as Adam's mother does in the picture. When she gets up and runs away with the blanket over her head, she gives Dad an ideal opportunity to **comment** on her silliness and Adam repeats what his father says. Keep finding new unexpected things to do to keep those comments coming!

When Adam's mom does the unexpected, she gives him a new reason to communicate – to comment on her silliness.

- Once your child is playing the game and frequently taking turns, encourage him to **exchange roles** with you. If you have been hiding him under the blanket, try to get him to hide *you* under the blanket. When you're hiding, you won't be able to show him what to do. So if possible, involve his other parent, grandparent, sister, brother or babysitter in the play. If your child needs a cue, this third person can take on the role of "Helper," saying, "Where's Mommy?" and starting to pull the blanket off your head.

- **Help your child start the game on his own.** Leave the "hiding" blanket conveniently in sight and drop a hint, such as, "Oh, look, the hiding blanket."

- **Let your child try out his new communication skills in other games and activities.** Hide behind the curtain, look for hidden toys or wave "hi" to people at your window. Find a book that asks the same question as you did in the game, such as *Where's Spot* by E. Hill.

- **When your child knows the game well, include other family members.** Bring in a sibling or Grandma, then ask your child who should hide under the blanket, "Grandma or Annie?" Remember to explain exactly how you've been playing the game to the new person so that he or she can offer the same opportunities for your child to communicate.

Hide-and-Go-Seek

When your child is at the Early Communicator or Partner stage, he may be ready to move on from playing Peek-a-boo to playing Hide-and-Go-Seek. Like Peek-a-Boo, Hide-and-Go-Seek gives your child a chance to squeeze into tight spots or be covered with pillows and blankets. But Hide-and-Go-Seek offers your child the opportunity to take more turns.

Hide-and-Go-Seek at the Early Communicator and Partner stages

Let your child learn this game by being the one who hides first – there are fewer demands on the person who hides. Help him hide behind the sofa, under a chair or behind a curtain. Count slowly to ten and then say, "I'm coming" or "Where's (*your child's name*)?" Then find your child. Later, you and your child can switch roles, giving him the chance to be the "seeker." When you begin playing this game, you will need a third person to model your child's turns for him.

What you can expect

When it's your child's turn you can expect him to learn to do some of the following:

- hide and then seek
- start the game by counting
- tell the "hider" that he is coming (by repeating your model or using his own words)
- tell the "hider" that he's been found (e.g., "I got you" or "I found you")
- announce whose turn it is to hide and whose to seek
- complete fill-in-the-blanks with words
- answer questions with words and gestures
- ask Yes/No, "Where" and "Who" questions (at the Partner stage)
- comment

What you can do

- **Provide models of your child's turns.** For example, when you are searching for your child, use the words that he can say when it's his turn to be the "seeker" – e.g., "Where are you?" or "I see you." When your child is seeking, have a third person go with him. He can say things "as your child would if he could" – e.g., "Where's my Mommy?" and "Is Mommy in the kitchen?" This person can also hide with your child, saying something like, "You found me!" when he is discovered.

- **Give the right cues to help your child take his turns.** At first your child may need **physical help** both to remain hidden and to search for the "hider." Once your child is familiar with the game, give less explicit cues. Wait for your child to **fill in the blanks** to complete comments like "Mommy's not in the . . .," as you open the bedroom door. Ask **questions** at his level (e.g., "Do you see Mommy?" for a child at the Early Communicator stage or "Who's hiding?" for the child at the Partner stage). As your child progresses, give **hints** like "I hear Mommy" or "Mommy's not in the kitchen." Your child may also need **instructions,** such as "Start counting," or **speaking instructions** such as, "Say, 'I'm coming.'"

- As your child learns to participate in the game, **make it more complex**. **Pretend** that you can't find your child and search in different rooms, calling out "Mommy is looking in the kitchen. No (*your child's name*). Mommy is looking behind the door. No (*your child's name*)." When you finally find your child, say, "There you are" or " I see you."

- When your child is very familiar with the game, **exchange roles** so that he has a turn being the "seeker." There are more opportunities for verbal turns in this role. Encourage your child to use the same script that you used when you looked for him.

Tickles

Many young children enjoy People Games that involve some kind of touch and deep pressure, such as tickling, tapping, stroking or hugging. These kinds of games are especially appealing to children who actively seek these sensations. Firm touch or deep pressure can have a calming effect on some children. Instead of tickling your child, try giving him some firm but gentle pushes above his tummy.

It's fun to give **and** *get tickles. Get face-to-face with your child when you tickle so you can see each other's reactions.*

Hold your hands in the tickle position and, in an animated voice, say, "Tickles!" Pause so your child can take a turn and then give him tickles in a playful way, saying, "Tickle, tickle, tickle!"

Make sure that you and your child are face-to-face when you play Tickles. If your child is sitting on a chair, kneel in front of him. If he is lying on the bed, lie sideways facing each other or lean over him so that you are face-to-face.

Tickles at the Own Agenda stage

What you can expect

The Tickle Game will be short in the beginning. Your child may run away after his first tickle. But later you can expect him to do some of the following:

- look briefly at you
- reach for your hand
- smile and laugh

What you can do

- **Create excitement about the Tickle Game** by being very animated and tickling your child briefly but with gusto!

- **Repeat giving tickles**, gradually waiting longer with your hands in "tickle position" before you tickle your child again. This gives him an opportunity to smile, look at you or start to pull your hand towards him. Remember that he may do just one of those things, all of those things or even something else altogether. Perhaps he will move his body towards you or start to laugh.

- **Treat any reaction from your child as if he has asked you to tickle him.** When you find out how your child is taking his turn, you can give him cues so that he will take the same turn again. For example, if he pulled your hand down, make sure you position your hand so that he has an opportunity to pull it again.

Daddy waits for a smile and a reach before giving tickles.

Tickles at the Requester stage

What you can expect

At this stage, expect your child to ask you for tickles, probably by pulling your hand. Your child may start asking for more after he's played the game a few times, but only if you give him the opportunity by pausing and looking expectant. As your child progresses, he will play longer and take other kinds of turns.

When it is your child's turn, expect him to learn to do some of the following:

- look at you
- make a sound or gesture to ask for tickles
- smile or laugh
- guide your fingers when you count, then imitate your counting on his own fingers and finally complete the counting sequence by holding up the next finger on his own hand
- perform an action to indicate where he wants his tickle (e.g., lifting up his arm for a tickle under his arm)

What you can do

Lynsey counts on her mother's fingers before she gets tickles.

- **Add more turns to the Tickle game by counting to three,** both aloud and on your fingers, before you tickle your child. At first, you need to provide exaggerated models of finger counting. Then, **wait** a bit for your child to imitate you. If he doesn't, he may need **physical help** in raising his fingers. (If your child raises *your* fingers for you in anticipation of what you will do next, let this be his turn.) Finally, encourage him to **fill in the blanks** by raising three fingers on his own hand after you count "One, two . . . ." If your child doesn't hold up three fingers, prompt him by holding up your three fingers and repeating, "One, two . . . ." Wait for him to copy you. As soon as your child takes his turn, give him the tickles.

- **Add another opportunity for your child to tell you that he wants you to continue.** For instance, you can ask him if he wants to continue playing by saying, "More?" or "Again?" and model a head nod for "yes" or a head shake for "no." Or you can teach the hand sign for "more."

- **Give your child tickles in new places,** like on his nose, under his arms or on his legs. Exaggerate the names of his body parts before you tickle them. Then, pause before continuing the game to give your child a chance to tell you where he wants a tickle by lifting his arm or leg.

- After you've been tickling different parts of his body a while, try to **introduce a choice between two**. If you say, "Tickle *nose* or tickle *arm?*" and your child lifts his arm, you will know that he has learned the meaning of those words. He has also learned to communicate not just to request but also to respond to you.

- **Change the way your child requests.** With repeated exaggerated models, he may start to say "Ti . . ." when he pulls your hand towards him for a tickle, or make the tickle gesture or hand sign for "more."

Tickles at the Early Communicator stage

What you can expect

Your child likes to give and get tickles and can play the game for a long time.

When it is your child's turn, expect him to learn to do some of the following:
- ask for tickles consistently with gestures or words
- complete fill-in-the-blanks, such as "I want . . . (tickles)"
- answer choice questions about what kind of tickles he wants, mainly by repeating the last word he hears, and answer Yes/No questions about where he wants them (e.g., "On your nose?")
- make one or two comments
- start a tickling game with you and others

What you can do

- **Provide models of his turns and then give the right cues to help him take his turns.** Say it "as he would if he could," such as "I want tickles" or "on my leg." To help your child learn to answer questions about where he wants his tickles, provide **visual cues** and use **fill-in-the-blank** opportunities. For example, point to a body part, like his arm, and say, "Tickle on Adam's . . .," and wait for him to say, "arm." Ask questions at his level such as, "Want a little tickle or a big tickle?" or a Yes/No question such as "Want another tickle?" Limit these questions and ask them at natural spots to prevent the game from becoming a test.

- **Expand the reasons for which your child is communicating by doing the unexpected and offering choices.** If your child asks for tickles on his arm, fool him by giving him some tickles on his head. Perhaps he'll correct your mistake by telling you that's not what he wanted. And offer choices that will help your child learn new words. For example, ask, "Do you want tickles on your nose or on your shoulder?" or, "Do you want a little tickle or a big tickle?"

- **Exchange roles** so that your child has a chance to give and get tickles. Sometimes it is easier for your child to exchange roles if he has a "tickler" – a tool that he can use to tickle others, such as a feather duster. The "tickler" also acts as a visual reminder of the game.

- At this stage, **it's time for the whole family to play**. Show others how you play the game and encourage them to play with your child as often as they can. If your child has a brother or sister, make sure he or she has a chance both to give tickles and receive them. To encourage your child to start tickling another member of the family, try a hint – "Daddy needs a tickle" – plus a visual cue, such as pointing to Daddy.

- **Let your child try out his new communication skills in similar games.** Tickle him first and then together tickle all his stuffed animals or dinosaurs, naming each of them as they get a tickle.

Tickles at the Partner stage

What you can expect

At this stage, you and your child will be taking more balanced turns. Both of you take turns tickling one another, and your child can answer and ask questions about the game.

When it is your child's turn, expect him to learn to do some of the following:
- answer more questions about the game
- tell you what to do – e.g., where to tickle him, who to tickle
- use his own words – e.g., to announce who he's going to tickle
- play imaginatively and with others

What you can do

- In addition to playing the game in the same way as you would for a child at the Early Communicator stage, **try asking "wh" questions**, such as, "What kind of tickle do you want?" "Where do you want a tickle?" or "Who gets a tickle?" However, remember not to bombard your child with questions. If he can't answer a question when you ask him, ask again and provide an emphasized model of the answer. For example, if he can't answer the question, "Who gets a tickle?" say, "Who gets a tickle? *Daddy* gets a tickle." You can then re-ask the question to give your child a chance to answer on his own.

- **You can introduce imaginary play** by tickling your child's stuffed animals and pretending that they are asking for "more tickles," "big tickles" or "tickles on their heads." There are many possibilities to extend the tickle game and avoid getting stuck doing the same thing over and over. At this stage, your child may even have ideas of his own on how to play.

Chase

Running Games are favourites with children who are always on the move. Chase is a running game in which you run after your child in an effort to catch him in your arms, or your child runs after you! After your child learns the game with you, it will be easier for him to include other children and play the game at the park or at school.

Chase at the Own Agenda stage

What you can expect

In the beginning, your child probably won't take any turns, but later you can expect him to do some of the following:

- start to look back at you while he is running
- try to continue running when you catch him by pushing your hand away
- laugh, smile and look back at you when you catch him

What you can do

- **Begin the game as your child is running away from you.** Call out his name, and say "Gonna get you" and point to him. Then run after him while repeating, "Run, Run, Run!" Make it very exciting and pretend you can't catch him. Then after a few seconds, catch him by scooping him up or embracing him with a big hug, and say, "Got you!" Hold onto your child a few seconds. Then say, "Run!" before you let him start running again.

- **Repeat the game** in this way. Gradually, your child will begin to look back at you, expecting you to chase him. To help him do this, **wait a little longer** before you let him go each time you play. You're waiting for a new turn – a look from your child, for example, that means, "Let me go!"

Chase at the Requester stage

What you can expect

At this stage, your child will probably include you in his running game and understand what he has to do to get you to chase him.

When it's your child's turn you can expect him to do some of the following:

- ask you to catch him by looking back at you while he is running
- laugh while he looks at you
- look at you and push your hand away when you catch him
- make a sound after you say, "Ready, set . . . !"

What you can do

- Play the game exactly as you would for a child at the Own Agenda stage, but now don't catch your child right away. **Wait for him to take his turn** by turning around and looking at you. When you catch him, expect him to push your hand away to let you know he wants to start running again.

- When your child is familiar with the game, **add another opportunity for him to communicate** when you catch him. You can say "Ready, set, go!" before you release him and, as he becomes familiar with the turns in the game, give a partial model (i.e., "Ready, set . . ."). Wait for your child to complete the phrase with a sound or a movement.

Chase at the Early Communicator stage

At this stage, your child learns how to get you to chase him by copying your model. You can say "Run," "Get me" or "Ready, set, go!" to start the game. It doesn't matter which you choose as long as you are consistent.

What you can expect

When it's your child's turn you can expect him to learn to do some of the following:

- start the game of Chase by looking at you and saying "Run!" or "Get me!"
- repeat what you say to keep the game going
- complete a fill-in-the-blanks to keep the game going, such as "Ready, set – go!"
- comment on the game at first using your verbal models and eventually using his own words
- answer choice questions, such as "Do you want to run slow or fast?" and Yes/No questions, like "Do you want to chase Daddy?"

What you can do

- **Change the game to offer opportunities for new turns.** Start the game by saying, "Run!" "Get me!" or "Ready, set, go!" Run into different rooms in the house as you say, "Run! In the kitchen!" "Run! In the bathroom!" After you have played the game many times, you can offer your child a choice about where he wants to go: "Kitchen or bathroom?"

Or, turn the game of chase into an obstacle course. Block your child's way or put some pillows in his path. Then model a comment, like "Look! A box," "Uh oh" or something your child must say to continue the game, such as "Move!"

Benjamin's father changes the game by putting up a roadblock.

Ali's father changes the game by **becoming** the roadblock.

- **Exchange roles** with your child and let him chase *you*. Give your child a model of what he can say as the "chaser." Say, "Get Mommy!" and run away from your child. Soon he may start to say "Get Mommy!" too. If you include other people in the game, your child can learn to generalize his turn, saying "Get Daddy!" "Get Jesse!" etc.

Chase at the Partner stage

Chase for a child at the Partner stage is more elaborate than for a child at any other stage, since he can answer more kinds of questions and generate his own ideas.

What you can expect

When it is your child's turn expect him to learn to do some of the following:

- ask you to chase him
- answer your questions (e.g., "Do you want to chase me?")
- copy your models
- comment spontaneously
- ask questions

What you can do

- The game provides many opportunities for your child to communicate for reasons other than asking you to chase him or to let him go. If you **set up an obstacle course,** he can call out the names of the obstacles as you chase him around a plant, over the bed or from room to room. He may be able to suggest new things to add to your course or how the course should be run.

- If your child is ready, **include some imaginary play**. Instead of being Daddy chasing after him, you can become a character from a favourite book (e.g., the Big Bad Wolf) or a scary dinosaur. Pretend your child is a little pig or a tiny dinosaur that you want to eat for dinner. Then change roles and let your child try to catch you for *his* dinner.

Horsey Ride

In Horsey Ride your child gets on your shoulders or, if he likes the feeling of deep pressure, lies tummy-down on your back for a "ride." When you stop, his turn is to ask you to start again. Eventually, your child can tell you when to stop *and* when to go.

Horsey Ride at the Own Agenda stage

What you can expect

Just as in all the games, the turns your child takes will change as he plays the game over and over. Initially, he may get off his "horse" right away, but later you can expect him to do some of the following:
- laugh or smile during the ride
- move his body when the "horsey" stops
- make a sound when the "horsey" stops

What you can do

- **Create anticipation at the beginning** by getting down on all fours and saying "Horsey!" with excitement. If you neigh, you'll probably get his attention.

- At first, simply **let your child enjoy the ride.** Repeat the game, saying "Go, go, go" as you move forward, and then "Stop." Gradually increase the time that you wait so that your child can indicate he wants you to "go." If your child doesn't do anything, try moving your body a little bit forward and then stop.

Horsey Ride at the Requester stage

What you can expect

When it's your child's turn you can expect him to learn to do some of the following:
- laugh or smile during the ride
- move his body when "horsey" stops
- tap the "horsey" to make it go
- say something that sounds like "Go" when the "horsey" stops

What you can do

- Play the game in the same way as you do with a child at the Own Agenda stage, except **wait a bit longer** for your child to take his turn when the "horsey" stops.

Horsey Ride at the Early Communicator stage

What you can expect

When it's your child's turn you can expect him to learn to do some of the following:
- tell you to "Go" and "Stop," first by repeating what you say and then on his own
- make a choice (e.g., "Slow or fast")
- start the game by saying "horsey" or pushing you into "horsey" position
- comment on something new
- answer a Yes/No question, like "Do you want another ride?"

What you can do

- **Provide verbal models** of "Go!" and "Stop." Try giving models that will make it easier for your child to **fill in the blanks,** e.g., "Daddy – go! Daddy – stop!"

- **Expand the game** by making the "horsey" go faster and slower, and go from room to room. Then offer your child choices, such as "Do you want to go slow or fast?" or "Kitchen or bedroom?" Or, put obstacles in the horsey's way to encourage your child to comment on the new situation (e.g., "Uh oh!" or "Look! A fence.") or to tell you how to proceed (e.g., "Jump!").

Horsey Ride at the Partner stage

What you can expect

When it's your child's turn you can expect him to learn to do some of the following:
- answer questions about the game (e.g., "Where do you want to ride?")
- tell you what to do (e.g., "Go faster, Daddy" or "Whoa! Slow down, horsey!")
- share his own ideas by commenting (e.g., "Nice horsey" or "Silly horsey")

What you can do

The standard Horsey Ride becomes a more elaborate game at this stage. You can introduce **imaginary play** into the game. Your child may enjoy pretending he is riding his horse to school or that his horse is thirsty and needs a drink. Remember that your models and comments will help your child think up new ideas just as much, if not more so, than would asking lots of questions. For example, if you say "This horsey is so tired," your child may say, "Sleep horsey." However, if you say "What should the horsey do?" the game could possibly end quickly if your child can't find an answer.

Up-and-Down

In Up-and-Down games, you toss your child in the air, raise him up on your knees or give him a ride on your legs and then bring him down again. As you will see, there are many variations of Up-and-Down. If your child enjoys motion, he will probably enjoy at least one of these games.

Up-and-Down at the Own Agenda stage

What you can expect

At this stage, your child may not take any turns. At first he may run away after one toss up and down. Later you can expect him to do the following:

- look at you when you toss him up in the air
- look at you when you put him down
- reach up to ask for more

What you can do

- **Get your child's attention** and then begin the game. Hold out your arms when you know that your child is looking at you and say, "Up?" Pick up your child and then toss him above your head, saying, "Up!" Place him back on the ground and put your arms out towards him, asking, "Up?" Even if he doesn't respond, pick him up, saying, "Up," and continue to play the game the same way. Don't wait too long at first because your child won't yet know what to do.

- Each time you play the game, **wait longer** before you pick up your child. Cue your child to reach or look at you by extending your arms to him.

Up-and-Down at the Requester stage

What you can expect

When it's your child's turn you can expect him to learn to do some of the following:

- look at you and reach up
- make a sound directed at you
- look at you to get you to put him down
- count on your fingers
- imitate you by counting on his own fingers

What you can do

- At the beginning of the game, **add counting:** "One, two, three – up!" (See Tickles at the Requester stage, on page 171, for information on how to add counting to the game.) Counting prepares your child for the fun that will follow and creates opportunities for more turns. If your child does not copy your finger counting, help him by physically guiding his fingers as you say each number.

Up-and-Down at the Early Communicator stage

What you can expect

When it is your child's turn, expect him to learn to do some of the following:

- look at you and ask to go "up" with a word
- look at you and ask to go "down" with a word
- copy the finger counting and repeat the numbers to keep the game going
- complete several fill-in-the-blanks when counting

What you can do

- If your child is starting to echo, **help him take his turn verbally by encouraging him to fill-in-the-blanks** after you count, "One, two, ..." Let him know that you expect him to take a turn by **slowing down** before you count "three," and waiting to give him an opportunity to say the word. Later, when your child knows the game well, he may take several turns, filling in the blanks for each number. Also include some carrier phrases like "I want . . . " in the game. Gradually, say less so your child can complete the phrase on his own.

- **Add new actions to the game so your child can take new turns.** Give your child a spin instead of a toss. Then you can offer a choice within the game: "Up or a spin?"

- **Do the unexpected.** When your child tells you that he wants to go down, leave him in the air or put him down in a new place, such as on the bed or the couch.

Up-and-Down at the Partner stage

What you can do

- Adapt the game so that your child has many opportunities to take verbal turns. For example, you can lower him to the ground very slowly a few times and then do it quickly, modelling the words that describe what you are doing. Then offer your child the choice, "Do you want to go slow or fast?" You can lift your child high above your head and then ask, "Do you want to go very high or not too high?"

- Introduce imaginary play by pretending that your child is a flying bird or an airplane. Model the sounds that birds and planes make as well as words that your child can use in imaginary play, such as, "Plane's coming down. Oh no! A crash!"

Other People Games for all stages

Horsey! Up and Down

This is exactly the same game as "Up-and-Down" except that your child gets on your back for his up-and-down ride.

Ring-Around-a-Rosy

Ring-Around-a-Rosy is a chant that provides opportunities for your child to learn and practise the words "up" and "down."

The words to the chant are:

    Ring-Around-a-Rosy

    A pocketful of posie

    Husha, husha, we all fall (*pause*) down.

You can change the words to something simpler:

    Round and round and round and round

    We all fall down!

    Then, Let's get up!

Head stands

If your child likes to put his head down and his bottom up, turn this into a People Game. When he puts his head down on the couch, try lifting his legs. Say "up" when you lift them and "down" as you lower them.

Up-and-Over (Flips)

Invite your child to play Up-and-Over by extending your arms and saying the game's name. Hold your child's hands as he stands opposite you. Then help your child climb up your legs, finally flipping him over.

One, Two, Three – Swing!

Play One, Two, Three – Swing! the same way as you play Up-and-Down, except instead of tossing your child over your head, swing him around by his arms saying, "One, two, three – (*pause*) swing!" (or "go" or "whee!"). If you are already saying, "One, two, three" in other games, try another repetitive phrase, such as "Ready, set – swing!" or make one up using your child's name – e.g., "Adam's going up, up, up" and "Adam's going down, down, down!"

You can try this game on a real swing. Some children become very interactive and attentive when they are in swings. (See Chapter 11, page 395 for how to use swings in People Games.)

Your child may enjoy flips!

You can play People Games on swings if you provide an opportunity for your child to do or say something before giving him a push.

One, Two, Three – Swing! between two people

One, Two, Three – Swing! is fun to play when your child walks between you and another big person. Hold your child's hands, and lift him into the air as you say, "One, two, three – (*pause*) swing! or "One, two three – up!" Again, if you are counting in other games, change "One, two, three – up" to something new: "It's time to – swing" or "Here we go – up!"

Tug of War (One, Two, Three – Pull!)

If your child likes to hold onto things, a game of tug of war not only satisfies this need but also helps him to interact and communicate. To play, you each hold an end of a towel or a blanket, depending on which your child prefers. Say, "One, two, three – (*pause*) pull!" and then pull the material gently but firmly.

One, Two, Three – Jump!

One, Two, Three – Jump! is played the same as way as Up-and-Down. But instead of tossing your child above your head, take your child's hand and jump up and down together, saying, "One, two, three – jump!" If your child likes jumping, you may want to get a mini-trampoline, which can be found in sporting goods stores. If your child uses the trampoline, make sure that you interrupt his jumping so that he has an opportunity to request more.

The Big Ball game

A ball that is big enough for your child to sit on is ideal for playing People Games. Your child can sit on the ball, lie across it on his tummy or kneel on it while you support him. Bounce the ball gently and say, "Ready, set – go!" "One, two, three – bounce" or "Bouncey, bouncey on the – ball!" Provide opportunities for your child to take the turns appropriate for his stage of communication.

Pillow Mountain

This game provides a variety of stimulation – running, jumping and the feeling of pressure on the body.

Together with your child, build a mountain out of pillows by piling pillows one on top of the other. As you build, count each pillow, holding your fingers up to indicate each number. Then say, "Let's jump!" and help your child jump into the pillows. You can also help your child take a running start. There are several places you can interrupt the action to give your child a turn as soon as he knows the game. If he's at the **Requester** stage, his turns can be to help build the "mountain" and then jump; if he's at the **Early Communicator** stage, he can fill in a blank after you say, "Ready, set, . . . !" A child at the **Partner** stage can be encouraged to tell you how high to make the mountain and whose turn it is to jump first.

Games to help your child understand simple commands

Children at the **Own Agenda** or **Requester** stages of communication are just learning to understand what you say. You can help your child learn to respond to some basic one-step commands by making games out of everyday directions. If you have a positive attitude to teaching, these games can become just as much fun as the other ones that we looked at. Play the games using the Helper's Rule: "Ask once and wait. Then ask again, adding help."

Come Here game

Begin the game as your child is running away from you. When he is not too far away, call out his name and say, "(*Your child's name*), come here!" To help your child respond, have another adult guide your child to you. Later on, your child can run back-and-forth between you and the other person. If you need to motivate your child to come to you, let him see that you are holding a treat or a favourite toy. As soon as your child comes to you, praise him, hug him, give him a toss in the air or give him the treat or toy.

Fade out the physical help and the treat as soon as you can. Then try calling your child when he is farther away from you.

Use other opportunities during the day to practise his response to "come here." For example, when lunch is ready, call his name and say, "Come here," even if you usually go and get him or bring his lunch to him.

Silly Sit Down

In this game, you teach your child to sit down and then turn this action into a game. To start, bring your child to a soft chair, a swivel chair or sofa and ask him to sit down. If he doesn't respond, ask again and then help him sit down. When he does, cheer for him, bounce him on the cushion, or spin him around if the chair swivels. Do this several times during the day, gradually reducing the amount of help you give your child.

Once your child learns to sit down after you tell him, you can make the game a lot more fun. Join in with your child when you play. For example, say, "Sit down" and then race your child to a chair, sit down together in many different places or let your child sit on top of you. By turning sitting down into a game, your child can enjoy learning to follow an important direction while having fun. And if you introduce "sit down" naturally into his day, such as asking him to "sit down" for lunch or "sit down" to watch TV, he'll start to generalize his new learning.

Summary

At the beginning of this chapter we said that "everything your child needs to know about communication can be learned in a People Game." In a People Game, just as in a conversation, your child must stay on topic, take his turn and respond to the person he is playing with. To help your child communicate, structure your People Games using the R.O.C.K. guidelines. Repeat what you do and say each time you play; play the games often; give your child the opportunity to show you the turns he can take; and cue him to take those turns, when possible using natural cues that don't interrupt the flow of the game. Most important of all – keep the games fun!

Not all children learn to talk in People Games. However, they do learn a lot about the back-and-forth nature of interaction. Best of all, your child won't even realize that he is doing more than simply having a good time with his favourite person – you.

Help Your Child Understand What You Say

For your child to understand the connection between words and the real world, he must first understand what's happening around him. But understanding the world isn't always easy for your child. Because processing information can be difficult for him, you and he may develop different impressions of a situation. For example, if your child lines up his toys because he likes to look at the pattern formed, his understanding of what "playing with toys" means is probably different from yours.

Even when your child does understand the situation, he may not understand the words that go along with it.

Raphael seems to understand the meaning of "go into school."

In another situation, the words "go into" don't mean anything to Raphael.

It looked like Raphael understood what his mother said when the car pulled into the school parking lot, but it's more likely that Raphael knew what to do because he had done it many times before. By building repetition and predictability into his life, Raphael's parents have helped him make sense of the situation. Now, they must help him make sense of the *words* in the situation, too.

In this chapter you will learn how you can increase your child's comprehension of what people do *and* say by adjusting how you talk to him.

This man speaks to the tourists quickly, using long sentences. They are having difficulty understanding him.

Imagine you are a tourist lost in a foreign country and you ask someone for directions. If this person answers in his own language, you probably won't understand him. But as soon as he sees that you have no idea what he's talking about, he may automatically make some adjustments to what he says. He may help you understand his directions by **saying less** – replacing his long, complex sentences with short, simple ones – and by **stressing** only the key words you need to understand. He can also **slow** down his rate of talking, **show** you the route on a map, and **point** you in the right direction. If you still don't understand, he can **repeat** the important words and gestures over and over until you do. After all this, you can find your way and even learn to say a word or two in a new language!

Now, the man changes the way he talks to the tourists. He helps them understand his directions by saying less, repeating and emphasizing a few key words, slowing down his speech, and showing the tourists the way by pointing and using the map.

Your child may experience the same frustrations as someone trying to understand a foreign language. In Chapter 1, we discussed how most children with language delays have difficulty "taking in" what they hear. This means that they have difficulty:

- understanding what you say
- listening to you when there are other sights and sounds
- organizing what they hear

*Jeremy doesn't understand
what his mother says.*

Jeremy, you need to put those things away now so that we can eat lunch.

Even when your child knows the meaning of a particular word in one situation, he may not understand what it means in another context. This is because your child tends to associate a single meaning with a particular word.

Jenny, go get on your coat.

*Jenny has learned that "on" means
"on top of." Now she thinks that
"on" has only one meaning.*

Say Less and Stress, Go Slow and Show!

To help your child understand what you say, you can make the same kind of adjustments that you would for someone who is learning a new language.

Jeremy's mother makes the same adjustments to what she says as we do for anyone learning to speak a new language. She doesn't use a lot of words to tell Jeremy what to do. Instead of saying, "Put everything in here," she uses specific names ("toys" and "in the box"). When she repeats and stresses these important words several times, while showing him the toys and the box, Jeremy finally gets the message.

To help remember how to adjust what you say to make it easier for your child to understand, use the following rhyme:

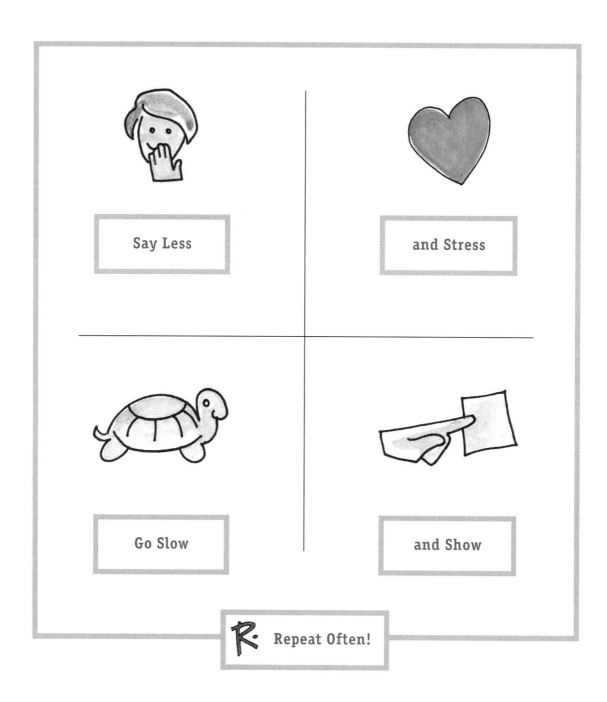

Say Less

- Simplify what you say
- Use short, clear labels and sentences

Simplify what you say

"Saying less" means that you talk to your child at his level of understanding, which depends on his stage of communication. Give all instructions in clear, simple words. Most often you need to give a visual cue along with the instructions. For example, when it's your child's bedtime, say "Time for bed" and show him his pajamas.

Use short, clear labels and sentences

As a general rule, use short, clear labels or sentences that give your child the most essential information. If he is just starting to understand speech, use single words to label the objects, people and actions that he shows an interest in. Try not to delay before labelling. If you say "Juice" after your child's attention has shifted to something else, your word loses its meaning. For children with better comprehension, speak in sentences, but never use ones that are long, complex or ambiguous.

Christopher can't understand what his father says.

When his father uses a simple sentence and shows Christopher what he is talking about, Christopher figures out exactly what to do.

Stress

- Exaggerate key words
- Put key words at the ends of your sentences
- Use FUN words

Exaggerate key words

By stressing key words, you catch your child's attention and make the important words stand out. To stress certain words, say them in a louder voice or using an exaggerated tone. Emphasize the words in the way that seems most natural.

Each child reacts differently to high levels of animation. A more passive child who seems to "tune you out" usually responds better to a louder, animated voice. However, there are also passive children who will withdraw or become distressed if you use too forceful a voice. You'll know what is best for your child by his reaction to what you do.

Put key words at the ends of your sentences

Because your child remembers the last thing he hears, putting important or key words at the ends of your sentences draws his attention to these words and makes them easier to recall. By making your child notice important words, you can then help him understand them too.

Once your child *understands* the key words, it is no longer necessary to place them at the ends of sentences. You want your child to understand the meanings of words no matter where they fall in a sentence. For more on word order, see Chapter 2, page 82.

Go Slow

- Pause between words and phrases
- Be natural

Pause between words and phrases

If you pause between words or phrases, you give your child time both to process the things that he hears and to come up with a response. To make sure that your child can make sense of what you say, first say the whole sentence as you normally would, and then repeat the same sentence with pauses that make key words stand out. You can do this by using **buildups** and **breakdowns**, which are discussed later in this chapter.

Be natural

Try to speak as naturally as possible to help your child understand the meaning of what you say. You want to avoid losing the natural rhythms and intonations that help your child understand speech. If you speak too slowly or separate words that work as a unit, such as "Come here," "Thank you," or "I want," your child may find you more difficult to understand, not easier. And if you sound too robot-like, your child may sound the same way when he eventually copies your model.

Show

- Show with real objects
- Show with actions and gestures
- Show with pictures
- Show with the printed word

Since your child learns best when he can see what you're talking about, combining what you say with **visual cues** – real objects, actions, gestures, pictures or the printed word – increases your child's ability to make sense of your words. These visual cues stay in his sight long after the spoken word is gone. (See Chapter 7 for more on visual cues.)

Show with real objects

At first, your child may need to see real objects to make the connection between words and things. For example, when you tell him that it's time to go in the car, show him your car keys. When it's time to go to bed, show him his pajamas.

Show with actions and gestures

If your child doesn't understand your words, then actions and gestures will show him exactly what you mean. For example, when you ask your child if he wants something to drink, pretend you are holding a glass in one hand. Then, bring your hand to your mouth as if you were actually drinking. You can also help your child make sense of his world by pointing to objects, people or places when you talk about them. Your meaning will be clearer if you use gestures, such as nodding your head up and down for "yes" and shaking it from side to side for "no," as well as by exaggerating your facial expressions, particularly smiles and frowns. Your child will notice the looks on your face best if you and he are face-to-face.

Just say "no" – and show it too!

Show with pictures

Pictures can help your child understand what you are talking about when the real things aren't available. For example, a picture of juice on the refrigerator door tells your child what's inside. Pictures can also show your child what he will be doing during his day. They can even show him how he should behave in certain situations.

Show with the printed word

Some children are interested in the printed word at an early age. Reading gives your child a new way to get information, and eventually the printed word can also help him express himself. Even if your child can't read yet, present printed words along with pictures so that your child can begin to make the connection between the two.

If your child sees names printed over pictures in a family album, he may start to recognize the names and "read" them.

 ## Repeat Often

Give your child a chance to hear new words used as often as possible and in many different situations throughout the day. For example, if your child has learned to understand "up" in a People Game, try to use that word at other times, as in "Let's go *up*" when you're climbing stairs, or in a song that includes the word, such as "A Little Bit *Up*." (See Chapter 9, page 316 for the words to this song.)

The next section describes how to adapt the guidelines – **Say Less and Stress, Go Slow and Show!** – for your child's stage of communication.

How to adjust what you say at the Own Agenda and Requester stages

Say Less

- Label objects, people, actions and events
- Use the specific names of people, objects and actions
- Use your child's name when you talk to him

Stress

- Use FUN words

Go Slow

- Pause between words
- Be natural

Show

- Show with real objects
- Show with actions, gestures and exaggerated facial expressions
- Show with pictures

Label objects, people, actions and events

Label what your child looks at or does with one or two simple words. Labelling not only helps him make the connection between words and things, but also gives him verbal models that he can eventually use. When you label, make sure you don't leave out extra words like "a" and "the." These words help your child understand that an important word comes next.

Instead of giving Carl the name of what he's looking at (pizza), Carl's mother talks about the juice. This is confusing for him.

When Carl's mother talks about what he's interested in, she helps him understand what "pizza" means.

Use the specific names of people, objects and actions

Avoid words like "it," "s/he," "this" and "there" because they are imprecise. Instead, call things that your child shows an interest in by their proper names. The words "cookie," "books" and "Joanne" give your child more information than the words "it," "them" and "she."

Rebecca's mother speaks to her using as few words as possible, emphasizing the word "open" because it describes what Rebecca is interested in.

Use your child's name when you talk to him

The word "you" can be confusing for your child to understand because it refers to many different people. Calling your child by his proper name avoids confusing him and also helps him learn his name. Instead of saying, "Mommy loves you," say "Mommy loves Matthew."

Use FUN words

FUN words, like the animal sounds "Moo" and "Meow," and the frequently used "OK,"are very appealing to all children. Most FUN words are easy to remember and understand because they are associated with specific objects, actions and intonation patterns. FUN words are even easier to understand if you exaggerate what you say *and* do. For example, if you say "Whee!" and bring your hand down as if it were sliding every time your child goes down a slide, he may soon associate the FUN word "Whee!" with going down the slide.

Here are some other FUN words and associated actions that your child may like:

- **bye, bye!** (wave)
- **uh oh!** or **oops!** (bring hand to head)
- **ouch!** (exaggerate a pained look on your face; rub the part of the body that you or your child hurt)
- **yucky!** (exaggerate a disgusted look on your face)
- **yummy!** (rub your tummy)
- **whee!** (sweep your hand down as if it were going down a slide)

FUN words like "uh oh" are fun to listen to, easy to understand and easy to repeat.

Sometimes quickly repeating the same word over and over in an excited way can catch your child's attention. It is much more fun for your child if you say "Run! Run! Run!" or "Up! Up! Up!" with lots of animation in your voice than if you say the same words only once. Repeat these words in rapid succession to emphasize them and motivate your child.

Kelsi's father creates enthusiasm by rapidly repeating "up" over and over.

Show with real objects

As you say the names of things that are important to your child, show him the real objects that match the words. For example, hold up his book as you say "book," or hold up your child's pajamas as you say "pajamas." If your child is a hands-on learner, let him touch and hold the object. Eventually, you can stop showing him the objects and wait to see if he understands what you say without the visual cue. When he no longer needs to see the object in order to understand, you can use speech by itself.

Corey's mother shows him the book to help him understand what she's saying.

Show with actions, gestures and exaggerated facial expressions

Add actions, gestures and exaggerated facial expressions to your words to show your child what you mean. Actions and gestures include acting out the meaning of the words, using hand signs and pointing to things. Keep your actions big and obvious so that your child notices what you are doing. Be face-to-face when you perform actions so that he can see you. Some signs and gestures that are helpful for your child's understanding at this stage are illustrated below.

Yes and No
Exaggerated head-nods up and down for "yes" and headshakes from side to side for "no."

Finished
Slide one hand over upturned palm of the other hand.

Hi and Bye
Wave hand

Come (to me)
Hand wave inward (beckoning)

Up
Point index finger up

Down
Point index finger down

Point to places and objects that catch your child's attention to help him match your words to real things. You can also place your child's hand on what he's looking at to guarantee that he sees what you're talking about. This technique usually works best if you follow his interests, rather than making him follow yours.

In addition to pointing to things you talk about, pointing to your mouth can help your child understand more about speech. Pointing to your mouth and exaggerating the way you make some sounds draws your child's attention to the way you speak so he can see how to do it himself.

Show with pictures

Take some photographs of your child's favourite foods, toys and people and show these photos to your child when you talk about these things. If he likes videos, show him the picture on the video case and say the name of the video before you play it in the VCR. In this way, your child will start to understand that pictures can stand for things and that the thing and the picture have the same name.

When her mother shows her a picture of juice, Madeline starts to understand what's inside the fridge.

How to adjust what you say at the Early Communicator stage

Say Less

- Use grammatically correct English in simple sentences
- Label objects, people, actions and events
- Say the names of people after you use pronouns

Stress

- Use buildups and breakdowns
- Use FUN words

Go Slow

- Talk to your child in two ways:
  - one way to help him understand
  - one way to help him talk

Show

- Show with objects, gestures and pictures

Use grammatically correct English in simple sentences

Leaving in articles like "a" and "the" allows your child to hear the natural rhythms of speech, helping to convey the meaning of sentences. For example, when you talk to your child say, "You're a funny boy!" rather than "You're funny boy!"

Label objects, people, actions and events

Labelling what your child looks at or does helps him make the connection between words and things and provides a verbal model that he can eventually use himself.

Say the names of people after you use pronouns

Pronouns, especially the words "I," "me" and "you," can be tricky. Your child may repeat these pronouns just as he hears them without understanding what they mean. You may have noticed that when he asks for a drink, he may say, "You want a drink" instead of "I want a drink."

We have looked at how giving your child a model from his point of view, or saying it "as he would if he could," helps him learn what pronouns to use. But he also needs help understanding what the pronouns *mean*. To help clear up the meaning of words like "I," "me" and "you," use the correct pronoun and then add your child's name or the name of the person to whom you are talking. For example, say, "*You*, Adam, are going to school." To avoid confusion between providing a model of what your child should say and clarifying the meaning of pronouns, try choosing a special time to work on helping him *understand* these specific words. Mealtime is ideal because your child has the benefit of seeing how you use pronouns when you speak to other family members.

Jerry's parents help him understand what "you" and "I" mean by using names after they use pronouns.

Use buildups and breakdowns

Remember that your child is a "gestalt learner" (see Chapter 1, page 15). This means that he may understand a whole sentence as a unit, but not the individual words. Two techniques – called buildups and breakdowns – can help your child understand what each word in a sentence means and how the words fit together.

- **In a buildup, start by saying each part of the sentence and then "build up" the parts into the complete sentence.** For example: "Hat *(point to hat)*. Put on *(gesture)*. Put on the hat." Buildups help your child understand each word in the sentence. They also show a child who is using only single words how he can put two words together, or a child who is using two words how he can put three words together.

To help your child understand each word, start with one word and then build those words up into a short sentence.

- **A breakdown starts with the whole sentence and then breaks it down into its parts.** For example: "Take your spoon and eat the cereal. Take spoon. Spoon (*point to spoon*). Eat cereal (*point to cereal bowl*). Cereal (*gesture or point to bowl*)." Most of the time, you use a combination of buildups and breakdowns.

Danny's mother starts by saying the whole sentence and then breaks it down into smaller parts, pointing to what she is talking about. Then, she builds the last part of the sentence up again ("Eat the cereal").

Talk to your child in two ways

You should always say things "as your child would if he could" when he is motivated to talk but doesn't have the right words. But what about all the other times when you don't expect your child to say anything? Then you need to talk in a second way – to help him understand what the words mean. When helping your child understand what you say, use comments and labels that give him information, but not ones that you necessarily expect him to repeat.

Justin's mother helps him understand that things have names.

Now, Justin's mother is helping him ask for juice by emphasizing the words that Justin can use to request.

Show with objects, gestures and pictures

As your child develops, you can use more and more visual cues to help him understand his world. Pictures – either photographs, line drawings or even picture symbols– can help you explain what you are saying when the real things aren't in sight. Pictures can also explain the events in your child's day and the way people feel (see Chapter 7).

Pointing can also focus your child's attention on what you're saying. Besides pointing to objects and people close to your child, try pointing to objects, people and events that may be some distance away. While pointing is most effective when you follow your child's lead, at this stage you can also begin to point to things your child may not have noticed on his own.

How to adjust what you say at the Partner stage

- Talk to your child in two ways:
  - one way to help him understand
  - one way to help him talk
- Use buildups and breakdowns
- Repeat what your child says, correcting any mistakes
- Offer your own comments and ideas
- Show with Picture Schedules, Choice Boards and Personal Stories

Talk to your child in two ways:

- **Talk to your child to help him understand.** A child at the Partner stage understands many kinds of words in a variety of sentences. Unless he has a great deal of difficulty with the actual production of speech, he talks and can have short conversations. However, these conversations can break down when he doesn't understand you.

  If your child doesn't understand what you say, think of an easier way to send your message or to ask your question. Remember how Jerry's father helped him understand what the girl in the park said.

Jerry's father helps him understand what the girl says by simplifying it.

Christopher doesn't understand what his father means . . .

. . . so his father says exactly what he means in a way that Christopher can understand – by being clear and specific.

- **Talk to your child to help him talk.** Remember that even Partners still frequently rely on your verbal models to express themselves. When your child can't find the right words or makes mistakes, you need to help him by saying the words from his point of view – by saying it "as he would if he could!"

Use buildups and breakdowns

While he can understand longer sentences, your child still may use whole chunks that he has memorized without knowing the meaning of the words. So, you need to break sentences down and then build them up again to show him how the words go together. (See buildups and breakdowns at the Early Communicator stage for a more detailed explanation.)

As your child progresses, use buildups and breakdowns to help him understand more abstract words as well: connecting words (e.g., "because"), prepositions (e.g., "after") and some question words (e.g., "how?" and "why?").

Brian's father uses a buildup to help him understand "because."

Brian's father tells him what to do ("Put on your jacket"). Then he tells him why he should do it ("It's cold outside"). Finally, he shows him how the word "because" links the two sentences together.

Show with Picture Schedules, Choice Boards and Personal Stories

Your child can benefit from all kinds of visual cues, like Picture Schedules, Choice Boards and Personal Stories, which are explained in Chapter 7. Picture Schedules and Choice Boards are both tools that you can make with pictures and paste that will help your child understand what he can do during the day and within activities. Pictures can also make abstract concepts, like the past, the future and human emotions, more concrete for your child, while Personal Stories can help him understand what's happening in confusing situations.

Summary

Most children with ASD have difficulties understanding what people say. You can help your child make sense of words by adjusting the way you talk. Say less when you talk to him. Speak to him in short sentences that describe what's happening around him. Make the words that you want him to understand (and eventually say) stand out by slowing down before you say them and exaggerating them. Finally, use your child's strength – his interest in all things visual – to help him understand and organize events and people, both what they say and what they do.

Use Visual Helpers

7

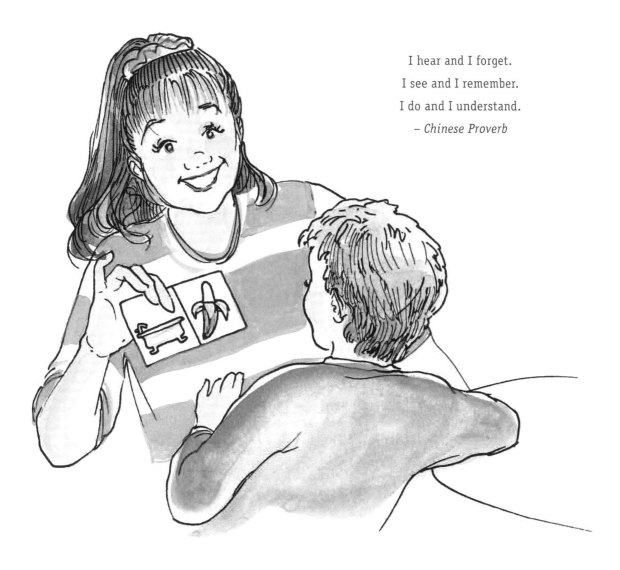

I hear and I forget.
I see and I remember.
I do and I understand.
– *Chinese Proverb*

Albert has no idea what his mother is saying . . .

. . . until she shows him a picture of what she's talking about.

Most children with ASD are visual learners – they learn best by looking. Most visual learners enjoy toys like puzzles and shape sorters because they can *see* how to use them. They like to watch videos and television shows, especially cartoons or Wheel of Fortune. Some visual learners are also fascinated by letters and numbers and may surprise you by reading a few words they haven't been taught.

Why do some children learn better visually? When you say a word it is over in a millisecond – too soon for a child who has difficulty processing speech. So your child concentrates on the things that he *can* understand – things he can see. Unlike the spoken word, things that your child looks at, such as objects, photographs, pictures, line drawings and printed words, last for a long time. When your child looks at a picture, he continues to receive the information presented in it for as long as he looks at it.

Most of us use "Visual Helpers" all the time: for example, an arrow on a street sign tells us which direction to drive, a calendar helps us plan our week and referring to notes on cue cards makes giving a speech a lot easier. We all use these sorts of visual aids to enhance our understanding of the world, and to help organize information and express ourselves. Your child can also benefit from information that is presented in a visual way.

In this chapter you will find out how you can take advantage of your child's strength as a visual learner. First, we will look at how you can create special aids, called "Visual Helpers," using the things your child sees – objects, pictures and the printed word. These Visual Helpers will help your child understand what is going on around him and express himself. In the second part of the chapter, you will learn how you and your child can use Visual Helpers at each stage of communication. Many of the ideas are adapted from Linda Hodgdon's excellent book, *Visual Strategies for Improving Communication*. (See references p. 422)

How to create Visual Helpers

You can make Visual Helpers, like Choice Boards, Picture Schedules, Self-Help Boards or Communication Books, using real objects, colour photographs, coloured or black and white line drawings and the printed word. Some of these things will work better for your child than others. When making your Visual Helpers, you'll need to consider your child's preferences and his ability to understand different types of pictures, but finding out which ones work best will also take some experimenting. Here are the kinds of things you can use to make Visual Helpers listed in order from easiest to hardest to understand.

If your child is not ready for pictures, use real objects as Visual Helpers.

Real objects

Often children at the Own Agenda and Requester stages do not understand pictures or photographs, and are not interested in looking at books or photo albums. If this is true for your child, then Visual Helpers made from pictures and photographs may not be too helpful. Your child will benefit more from seeing the real objects themselves. For example, if you want to tell your child that he's about to get a drink, showing him a picture of a glass of juice may not mean anything to him. But, if you hold up an empty cup, he may realize what you are trying to say. Sometimes the real object may not be available or it may be too big to use. When this happens, you can try to find a toy or an object that looks like the real thing or that can represent the real thing. For example, you can use a toy swing to stand for the park. Be aware, however, that some children find toys confusing and will actually understand pictures better.

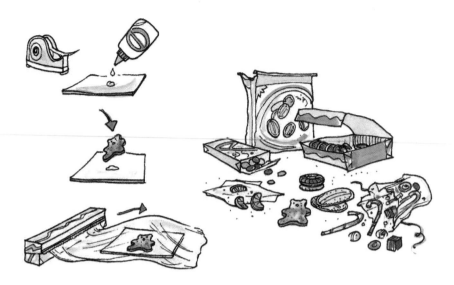

To help your child make the transition to understanding pictures, try attaching a real object to a piece of cardboard and covering it with transparent plastic wrap.

Colour photographs

Many young children with ASD enjoy looking at colour photographs. They look at pictures of real people in the family photo album or examine the animals and objects on the packaging of toys or on cereal boxes. If photographs hold your child's attention, he will benefit from Visual Helpers made with realistic photographs. You can buy pictures of familiar foods or objects at some children's bookstores or toy stores. Or, get out your camera and take pictures of the things and people that are important to your child! If you decide to take your own photos, zoom in on what you want your child to focus on so that the photograph doesn't have any unnecessary information. For example, if you want a Visual Helper of a specific toy, take a picture of only that toy, rather than one of your child playing with the toy. For children who are just starting to get interested in photographs, use large photographs (5" X 3"). You can also cut out photographs and labels from magazines, catalogues and the packaging of toys and foods.

computer

Your child may understand photographs before he understands line drawings. To help him understand drawings, try putting one in the corner of the photo.

Line drawings

Unlike photographs, line drawings don't always look exactly like the real thing. But drawings can be easier to use because they are less costly and more readily available. In addition, drawings can be general, while a photograph is always specific. For example, if you use a photo to show your child which article of clothing to put on, he may insist on wearing the exact same T-shirt he sees in the photograph. But if you show him a drawing, he'll know that he has to put on *a* T-shirt, but he won't think about one T-shirt in particular.

You can take realistic photographs right off the packages of your child's favourite foods.

　　If your child looks at drawings in books or likes to line up his toys, he could be ready for line drawings. You can buy computer programs and books of line drawings in specialty stores and some pictures are available on the Internet. You don't have to be a great artist to draw a few simple pictures yourself! Most speech language pathologists know about or have access to a wide variety of line drawings.

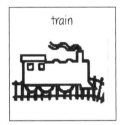

These pictures are from a commercially available book called "The Picture Communication Symbols Book" by Mayer-Johnson.

Visual Helpers can help your child understand information

Visual Helpers can help your child understand different kinds of information. They can show him:

- the choices he has
- what's going to happen
- the past and the future
- his feelings and the feelings of others
- how to do things independently
- what he needs to know about difficult situations

Visual Helpers can help your child understand the choices he has

One of the simplest Visual Helpers is the Choice Board. A Choice Board shows your child pictures of food, toys and activities that he can choose from. By giving or showing you a picture on the board, your child can make his choice.

Choice Boards can be made using objects or pictures. If you use objects, there are several ways to display them: you can put the objects in clear plastic bags with locking tops and attach them to a display board or a string, or you can place them in a divided shoebox. You may want to try putting objects in the transparent pockets of a shoebag (see picture on page 220).

If you use pictures, you can attach them to a sturdy piece of paper or cardboard. Use Velcro fasteners so that you can change the pictures when you want to offer new choices.

How many objects or pictures go on the Choice Board and how your child makes his choice will depend on his stage of communication. Until he understands how to make a choice, limit the number of choices to two. After your child is experienced at using a Choice Board, you can put the pictures of his choices in a book that he can carry with him. This way, he can make choices wherever he goes.

train

bubbles

This is a two-part Choice Board, using pictures.

I want

train

lunch

video

puzzle

By adding "I want" to the Choice Board, your child can learn how sentences are made.

The No Sign

Sometimes a choice is not available – you may have no more cookies left in your cupboard or someone ate the last banana. You can let your child see that a choice is not available by using the **No Sign**. The No Sign is a circle with a slash going through it diagonally, like the one used in No Smoking signs. You can make your own No Sign by drawing the symbol on a transparent piece of plastic or cutting it out of paper, and then placing it over the picture of the choice that is unavailable.

train   bubbles   puzzle   video

Watching a video is not a choice today!

Your child's choices are sometimes limited when it comes to his behaviour. For example, if he does something that is harmful to himself or to others, you need to show him that this action isn't an option. It's best to focus on the positive, even though you might think it would be helpful to put the **No Sign** over a picture of the unacceptable behavior. If your child can still see the picture of something like hitting, he might ignore the No Sign. So, show your child pictures of what he's supposed to do. For example, if you want him to stop hitting, show him a picture of a child with his hands down. You may also have to physically stop him from hitting. Then point to the picture of what he could do instead, such as count to ten to calm down or get a book to read.

Instead of using this picture...

...show your child another behaviour that is acceptable

Adapted from L. Hodgdon, *Visual Strategies for Improving Communication*. (Troy, MI: QuirkRoberts, 1995).

Visual Helpers can help your child understand what's going to happen

When you use words to tell your child what he's going to do during the day, he may not understand much of what you say. It must be scary not knowing what's going to happen next! But if you use a **Picture Schedule**, you can help your child better understand and anticipate the events in his life. Picture Schedules use objects or pictures to show your child what's in store. They can be very simple or longer and more detailed.

Simple Object or Picture Schedules can show:

- an object or a picture of a person or a place that represents what your child is going to do
- two objects or pictures that tell your child what he is going to do over a short period of time – e.g., "First banana. Then bubbles." This kind of schedule is called a First/Then Board. The mother on the first page of this chapter is using a First/Then Board with her son.

The first Picture Schedule is usually a First/Then board.

More detailed Picture Schedules and Self-Help Boards can show:

- four or five pictures or objects of what your child is going to do all through the day
- four or five pictures of the individual steps in an activity, such as pictures of each item of clothing your child needs to put on when he gets dressed or the series of actions he needs to perform when he washes his hands
- pictures of a few of the important events of your child's entire week

Make an Object Schedule by placing four or five objects that represent your child's daily activities in something like the transparent pockets of a shoebag.

Make a Picture Schedule by attaching pictures to a board horizontally or vertically. If your child is interested in the printed word, you may want to attach the pictures horizontally from left to right so that he can get used to the way he will eventually read. Otherwise, you need to experiment to see which presentation style your child prefers. Then, be consistent in all his Picture Schedules. For Picture Schedules that change depending on the day, attach the pictures with Velcro fasteners or tape, and for schedules that are permanent, like washing hands and brushing teeth, paste the pictures right onto the board.

This Picture Schedule shows your child his morning routine.

This Self-Help Board shows each step of getting dressed.

Another way to make a Picture Schedule is by placing pictures in pockets and attaching them to a display board.

Visual Helpers can help your child understand the past and the future

Since your child understands what he sees better than what he hears, imagine the difficulty he has when you talk about the past or the future, abstract things that are impossible to see. Visual Helpers can show your child what you mean when you talk about these abstract ideas.

Create a **"Finished" or "All Done" container** to help your child "see the past." Print "finished" or "all done" on a box, an empty container or a special pocket, like a letter envelope. To show your child that an activity is over, place objects or pictures in the box as soon as the activity is completed. If your schedule is made with pockets, simply turn the card backwards in the pocket when the activity is done. (See the discussion on how to use the "All done" container in the section on Visual Helpers for your child's stage.)

Your child can see what he's done when he puts the picture or the object of the finished activity into the "All done" container.

Keep a **Picture Diary** to help your child understand what you mean when you talk about things he's done. A Picture Diary can be a single picture or a booklet of drawings, photographs or souvenirs from places your child has been, like his preschool, homes of family members or the swimming pool where he takes lessons. By keeping a Picture Diary, you give your child a visual record of what's happened in his life, which can help him understand you when you talk about what he's done. Pictures in a Picture Diary also help your child remember what happened in the past and may remind him of something that he can share with you.

Carl's teacher sent home a picture of what Carl did at school, giving him and his mother something to talk about.

Show your child a picture to prepare him for visits to places you go to frequently. Before you leave home, show your child the picture and talk about the place he is going. For example, if you are planning to take your child to a movie, show him the movie's advertisement in the newspaper ahead of time.

If your child routinely goes to a babysitter, daycare or preschool, keeping a **Communication Book** is a good idea. In the Communication Book you and your child's other caregiver report through pictures and brief notes the things that your child does. Your child carries the book back and forth, enabling you and the other caregiver to communicate with him about what he experienced when you weren't there.

Your child's teacher can circle pictures of what your child does each day on a sheet like this.

By looking at Amanda's Communication Book, her teacher can talk about the trip Amanda took to the flower store with her father.

Visual Helpers can help your child understand his feelings and the feelings of others

We use facial expressions all the time to express our feelings. Smiling lets others know that we are happy, hanging our heads down tells them we're sad and raising our voices can mean that we're angry. However, your child may miss these clues about how you are feeling. He may not understand what you mean when you say you are "happy," "sad" or "mad." But if you show him pictures representing these emotions, your child has more time to understand what you're talking about. Label the pictures as you show them to your child so that he learns the names of different feelings. You can also write a picture story about feelings (see pages 247–248). Eventually, your child may point to or give you a picture to let you know how he feels.

Visual Helpers can show your child how to do things independently

When your child uses Visual Helpers like Self-Help Boards, he becomes less dependent on you to instruct him on how to do things like wash his hands, brush his teeth or even deal with his anger. Visual Helpers can also help your child organize his life so that he can do other things on his own. For example, you can show your child where to put his clothes, toys and books by labelling shelves, closets and cupboards with a picture and a word. By using these labels, your child will be able to put things away by himself and maybe even learn to read a word or two. (For other ideas about using the printed word, see Chapter 10, pages 355–360.)

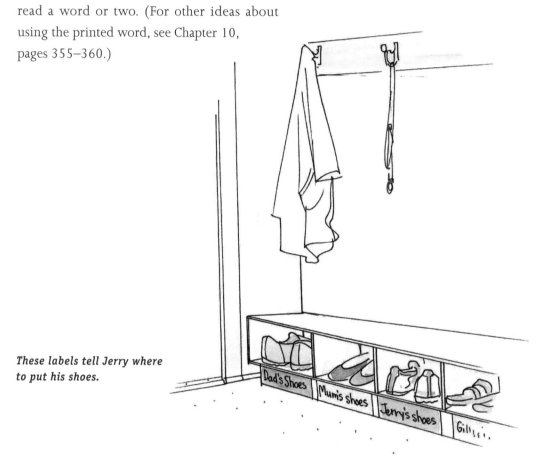

These labels tell Jerry where to put his shoes.

Visual Helpers can show your child what he needs to know about difficult situations

Once your child understands simple stories (usually at the **Early Communicator** and **Partner** stages), you can write **Personal Stories** especially for him. These stories, written from your child's point of view, help him understand what people do and say in confusing situations. In addition, the stories suggest to your child something that he can try to do in the same situation. (See page 239 to learn how to write Personal Stories.)

Visual Helpers can help your child express himself

Visual Helpers can give your child another way to communicate while speech is developing or they can remind him what to say when he is already talking. Visual Helpers:

- let him make choices
- give him another way to say something, starting with requests
- remind him what to do and say

Visual Helpers let your child make choices

A Choice Board can be used to encourage your child to initiate communication on his own. Instead of constantly asking your child what he wants, you can teach him to initiate communication by pointing to a picture on the Choice Board or getting a picture or object and then giving it to you. Once your child is interactive and verbal, the pictures and words on the Choice Board will remind him to ask you for things that he wants.

   You can also use a Choice Board to help your child respond to your questions. When you present your child with the choices on the board, you can ask him what he wants and wait for him to respond by pointing to the picture or saying the word. Depending on your child's stage, you will ask him to make choices in different ways. For example, you can give choices by showing and naming the two choices (e.g., "bread or cookie?"), asking "What do you want?" and waiting for your child to respond, or asking a Yes/No question, such as "Do you want cheese?"

Visual Helpers give your child another way to say something

It can take a long time for speech to develop. In the meantime, your child needs to learn other ways to communicate. Exchanging a picture or object for things he wants or pointing to pictures on a board are clearer ways for your child to communicate than pulling or leading. Your child also starts to understand that pictures, like words, can stand for or symbolize the real thing. Remember, Picture/Object Exchange and pointing to pictures aren't permanent alternatives to speech. In fact, they can actually *assist* in the development of speech. For those children who continue to find speech difficult, picture communication is a good introduction to alternative forms of communication.

Visual Helpers can remind your child what to say and do

Every time you use Visual Helpers, you should say exactly the same things. Because of the repetition, your child may eventually start repeating some words. Soon the pictures may simply cue your child to say words he has learned. You may even hear him talking himself through an activity as he looks at the pictures!

Picture Schedules for routines are meant to give your child independence. Eventually, you won't even be in the room when your child uses them. However, while your child is still learning to use his Picture Schedule to do the routine, you can take advantage of the opportunity to promote two-way communication. For example, once your child has put on his pants in a dressing routine, show him his Picture Schedule and let him tell you which item of clothing he needs to put on next. You can say something like, "First, put on pants. Then put on . . . ," and wait for him to fill in the blank. However, as soon as your child is able to do a part of the routine on his own, let the pictures give all the instructions.

Cue Cards provide another reminder of what your child can say. Cue Cards are just what you'd think – cards that have a picture and words or sentences that cue your child to say something. Cue Cards that have "I want," "I have" and "I see" printed on them can remind your child how to ask you for things or make a comment. Cue Cards can also give your child a whole sentence to say, such as "What did you do today?" (We'll find out more about Cue Cards when we talk about the children at the Early Communicator and Partner stages.)

Tips on using Visual Helpers

- Put Visual Helpers in the places where they will be used
- Add the printed word
- Watch what you say
- Draw your child's attention to the pictures

The picture of the swings lets your child know where he's going before he goes there.

Your child will be able to make on-the-spot choices when you put pictures of his favourite foods on the refrigerator door.

Put Visual Helpers in the places where they will be used

Visual Helpers can't help your child unless he sees them when he needs them. So put Visual Helpers where they make sense. For example, put pictures of juice or milk on the refrigerator door or pictures of toys on the outside of toy cupboards. Place the pictures at your child's eye level using tape or Velcro. For the refrigerator door, try gluing pictures onto magnets.

Add the printed word

Even if your child doesn't read yet, add the printed word by labelling pictures. This way, your child can start to see the connection between pictures and the printed word. You don't need to print everything that you say, just the important words. While there is no rule about using lower case or upper case, it makes sense to print the words in lower case letters, the way your child will see them in books.

Watch what you say

Try to say the same thing every time you talk about a picture, but don't say too much. Use clear, simple sentences.

There are some guidelines about when to talk and when not to talk: during **self-help routines**, like teeth brushing and hand washing, describe each step while your child learns the routine. Then let the pictures do most of the talking! You can still use self-help routines as an opportunity for communication, but you don't want your child to become dependent on your instructions.

When looking at the daily Picture Schedule, always talk to your child about his plans for the day or, at the end of the day, about what he's accomplished. You can talk about what other family members are doing as well. And remember that any time is a good time for conversation if your child is able to have one.

Draw your child's attention to the Visual Helpers

Don't expect your child to use Visual Helpers as soon as you put them out. You need to draw his attention to the pictures by bringing them into his line of sight and pointing to them with a steady finger as you talk about them. You can also guide his hand to touch or point to the pictures.

If you are using pictures to help your child do an activity or routine, you need to point to a specific picture *each* time he is about to do one step of the activity. For example, if he is using a bath-time schedule, point to the picture of the first step in the routine, which may be turning on the water. After you have turned on the water, direct your child's attention to the picture illustrating the second step of the routine and so on until you have completed all the steps.

The picture of the cookies is at the child's eye level, not the adult's.

This little boy's father helps him understand the bathtime routine step-by-step.

Use Visual Helpers at your child's communication stage

The following section gives suggestions on how to use Visual Helpers for children at all four stages. If your child is interested in pictures, he may be ready for some of the suggestions given for a child at a more advanced stage.

Visual Helpers for the child at the Own Agenda stage

At this stage, it is best to use real objects, realistic photographs and labels from food and toy packages. These Visual Helpers can help your child understand what you say and give him a way to express himself.

Visual Helpers can help your child understand his world

Use real objects to help your child make sense of what is about to happen

You can show your child objects, such as a juice pitcher, his pajamas or a book to help him anticipate what is going to happen. Show your child an object that he can associate with a routine or activity – the cereal box before breakfast or his rubber duckie before his bath. Sometimes you can use a specific object to represent an activity, so that every time your child sees that one object, he associates it with a specific event. For example, if you bring out the same empty cup every time you say "Juice" your child may start to connect that specific cup with getting a drink of juice. You can use different objects to represent other activities: a special spoon to indicate mealtime, a bar of soap to stand for bathtime or your car keys to let your child know that it's time to go for a drive. Eventually, he may bring you one of these objects on his own to ask you to do something.

Every time Billy's mother takes him in the car, she shows him the keys and says, "Go!" Then one day, Billy brings her the keys and says, "Go!"

Use an Object Schedule to help your child understand what's going to happen

Once your child can concentrate on objects, make an Object Schedule with four or five objects to help him understand what he's going to do at different times of the day, such as in the morning or before bed at night. Show him the object that represents the activity and tell him what's about to happen. For example, before helping your child get dressed, show him a shirt and say "Get dressed!" Let your child handle the object if he can do so without getting too distracted. He may even take the object to where the activity takes place. When he has completed the activity, help him put the object in the "All done" container and say "All done!"

Rebecca likes to take the cup from her Object Schedule to the counter where she has breakfast.

Use real objects to signal to your child what he should do next

Sometimes your child doesn't want to leave one activity for another because he doesn't know what to expect next. But if you give your child an object that he can associate with the next activity, he will be able to change from one activity to another more easily. For example, give him a ball before he goes outside or an audio casette to play in the car before leaving the park. This strategy can be very helpful in a preschool setting, where your child may not want to leave an activity because he is enjoying himself. If your child's teacher hands him something that can remind him about how much he likes another activity, like giving him a paintbrush before guiding him to the easel, he will have less trouble starting something new.

Introduce a few large photographs and labels from packages to help your child understand what choices he has

If your child is ready for pictures, use large (3" X 5" or bigger) coloured photographs or cut pictures from packages of cereal, snacks or toys. Place photos of two things that your child likes to eat on the refrigerator door or on a kitchen cupboard. Make sure that the pictures are at your child's eye level. Choose motivating things that he will want frequently during the day.

When your child approaches the place where the motivating item is kept, point to the picture and say its name. If your child is interested in the picture, try taking his hand and guiding him to touch the picture while you say the word. Then, give him the item shown in the picture.

Visual Helpers can help your child express himself

Use objects to help your child make choices

When you first start offering choices, offer something you know your child likes and something he's not interested in. Hold up the two things for your child to choose between. You may have to move around to get your child to look at the choices. He won't send a message directly to you, but he may reach or look at one thing. Treat this reach or look as if he has made a choice. Quickly, help him touch the object he chose and then give it to him.

Teach Object Exchange to help your child ask you for things by communicating directly to you

This technique is exactly like Picture Exchange, except instead of pictures, your child gives you objects in exchange for what he wants. You will need a third person to teach Object Exchange.

Here's how it works. First, make sure your child wants the item you are going to teach him to ask for. For example, after he has had a salty treat, bring out the juice because he'll probably be thirsty. Sit at a table opposite your child. Let him see the juice on the table but don't let him have it. If he continues to grab for it, hold onto it. Put the cup in front of him, extend your open hand, and have another person guide his hand to pick the cup up and give it to you. As soon as he gives you the cup, act as though he has asked you for a drink. Say it "as he would if he could": "Juice!" At the same time, give him his drink in another cup. It may take several attempts before your child gets the idea of what he's supposed to do, so don't get discouraged. Try again later in the day or the next day. When your child starts giving you the cup consistently to get the juice, put the "asking" cup where your child can see and reach it, perhaps in the transparent pocket of a hanging shoebag. Later, you can attach the object to a picture to help your child make the connection between the real thing and the picture. While Object Exchange is limited, the idea of having to give you something to get something in return helps your child see the power of communicating directly to you.

You can try to teach your child Picture Exchange at this stage, even though he probably doesn't understand the pictures. As he gets more experience giving pictures and receiving specific foods or objects in return, he will eventually start to attach meanings to individual pictures.

Aaron gives his mother a special cup to ask her for a drink.

Visual Helpers for the child at the Requester stage

At this stage, use objects and realistic pictures, such as large (3" x 5" or bigger) coloured photographs, or cut pictures from the boxes or packages of cereals, snacks or toys.

Visual Helpers can help your child understand his world

Use a First/Then Board to help your child understand what's going to happen to him (within the next hour)

At this stage you can make a First/Then Board using either objects or pictures. To make matters simpler, we'll talk about First/Then Boards using pictures. To make one, find two pictures to represent what your child is going to do in a short time span. For example, one picture might be of a toy, like a puzzle that he is going to play with, and the other might be a picture of a treat that he can have after he plays. Attach the two pictures vertically or horizontally onto a board. As you show your child the pictures, help him to touch each one as you explain to him, "First, puzzle. Then, grapes." Make the second activity on the board the best one, so that your child has something to look forward to. Pick an easy puzzle with only a few pieces or have the puzzle almost completed. Let your child take the picture (or miniature object) with him to the first activity and once he's finished playing, help him return the picture or object to the "all done" container. Then show him the picture of the grapes again, saying, "grapes." Help your child touch the picture when you say the word, and then give him his treat.

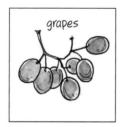

This is a First/Then Board made out of pictures. You could show your child the same thing using objects – a puzzle piece and toy grapes.

Use longer Picture Schedules when your child is ready

Once your child understands how the First/Then Board works, add one or two more pictures or objects to help him understand what he's going to do over a longer period of time. Your child may even be ready for a Picture Schedule showing him the steps of a routine, such as getting dressed or washing hands. (See Chapter 8, page 274 for more on using Picture Schedules in routines.)

Use a single picture to help your child understand where he's going

Show your child photographs of familiar people and places before you visit them. Use simple language to describe what's going to happen: "Granma's. Go Granma's."

Visual Helpers can help your child express himself

Teach your child Picture or Object Exchange to make requests

The Picture Exchange Communication System (PECS) teaches your child to ask you for things he wants, like food or a toy, by giving you a picture of something in exchange for the real thing. (Picture Exchange is learned the same way as Object Exchange. See the description of Object Exchange for a child at the Own Agenda stage on page 233.) At first, your child will need physical assistance to learn how to

If you have pictures of familiar people and places, you can prepare your child for visits.

exchange the picture for something he wants, like a raisin or a cookie. Gradually, he will learn how to exchange a few pictures without any help and without you cueing him. As soon as your child gives you the picture, make sure you say it "as he would if he could." For example, if your child gives you a picture of juice, say "Juice."

Here's another tip: when teaching Picture Exchange, ensure that your child gets a lot of practice exchanging pictures by offering the treats **bit by bit**. If your child likes raisins, exchange a raisin for a picture one by one. Break chips and cookies into smaller pieces and cut fruits, like apples and bananas, into sections. It is beyond the scope of this book to explain in detail the Picture Exchange Communication System. An experienced professional, such as a speech language pathologist, a special education teacher or a psychologist, can help you implement PECS. If your child resists Picture Exchange, try Object Exchange.

Kevin's mother physically helps him to give his father a picture before he learns to do it on his own.

Use a Choice Board to help your child respond when you ask him what he wants

Your child can use a Choice Board both to initiate and respond. When he initiates, he chooses a picture or object all on his own, and when he responds he chooses a picture or object in answer to a question. When you offer your child a choice, he may respond by reaching or touching one of the objects or pictures. If he doesn't do this on his own, guide his hand to tap the object or picture that you think he would choose and then give him his choice immediately.

Visual Helpers for the child at the Early Communicator stage

Your child is probably still very attracted to photographs, lettering on labels and large realistic coloured drawings. At this stage, if your child uses a variety of pictures, it is probably more practical to begin using drawings that are approximately 2" X 2".

Visual Helpers can help your child understand his world

Use the Choice Board to show your child what is available and what is not

As your child's ability to understand pictures increases, so does the number of choices available on the Choice Board. He's making more choices and using the board mainly to tell you what he wants, either by giving you pictures, saying a word or pointing.

Sometimes, however, a certain choice is not available. For example, you may not want your child to have the option of watching TV any time he wants. Help him understand when a choice is not available by introducing the No Sign (see page 219). Start with a choice that your child can see is unavailable. For example, if there are no more cookies, say, "No cookies" and let your child look into the empty box. Exaggerate the fact that the box is empty. Turn it over and shake it as you repeat "No cookies." Then put the No Sign over the picture of the cookies on the Choice Board, saying, "No cookies." It may take a few explanations in simple words, like "No cookies" or "No TV," before your child understands what the symbol means.

Sasha's mother lets him see that there are no more cookies in the box, so he understands that this is not a choice.

If your child has any behaviour problems, such as biting or hitting, remember to focus on the positive and use pictures that show him what an acceptable thing to do is. Describe what the pictures mean in simple short sentences and give him any physical help he needs to change his behaviour until he can do it on his own.

Visual Helpers show your child what he should do.

Use Picture Schedules and Self-Help Boards to help your child understand the events of his day and the steps in a difficult routine

If your child has no previous experience with Picture Schedules, start with a First/Then Board and use it in the same way as described for the child at the Requester stage (see page 234). It will not be long before you can add more activities to the board to show him what he's going to do all through the day.

This board shows your child what he is going to do during his whole day.

When the pictures show the steps in a difficult routine, your child may use the pictures more readily if each picture is placed at the spot where he performs the step in real life. For example, in a hand-washing routine, put the picture of the soap above the real soap, the picture of the hands getting dried above the towel and the picture of the water above the taps. As your child progresses, you can put all the pictures on a single Picture Board. Some children have no difficulty completing an action and then referring back to the board to see what the next step is. Once again, you will need to experiment to see what is right for your child.

It helps if you put the pictures where your child needs them.

Add a "finished" place to the Picture Schedule to help your child understand the past

Every time your child finishes an activity on his board, encourage him to put the picture of the completed action into a special container or envelope. Say the name of the action and "all done" or "finished" (e.g., "Bath finished"). He may need some hand-over-hand assistance to learn how to do this.

Use Visual Helpers to show your child what he needs to know about difficult situations

Write short **Personal Stories** for your child. These stories are written especially for your child to help him learn what to say and do in different situations. If you follow these guidelines, you can write Personal Stories for just about anything you want to help your child understand or do.

> ## Guide for writing Personal Stories*
>
> 1. Identify who and what the story is about.
>
> 2. Write from your child's point of view.
>
> 3. Describe what people do and/or say in the situation.
>
> 4. Give your child something to try to do and/or say in the situation.

Here is an example of a Personal Story that tells an Early Communicator what happens when a visitor comes to his house.

What I Can Do When a Visitor Comes

---

* adapted from C. Gray. "Teaching Children with Autism to 'Read' Social Situations." In *Teaching Children with Autism*, edited by K. Quill (Albany: Delmar, 1995).

Here is an example of a Personal Story to help an Early Communicator become potty trained.

I Can Try to Go Poo in the Toilet

My name is Jake. Sometimes, I need to poo.

Mommy goes poo in the toilet.

Daddy goes poo in the toilet.

Jesse goes poo in the toilet.

This is the toilet.

I will try to go poo in the toilet.

Visual Helpers can help your child express himself

At this stage, pictures can not only help your child to make requests, but also to ask and answer questions or to comment on something.

Use Cue Cards

- **Use Cue Cards to help your child make sentences.** With Cue Cards, you can help your child progress from communicating with a single picture during Picture Exchange to making a short "sentence." Print the words "I want" on a Cue Card and show your child how to put the picture of the item that he wants next to the words on the card. Then have him exchange the "sentence" for what he wants. If your child "echoes," use this opportunity to help him say the sentence after he makes it. As soon as he gives you the "I want" Cue Card and the picture, say it "as he would if he could" – e.g., "I want video." As your child progresses and becomes more interactive, he may no longer need to exchange the picture and the card – he can point to or say the sentence instead.

- **Use Cue Cards to help your child communicate for reasons beyond requesting** – such as answering questions and making comments. For example, if you are playing a game with your child and you want him to tell you whose turn it is, make "Your Turn/My turn" cards. These are simply two cards on which you print the words to indicate what he can say when it's his turn (e.g., "Jake's turn") and when it's your turn (e.g., "Mommy's turn"). Cue cards with question starters on them, such as "Where is…?" or "What is…?" can help remind your child what to say when he's looking for something or sees something he wants you to explain.

Cue Cards on the fridge can remind your child how to ask for a snack.

To use Cue Cards, hold the card up or point to it when you expect your child to speak. At first, provide an entire verbal model if needed, saying everything that is printed on the Cue Card and also taking your child's turn by filling in the blank. For example, if the Cue Card says "I see," say "I see" and point to something like a ball, completing the sentence by saying "ball." After giving the whole model several times, give your child a partial model, saying only, "I see . . ." and let him fill in the blank. When you feel he is ready, just say "I . . . " and let him fill in more blanks. Your goal is for the Cue Card to eventually remind your child that it's his turn to say something, without you needing to do or say anything at all. Remember, once your child starts talking, he doesn't have to stick to the script. It's better for him to say things his own way.

Cue cards remind Sujit to ask for a second helping, using his own words, which is even better than sticking to the script.

- **Use Cue Cards to help your child understand and talk about feelings.** Your child experiences happiness, sadness, anger, fear and excitement just like other children, but he may have difficulty understanding the "feeling words." However, you've probably already helped your child understand more about feelings than you thought. For example, when he gives you a hug, you may smile and say, "That makes Mommy happy." Or when he climbs up on top of the refrigerator, you may say in a stern voice, "Get down. Mommy's mad." In these examples, your body language, tone of voice and facial expressions all help your child understand how you feel, but he may need some extra help as well.

Begin with pictures of the earliest feeling words.

Put each picture on its own Cue Card. When you want to identify an emotion for your child, say the word and guide his hand to touch the Cue Card with the picture of the same emotion. You should always give your child an example of what is making him feel a certain way. For example, instead of simply saying, "Jake's sad," show and tell him what's making him sad – e.g., "The wheel's broken. Jake's sad." The best time to identify emotions with a Cue Card is when your child is experiencing them. Look at how Jake's mother follows his lead.

Jake loves Popsicles, especially purple ones, and gets very excited when his mother takes one out of the freezer. Every time his mother gives him one, she says, "Jake likes Popsicles. Jake's happy." Then she takes Jake's hand and touches a Cue Card with a happy face on it, repeating the word "happy." She does this over and over whenever Jake is really happy. One day, his mother gives Jake his Popsicle and waits. Jake grabs his mother's hand and makes her touch the Cue Card. As soon as she touches it, he says, "Jake's happy!"

Visual Helpers for the child at the Partner stage

At this stage, your child may be able to use all kinds of pictures and even get information from the printed word. If he is using a lot of Visual Helpers, it is more practical to use smaller drawings (2" X 2"). Your child is also becoming more independent. In self-help routines, like brushing his teeth or washing his hands, he may be following the pictures without you even being in the room.

Visual Helpers can help your child understand his world

Use Picture Schedules to help your child understand the events of his day, week and month

There are so many ways to use Visual Helpers at this stage. Many different Picture Schedules can show your child what to do all through the day, the week and the month. The concept of time can even be expressed through pictures.

A schedule that shows your child his **entire day** lets your child know what to expect and can be especially useful if he is reluctant to do something.

Every Thursday, Jerry's Grandma babysits for him while his mother goes to work. Whenever he arrives at Grandma's house, Jerry refuses to get out of the car and cries. He likes Grandma, but doesn't like it when his mother leaves him.

Jerry doesn't like being left at Grandma's house.

This Picture Schedule lets Jerry see that Daddy will take him home at the end of the day. *

A schedule for Jerry's day might go like this: "First Jerry's going to Grandma's house. Then Jerry's going to have lunch. Then Jerry's going to watch a video. Then Jerry's going to have a drink. Then Daddy's going to get Jerry and bring him home." This schedule may not solve the whole problem, but it will remind Jerry that he has a good time at Grandma's and that his father *always* picks him up at the end of the day.

The day can also be broken down into mini-schedules. A schedule for the **morning** might include "Go to the washroom. Take pajamas off. Have breakfast. Brush teeth." If your child has trouble getting dressed on his own, he can use a Picture Board showing each step of the routine – e.g., "Underpants on. T-shirt on. Pants on. Socks on."

A **weekly** or **monthly schedule** resembles a calendar with pictures of important events – swimming lessons, visits to friends or school – on the days they occur.

Picture Schedules can especially help your child in his preschool classroom. If he can consult his book or his board, he will know exactly what to do without needing help from his teacher.

Time is very abstract. So your child needs concrete examples of what happens at certain times of the day to understand how time works. For example, you might put a picture of a breakfast food beside "8:00 a.m." or a picture of the school bus beside "8:30 a.m." If your child is anticipating an upcoming event, like a movie or a trip to the zoo, show him how many "sleeps" he will have before that big day.

This calendar tells your child that there are three sleeps before the visit to the zoo.

---

* Adapted from L. Hodgdon, *Visual Strategies for Improving Communication,* (Troy, MI, QuirkRoberts, 1996).

Use Visual Helpers to help your child understand difficult situations

Personal Stories, described for the Early Communicator stage on pages 239 and 240, can be used for just about any situation where your child needs some suggestions about what to do or say. Think of something that is difficult for your child, refer to the guidelines and write the story.

Use Visual Helpers to show your child how to create something

Visual Helpers can show your child how to build or make something, from a tower to chocolate milk. Just print out the directions in words and pictures. Then help your child to follow them. (For more on following visual directions, see Chapter 8, pages 283–287.)

Visual Helpers can help your child express himself

Use Picture Diaries and Communication Books to talk about things your child has done

Your child may be very good at communicating about the things that he sees, but he can't see the things he has done earlier in the day. You can help him remember his past experiences by reminding him about specific things and asking him questions. However, if you ask question after question – e.g., "What did you see at the zoo? Who went to the zoo? Did you like the zoo?" – your conversation can quickly turn into a test.

Picture Diaries and Communication Books can remind your child what to tell you without you having to ask a lot of questions. As you look at the pictures, you can both comment on what you see. Here's a Picture Diary of a trip to the farm:

Amanda's mother lets her teacher know that Amanda bought some flowers with her father.

If your child attends a preschool, encourage his teacher to send home a Communication Book each day with a few pictures of what he does at school and a short note describing the pictures. If the teacher keeps this daily record, you'll have something to talk about with your child – e.g., "You played with Amy today. What did you make?"

Then you can put some pictures of the things that your child does at home in the Communication Book and he can take it back to school the next day to show his teacher. Make looking at your child's Communication Book part of his Picture Schedule, perhaps calling it "Talking Time," so that you both have an opportunity to discuss his activities.

Circling a picture on a photocopied sheet like this one is a quick way for your child's teacher to report on his day.

If your child's teacher sends home a record of who and what your child played with, you'll know just what to talk to him about.

Use Visual Helpers to help your child understand and talk about feelings

At this stage, your child is getting the idea of what the words "happy," "sad" and "mad" mean. You can also add "scared" to the list of feeling words. Use the "Feeling Cue Cards" to identify the emotions as your child experiences them (see page 242). Another way to help your child understand feelings is to create a Happy Book, a Sad Book, a Mad Book and a Scared Book with pictures of some of the things that make him feel these ways and suggestions for what to do when he feels "sad" or "mad."* (For more on making books for your child, see Chapter 10.)

* adapted from S. Freeman & L. Drake, *Teach Me Language*. (Langly, B.C: SKF Books, 1996).

Feeling Sad

When I am **sad**, I feel bad.

When I am **sad**, I don't feel **happy**.

I feel **sad** when my train is broken.

I feel **sad** when I get hurt.

When I am **sad** sometimes I cry.

I feel **sad** when Krista yells at me.

I need to tell Mommy or Daddy why I am **sad**.

When I feel **sad** and I cry, Mommy or Daddy gives me a hug.

I feel better.

Visual Helpers can also be great **problem solvers**. Think of a problem that your child has, get out a pen and paper and solve the problem visually. Look at what Briana's mother does when Briana has a problem.

Briana loves her sweatshirt with the pink hearts on it. One day, she and her mother are painting and Briana spills purple paint on her sweatshirt. Briana gets very upset and begins crying. Her mother decides to help Briana work through her problem with Visual Helpers. Here's how she presents the problem to Briana and then solves it visually.*

* adapted from J. Janzen, *Understanding the Nature of Autism.*
   (San Antonio: Therapy Skill Builders, 1996).

If you use Visual Helpers to solve problems with your child, prepare him for the possibility that the solution might not work. For example, in the case of Briana's sweatshirt, it is possible that the paint might not wash out. Briana's mother could suggest a back-up plan.

Use Cue Cards to explain how to use difficult words

Your child may need more specific teaching to understand and use certain words. For example, you can explain how to ask and answer questions that begin with "What?" "Who?" "Where?" and "When?" to your child through pictures and even a few printed words too. Prepare cards with the words "what," "who," "where" and "when" at the top. Underneath the words, paste or draw a few pictures that illustrate the kinds of responses these questions require. As you can see in the illustrations, "what" questions are answered with the name of an object, "where" questions with the name of a place, "who" questions with the name of a person and "when" questions with a time of day. Explain the cards to your child, giving him instructions: "Answer questions that begin with 'what' with the name of a thing," and so on. Give examples in addition to the ones on the cards. Have the cards readily available so that if your child has difficulty answering a question, you can point to the appropriate card to remind him of the right answer.

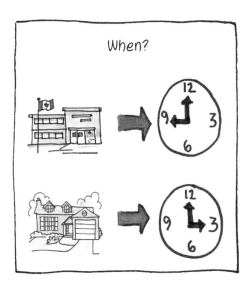

Use Cue Cards in conversations

Cue Cards can also give your child some reminders on how to start and stay in conversations. For example, a Cue Card can remind your child to say, "Hi. How are you?" If you're talking about plans for an upcoming event, you can make a Cue Card that helps your child talk about his plans – e.g., "Next week, I will . . . ."

If your child's understanding is good, Cue Cards can remind him about the rules of conversation by giving him instructions, such as "wait for an answer." Cue Cards can also remind him of what to say during play. For example, you can put sentences like "It's my turn" or "I like this game" on Cue Cards, as well as "No cheating!" or "I'm winning!" Place the Cue Cards on a game board or on the wall where your child can see them. Or move them in front of your child to remind him of what to say.

Cue Cards can help your child remember some of the rules of conversation.

Turn TV time into talking time

If your child is a visual learner, he probably loves watching TV and videos.

At first glance, watching TV may seem like a passive activity that allows few opportunities for your child to communicate. But you can turn TV-watching into an interactive experience by making some adaptations to the way you watch.

Watch TV with your child and use the pause button for videos

Most children like to watch the same videos over and over. When your child becomes very familiar with a video, he may start to anticipate his favourite parts. Use the pause button before one of these parts and focus your child's attention on what is about to happen. For example, in the video "Spot Goes to the Playground," just as Spot goes down the slide, the narrator says, "Whee!" Pause the video before Spot goes down the slide and say, "Spot is going down the slide." Wait and look expectant and then release the pause and say "Whee" with the voice on the video. Next time, maybe your child will take your cue and say "Whee" before you do.

Listen carefully to what your child imitates from a video and try to create some situations where he can generalize what he has learned.

This boy learns a FUN word from TV.

Then he has a chance to use it in real life!

Be interactive

If the characters on the video are singing and dancing, get up and sing and dance with your child!

Relate the TV information to the real world

Try to have some props identical to those on the video. For example, if a TV character fills a pail of water, have a pail out for your child. If you don't have real objects, use gestures to act out what the characters are doing.

Make your own video

If your child attends a preschool or a daycare, get permission to videotape the class singing songs or having a snack. Or find some cousins or children of friends and relatives and make your own movie about what your child can say when he meets someone new or wants a second helping at the dinner table. Your movies won't get an Oscar nomination, but by watching these activities performed by other children, your child will learn more about what he can say and do. Remember to write a script suitable for your child's stage of communication. Generally, use short simple sentences that your child can lift and re-use and include lots of carrier phrases and social language, like "Let's play" and "See you later." Children at the Partner stage can re-enact the video after watching it.

Use TV to interest your child in books

Many children's books have accompanying videos. For a child who does not show an interest in books, this may be a way to capture his attention.

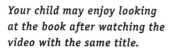

Your child may enjoy looking at the book after watching the video with the same title.

Use TV and videos to expand your child's thinking about feelings, the future and the past

If your child is at the Partner stage, you can use what's happening on videos to help him understand and talk about feelings. After a scary scene, describe how you felt. Next time, pause before the scene and alert your child to what's coming – "The monster is coming. I'm scared!" Talk about and encourage your child to talk about how the characters on television are feeling. Also talk about the things that make you and your child laugh. If your child doesn't mind, you can pause at certain key points in the video and ask him what is about to happen. When the video is over, talk about what you both have watched.

Use TV to interest your child in reading

Use the credits and the commercials to develop your child's interest in the printed word by pointing out a few words and explaining them so that your child can understand. If your child shows a great deal of interest in the credits, consider getting the closed caption option for your TV. Your child will be able both to see and hear what people are saying.

What about using the computer?

Like TV, computers can contribute to your child's learning because they present information visually and are fun to use. In addition, computers give your child repeated opportunities to practise the same words and concepts over and over. Many computer programs teach children vocabulary and provide an opportunity to listen and follow instructions. If your child is learning new vocabulary from the computer, make sure he has a chance to use these words in real life. If he has been identifying names of foods on the computer, serve him some of those foods or go shopping for them.

Though your child can learn a lot from computers, keep in mind that they don't replace interaction with people. So try to be with your child some of the time that he plays on the computer. Look for programs that are interactive, such as games where you and your child can each take turns. If your child is an early reader, try having little conversations on the computer that help him learn some social language. For example, type "Hi. How are you?" and show your child a print-out of the answer, "I am fine. How are you?" Then help him type out this response. Next, type "How old are you?" and show your child another print-out: "I am 5." As your child improves his computer skills, he will need less help from you to type his answers.

Summary

We all rely on Visual Helpers – calendars, daily schedules, street signs – to make sense of the world and organize our lives. The Visual Helpers described in this chapter are meant to lessen the confusion in your child's life by giving him information in a way that is easier for him to understand. Visual Helpers also give your child another way of expressing himself, and when he begins talking they can remind him what to say. There are many ways to use Visual Helpers: Choice Boards allow your child both to initiate and respond, Picture Schedules help your child understand what's going to happen and Cue Cards and Personal Stories suggest what your child can say and do without your help. The Visual Helpers we all use help us feel calm and relaxed, and they can do the same for your child.

R.O.C.K. in Your Routines

There are a lot of opportunities to learn about interaction and communication during the things that you and your child do every day.

Think of all the things that you and your child do in the morning. First, you both wake up. Next comes breakfast, and the cat may need breakfast too. After this your child needs to brush his teeth, get washed and get dressed. Then there are the breakfast dishes, and maybe a mad dash to work or a drive to daycare. All of this — and it's not even nine o'clock!

Though your morning may seem hectic and disorganized, there is actually a pattern to what you do. Getting up, getting dressed, and having breakfast are all examples of "daily routines": things that you and your child do in the exact same way every day. Daily routines can help your child make sense of his world because they are **repetitive** and **predictable**. The more times your child does something the same way, the clearer the meaning of what is happening becomes.

In this chapter, we will look at the ways in which the activities you do every day with your child – your daily routines – can increase his understanding of what you do and say, and how Visual Helpers can contribute to this understanding. We will also see that when you use R.O.C.K., daily routines become much like People Games: structured activities in which both you and your child have opportunities to take turns and interact.

R.O.C.K. in your daily routines

 ## Repeat what you say and do

Repeat what you say and do when you start the routine

The first step of any routine is to announce it by saying its name and doing something specific associated with it, like showing your child his pajamas before bedtime. If you begin routines with specific names or labels, your child will associate those words with the routine: "Bathtime" for having a bath or "Brush teeth" for brushing his teeth. It is important to be consistent in what you say and do. For example, if you say "Let's have lunch" one day and "Time to eat" another, your child won't learn to associate specific words with lunchtime. So, decide what labels you're going to attach to your routines and stick to those names. Printing the name of the routine on the top of a Picture Schedule may remind you to be consistent. As well, start your routines with the same action every time. For example, if you're telling your child it's lunchtime, you can either bring your hand to your mouth as if you were eating or hold up your child's plate. You may want to sing a special song at the beginning of a routine to help your child understand what is about to happen. There isn't one right way to start the routine, but once you decide what you're going to do, don't change it until your child is ready to learn something new.

lunch

If you print the name of the routine next to a picture, you'll be more likely to use the same words every day.

The second step of many routines is for your child to come to you so that you can do the routine together. Some children will come all on their own, while others may not come even after you call, "Come here." To get your child to respond to "Come here," use the Helper's Rule, described in Chapter 1. Call your child's name and say "Come here" once. Then wait. If he doesn't respond, call him again, physically guiding him over to the site of the routine.

In addition to "Come here," daily routines provide ideal opportunities for your child to learn to follow other simple directions in a natural, meaningful way. For example, some routines, like mealtimes, begin when your child sits down at the table, so in these routines your child can get a lot of practice responding to the direction "Sit down."

Repeat what you say and do during the routine

As with People Games, do the actions of the routine in the same way and order each time you do them until your child is very familiar with them. Keep what you say simple and consistent. Remember to "say less and stress, go slow and show." With practice, your child will start to understand how the routine works and will participate in it at his level of ability. Once your child can follow the routine without your help, you can vary it by introducing something new. For example, you can offer your child a choice or do something unexpected.

Repeat what you say and do when you end the routine

Just as your routines need beginnings, they also need clear endings. Always make the "finished" sign, saying "all done" or "finished," and then put the picture of whatever routine or part of the routine you've completed into the "finished" container. You may want to add, "Give me a hug," "Give me a kiss" or "Give me five" (done by slapping your open palm against your child's open palm) as a final step in your routine. In addition, you can develop other rituals to help your child understand that a routine is over. For example, to let your child know that he has heard the last story before bedtime, say, "The End. And now bed." You can sing a specific song or turn out the lights in the hallway before turning out his lights. No matter what you do, make sure you do it the same way each time.

If you end your routines by making the "finished" sign, your child will see that the activity is over.

Repeat the routine often with different people and in different places

It is easy for your child to become dependent on you being there to go through his routines with him. To help your child become more flexible and independent, try to find other people with whom he can do his routines. For example, maybe one day Grandma could have lunch with your child or the babysitter could give him his bath. If you get others involved, show them how to do the routine in the way that is most familiar to your child. They can use a Picture Schedule to keep what they do and say consistent. When your child is ready, let him do some routines without anyone's help.

Offer opportunities for your child to take a turn

Plan when you will offer your child a turn

The beauty of routines is that they are already broken down into small steps. Each of these steps gives your child an opportunity to take a turn. For example, think of bathtime. First you need to turn on the water to fill the tub. If your child can turn on the water, this can be his first turn. Next, your child needs to get undressed. He can take off his T-shirt – his second turn. Your child may want a toy to play with in the bath. His third turn can be choosing which toy he wants. Finally, he gets into the tub. When your child is in the bath you both can sing a song together: "This is the way Daddy washes my arm, washes my arm, washes my arm, when I am in the bath!" If you leave out the word "arm" after you sing the beginning of the song, your child can take yet another turn by filling in the blank with a word.

There are lots of things to do and say when getting washed!

Once you decide when you will offer your child a turn, be consistent. In the example above, this means that the next time you bathe your child, offer the turns at the same places – before you turn on the water, before he takes off his T-shirt, before he gets his bath toy and before the word "arm." Sometimes, you plan when your child should take a certain turn, but he takes a different turn at another time. He may do this because the new turn is more interesting to him or easier for him to do. Whatever the reason, follow his lead and include the new turn in the routine the next time you do it.

Plan what turns your child can take

The turns your child will take depend on his stage of communication and the specific routine. Because your child needs to understand what's happening before he can do things on his own, many of his first turns will be *actions*, responses to your directions and suggestions. For example, when your child washes his hands, you (or a Picture Schedule) can tell him to turn on the water and take some soap.

However, following directions is not the only kind of turn your child can take. You can balance your directions with opportunities for other kinds of turns, such as making comments or choices. Avoid giving your child too many directions in one routine, and don't give directions if your child no longer needs them.

Some routines, like mealtimes and bathtimes, are very social. In these routines, there will be more opportunities for your child to ask for things, make choices, fill in blanks, comment on the unexpected and have short conversations.

Offer new opportunities for turns as your child progresses

Naturally, you need to keep up with your child's progress. Once he has memorized a routine, add something new. For example, if you always give him his juice bit by bit, your child will get an opportunity to request "more," but nothing else. But, if you surprise him by giving him a drink he doesn't like, he has a chance to learn to say "no!" No matter what stage your child is at, there are always opportunities for him to learn something new in daily routines.

Cue your child to take his turn

Give explicit cues at first and then more natural ones once your child is familiar with the routine

The same guidelines that you use when playing People Games apply to bathtime, mealtime and even greeting a visitor at the door. At first, you need to do all the work, providing models of your child's turns for him or physically guiding him when necessary. Eventually, you do less: pausing and looking expectant may be enough to signal your child's turn.

Use Visual Helpers

Use Picture Schedules to show your child the routines of certain times of the day – for example, what he does in the morning before he goes to daycare – and for routines that your child has difficulty with. In difficult routines, the pictures show your child how the routine is done and will help him get through challenging spots. Visual Helpers can also remind your child what to *say* during routines. For example, at lunchtime, a Choice Board or a Cue Card with "I want" printed on it can remind your child how to tell you what he wants. And looking at a Picture Schedule of his whole day may make it easier for your child to tell you about what he's done or what he's going to do.

Engineer the situation

Once your child has learned the steps of a routine, you can give him an opportunity to take more turns by engineering the situation. You can put something he needs or wants where he can see it but not reach it or offer food bit by bit. The best way to encourage your child to comment is to introduce something new into familiar routines. The suggestions in Chapter 2, pages 68–81 will help you engineer the situation and make daily routines places where your child can always learn something new.

Keep it fun! Keep it going!

Though routines may be repetitive, they don't have to be boring! For example, most children will love bathtime if there are bubbles and toys in the water and you're singing songs or playing games.

Songs help make routines fun for you and your child.

Adding songs to routines is an easy way to make them more fun. Songs catch your child's attention and have actions that you can do together. In Chapter 9, we will look at how you can make up songs especially for your child. A special song can help your child learn some new actions or words, or help him through a difficult situation. For example, the father in the picture sings a song he has made up for his son to the tune of "London Bridge." The song is simple, with the same five words repeated over and over again – "Brian's pants are coming down" – but it makes potty training a little more fun.

In the same way that you can turn routines into fun activities, you can also turn fun activities into routines! Saying "goodbye" to mommy or daddy every day, greeting a babysitter or teacher, feeding a pet, visiting the doughnut shop or washing dishes can all be turned into enjoyable routines with predictable turns for you and your child.

Some routines can be extra difficult because of your child's sensory likes and dislikes. For example, it's often a challenge to turn mealtime into a fun activity if your child is a picky eater and sensitive to the smells of certain foods. Getting your child dressed may also be a challenge if he is over-sensitive to touch. But even difficult routines can provide an opportunity for your child to communicate directly to you. And, with some of the creative planning described in the next section, you can actually take those problem situations and change them into positive interactions between the two of you.

Anything you and your child do together every day can be turned into an interactive routine with turns for the both of you.

Adapt daily routines to your child's stage of communication

The following sections give you some ideas of how you can help your child learn to understand and participate in two daily routines – snacktime and getting dressed – by dividing the routines into small steps and making them more structured. You will find that snacktime, like all mealtimes, is one of the best and most natural places for you and your child to interact and work on communication goals. Getting dressed is more of a **self-help routine** in which the emphasis is on your child's understanding how to do the routine properly. However, after your child is able to get dressed independently, you can start to build communication opportunities into the routine and have little conversations. In the following pages, we will look at how you can adapt snacktime and getting dressed to your child's stage of communication – at the Own Agenda, Requester and Early Communicator stages. If your child is at the Partner stage, he may already know how to do these routines on his own, so we'll look at how you can make routines a time for conversation. Keep in mind that this is only a guide – you may have to do things a bit differently for your own child.

Routines for the child at the Own Agenda stage

At this stage, you do all the work in the beginning. You show your child how the routine works by taking his turns for him and physically helping him to do some parts of the routine. Then you need to figure out when you will wait for your child to show you how he's going to take his turn and when you will guide him through his turn. Most of the time, you will give him physical help for some of the actions in the routine, like turning on the water tap or wiping his hands. But you'll need to OWL and follow your child's lead to turn a reach or look into purposeful communication. Once your child is familiar with the routine, you can introduce something new for him to do.

What you can expect
At this stage you can expect your child to learn to:
- pay attention to the routine
- understand the steps of the routine
- intentionally interact with you

What you can do
- Provide verbal and physical models
- Give physical help (Use the "Helper's Rule" described in Chapter 1, page 40.)
- Wait for your child to take a turn
- Follow your child's lead
- Engineer the situation

Snack at the Own Agenda stage

Snack provides an ideal opportunity to help your child communicate intentionally to ask for his snack.

What you can expect

At this stage, you can expect your child to learn to:

• respond to "Come here" and "Sit down"
• ask for his snack using a gesture, object or picture

What you can do

You'll have to experiment to find out how your child can ask you for his snack – through Object or Picture Exchange, gestures or hand signs. Try Picture Exchange first. If your child doesn't catch on to the exchange, see if Object Exchange works better. Use miniature or toy objects, like play food, to represent favourite snacks. You can even attach the actual snack, like a potato chip, to a board and cover it with clear plastic wrap. (See Chapter 7, page 233 for an explanation of Object Exchange.) If exchanges don't work with your child, you can teach him a gesture, such as asking for his snack by holding out his hand, pushing a plate towards you or making a hand sign. Use the hand-over-hand method, as described for teaching Object or Picture Exchange, to teach these actions. Get someone to physically help your child to perform the action, like pushing the plate forwards, and then immediately give your child what he wants. The following table gives a step-by-step plan of a snack routine for a child at the Own Agenda stage.

Aaron learns Object Exchange at snacktime.

Snack: The steps of the routine at the Own Agenda stage

What you do	What you say	Your child's turn
Call your child by name and gesture for him to come to you. Use the Helper's Rule if your child doesn't respond.	"*(Your child's name)*! Come here!"	He may come or need some help.
Or, Show your child the cookie bag.	"Cookie!"	He may look at the bag or reach for it.
Point to the chair.	"Sit down." (Use the Helper's Rule if needed.)	He may sit down or need some help.
Give your child a small piece of the cookie.	"Cookie."	He eats the cookie.
You and another person can teach your child to exchange a toy cookie or a picture for the cookie (see Chapter 7, page 233).	"Cookie."	He gives you the object or picture with physical help.
Or, Use physical help to show your child how to hold his hand open with the palm up to ask for a cookie.	"Cookie."	He extends his hand with physical help.
Or, Show your child how to push his plate towards you to ask for a cookie. Give physical help.	"Cookie."	With physical help, he pushes his plate towards you.
Or, Show your child how to make the hand sign for cookie by giving physical help.	"Cookie."	He makes the sign with physical help.
Give your child a piece of the cookie as soon as he uses a picture, object, gesture or hand sign.	"Cookie."	He eats the cookie and reaches for another piece.
Repeat the physical help for Picture Exchange, hand signs or gesturing.	"Cookie."	He gives you the object or picture, makes a sign or extends his hand with physical help from you.

If you are using Picture or Object Exchange, when your child is ready, give a partial model instead of physical help. You can cue your child to give you the object or picture by opening your hand expectantly or touching your child's arm.

More for you to do

Follow your child's lead to get him to interact with you intentionally

At this stage, use all the Four "I"s – include your child's interest, imitate, intrude and interpret – to let your child see that his actions can influence you. In the following example, Shawn's father uses **intrude** to turn his son's behaviour into an interactive part of the routine.

Every time Shawn's father gives him a cookie, Shawn takes it and runs away to eat it alone on the living room sofa. One day, his father follows him to the couch and playfully intrudes by pretending to take a bite out of the cookie, saying "Yummy! Daddy's cookie." The first few times, Shawn doesn't like his father's intrusion. But soon he starts to think that what his father does is funny! Eventually, Shawn waits for his father to follow him to the couch, and even holds out the cookie for his father to take a pretend bite.

When Shawn's father intrudes and pretends to take a bite of the cookie, he makes it possible for Shawn to interact intentionally for the first time.

Yummy, Daddy's cookie!

Give him his snack bit by bit

If your child gets all his raisins at once or a whole cookie, he will only have one chance to ask you for what he wants. But, if you give him his snack bit by bit, there will be more opportunities for him to communicate to you.

Try a little "creative stupidity"

Pretend you can't open the juice, put a few cookies in the cereal box or hide a carrot in the cookie box. Remember that children love surprises and when parents make mistakes.

Jake's mother gets his attention when she pulls a carrot out of the cookie box.

Offer choices

Even though your child isn't directly telling you what his choice is, give him the choice anyway. Offer him something you know he likes and something that he doesn't care for. Hold up the preferred and less preferred choices and label them in a questioning tone. Your child will probably reach for the one he wants. As he reaches, name his choice and put the food up to your eyes so that your child will look at you. Then name his choice again while taking his hand and helping him touch the food that he has reached for or looked at before giving it to him.

Getting dressed at the Own Agenda stage

A child at the Own Agenda stage usually needs a lot of help getting dressed. He is just learning what is expected and trying to make sense of what you say.

What you can expect

At this stage, you can expect your child to learn to:

• follow the steps of the routine

• lift his arms and legs

• pull up his pants

• respond to "Give me hug"

What you can do

• Use the Helper's Rule (see Chapter 1, page 40)

• Follow his lead

• Be creatively stupid

When you put your child's clothes where he can see them, he has a visual reminder of what to do.

Getting dressed: The steps of the routine at the Own Agenda stage

What you do	What you say	Your child's turn
Lay his clothes on his bed and hold up his pants.	"(*Your child's name*)! Let's get dressed."	
Or, Call your child if he is not close to you. If he can see you, gesture for him to come to you. (Use the Helper's Rule if he needs it.)	"(*Your child's name*)! Come here."	He may come to you or need help.
Hold up his pants.	"Pants."	He may look at his pants.
Pause. Point to the pants.	"Put on your **pants**."	He may look at his pants or you.
Point to or touch your child's leg. Help him put on his pant leg if neccessry.	"One **leg**." (Use the Helper's Rule if he doesn't respond.)	He may lift his leg or need help.
Point to or touch your child's other leg. Help him put on his pant leg if necessary.	"The other **leg**." (Use the Helper's Rule if he doesn't respond.)	He may lift his leg.
Point to the pants. Get your child started by pulling his pants partway up.	"**Up**. Pull them **up**. Pull your pants **up**."(Use the Helper's Rule if he doesn't respond.)	He may pull up his pants.
Extend one of your arms and one of your child's arms over your heads.	"Yay! Your pants are on!"	He may look at you and smile.
Open your arms for a hug (use the Helper's Rule).	"(*Your child's name*)! Give me a hug (or kiss)."	He may hug or kiss you.
Repeat all the steps with the rest of your child's clothes.		
Make the "finished" sign.	"All done!"	He may look at you.

More for you to do

Use a Self-Help Board

While your child is probably not able to concentrate on a Self-Help Board, you can make one for yourself to help keep what you say and do consistent. Even if your child only glances at the pictures, it's a way for him to start connecting pictures with what he's doing.

Follow your child's lead to get him to intentionally interact with you

What do you do when your child doesn't fully co-operate? Let's look at what Rebecca's mother does when Rebecca has trouble getting dressed.

Rebecca's mother tries to make getting dressed more structured and repetitive for Rebecca in order to help her understand the steps in the routine and the words connected with it. But Rebecca keeps throwing herself on the bed, making getting dressed almost impossible! The next time Rebecca throws herself on the bed, her mother decides to follow Rebecca's lead instead of trying to finish the routine. So, she gives her daughter a few rolls back-and-forth. This is great fun for Rebecca! While Rebecca's laughing, her mother sees an opportunity to slip the T-shirt over her head. Right after she does, Rebecca falls back on the bed, so her mother rolls her again. Then Rebecca's mother quickly puts on the next item of clothing, and rolls her once again. Gradually, rolling on the bed becomes part of the routine, a reward for putting on any item of clothing.

Rebecca's mother finds that dressing Rebecca is easier when she follows Rebecca's lead.

Try a little "creative stupidity"

Since your child is just learning the routine, you may not want to do too many silly things at this stage. But as your child starts to participate in the routine – lifting his leg, glancing around to see which item of clothing comes next – try one or two of the ideas described in Chapter 2. For example, "accidentally" try to put your child's shirt on his legs or put Daddy's shoes on your child's feet. Being silly may get your child's attention.

Offer choices

If your child has a strong attachment to one item of clothing, offer him a choice between his favourite T-shirt and one he doesn't like to wear. If he reaches for his favourite, treat the reach as if he has told you what he wants – "Want red shirt!" – and physically guide his hand to touch that shirt. Then give him the T-shirt, saying, "Shirt." Shake your head as you put the other T-shirt down and say, "Not this shirt."

Routines for the child at the Requester stage

At this stage your child is pulling and leading you to the things he wants and is just starting to make sense of what you say and do. Routines provide an opportunity for him to learn how to replace pulling and leading with a more effective, symbolic form of communication.

What you can expect

At this stage you can expect your child to learn to:

- make requests with pictures, objects, gestures or sounds in the routine
- respond to some of your directions
- make choices
- refuse

What you can do

- Teach Picture or Object Exchange (described in Chapter 7)
- Provide verbal and physical models
- Give physical help using the "Helper's Rule" (see Chapter 1, page 40)
- Use natural cues as your child becomes familiar with the routine
- Follow your child's lead
- Engineer the situation

Snack at the Requester stage

Snack is a perfect routine for your child to learn Picture or Object Exchange.

What you can expect

At this stage you can expect your child to learn to:

- ask for his snack using a gesture, object, picture or sound
- respond to "come here," "sit down" or the name of the snack
- touch what he wants when you ask him to make a choice
- look at you before making a choice

What you can do

If you are using Picture Exchange at this stage, your child must be close to you to give you the picture. It works best if you keep the pictures in the kitchen where they will remind your child to ask for a snack. You can also set the stage by putting the snack where your child can see but not reach it – on a high counter or shelf. Or keep the snack in a cupboard with a childproof lock, and attach a picture of the snack to the cupboard door. This way, your child knows what's inside the cupboard but can't get his snack himself. He also can easily find the picture when he wants to exchange it.

The steps of the routine are on the next page. If your child is not ready for pictures, use objects instead.

Snack: the steps of the Picture Exchange routine at the Requester stage

What you do	What you say	Your child's turn
If your child does not know how to exchange a picture for something he wants, teach Picture Exchange (see Chapter 7, page 233).		
Or, If your child uses Picture Exchange, put the cookies where your child can see them and put the picture near the cookies (e.g., on the table or cupboard door).	Wait for your child to request on his own.	He may give you a picture of a cookie.
Take the picture. Give him a cookie.	"Cookie."	He may eat his cookie.
Make the hand sign for "finished." Later, help your child to make the "finished" sign.	"All done."	He may make the sign with your help.
Return the picture to its spot.	Nothing.	He's not responsible for putting the picture back.

More for you to do

Give your child his snack bit by bit

When you give your child his snack bit by bit, he gets a lot of practice asking for it over and over using either Picture or Object Exchange or gestures. Break foods, such as cookies, potato chips and cheese into many small pieces. Cut fruits like apples, oranges and bananas into little pieces as well.

Offer choices

Not many children at the Requester stage can make choices from pictures yet. So it's best to give your child a choice between two real foods, offering the preferred food last. If your child likes cookies better than celery, say "Do you want celery or a cookie?" If he likes celery better than cookies, say "Do you want a cookie or celery?" Once you think you know what your child wants, help him to touch the item before you give it to him, saying its name as he touches it. Then put the refused choice away while saying "No" in an exaggerated way.

Offer choices between two foods – one your child likes and one he doesn't like.

Getting dressed at the Requester stage

At this stage, the way you do the routine is very similar to the way that you do it for a child at the Own Agenda stage. (Refer to page 270 for the steps of the routine.) However, the difference now is that a Requester can respond to more of your directions and needs less help putting on items of clothing.

A Picture Schedule can help your child understand the steps of the routine. It will also keep what you do and say consistent.

What you can expect

At this stage you can expect your child to learn to:

- understand the names of some clothing items
- respond to your pointing and a few other gestures
- respond to "Come here," "Give me a hug" and other simple directions
- lift his arms and legs
- pull up his pants and socks

What you can do

- Wait and look expectant
- Use some "creative stupidity"
- Follow your child's lead if appropriate

Wait and look expectant

As soon as your child gets the idea of how the routine goes, don't do every step in the routine for him. He may surprise you by how much he can do on his own. For example, after he has on his T-shirt, name the next piece of clothing, but wait to see if your child can get it by himself.

Eric's mother waits for him to lift his arms all by himself.

Use some "creative stupidity" and give your child a new reason to communicate

As soon as your child understands the routine, make it interactive by engineering the situation. Try a little "creative stupidity": "accidentally" put his pants over his head or your head, put his shoes upside down on his feet, give him his Daddy's T-shirt or say "all done" without having put on his pants, his shirt or one of his socks.

Kevin likes it when his father is silly!

Eugene protests when his mother insists on putting his shoe on the wrong way.

Follow his lead if it's appropriate

By using the Four "I"s, you can get more interaction going. At the Own Agenda stage, Rebecca's mother included Rebecca's interests in the routine by turning Rebecca's favourite action, rolling on the bed, into a reward. And Shawn's father intruded to keep his son engaged. Following your child's lead is always appropriate if it keeps the routine going.

However, it is not always appropriate to follow your child's lead, particularly when his actions can't be adapted into the routine. For example, if your child hits you while you're dressing him or takes his clothes off after you put them on, you have to show him that these actions aren't part of the routine. Find out the reasons behind his actions: maybe your child doesn't like the clothing's material, or maybe he doesn't feel like getting dressed. In either case, you have to help your child finish the routine but without his negative behaviours. If your child doesn't like the clothing's material, try dressing him in something else. If he's just being stubborn, persist in the routine, praising him when he participates and saying something like "No hitting!" firmly but gently to tell him when his actions are not acceptable.

Routines for the child at the Early Communicator stage

Most routines go more smoothly now because your child knows what's expected and can understand a lot of what you say. He will probably communicate during routines in a variety of ways. He may ask for things using pictures, pointing, saying single words or repeating words and phrases after you use them. And, while he communicates mainly to get things he wants, he's starting to communicate for other reasons too. Whatever your child does, you can expect him to learn to progress in both how and why he communicates in routines.

What you can expect

At this stage you can expect your child to learn to:
- Understand the steps, gestures (including your pointing) and most of the words in his daily routines
- consistently request with pictures, gestures or words
- communicate for reasons beyond requesting:
  - to make choices
  - to refuse / protest
  - to respond to your directions
  - to comment
  - to answer simple questions (e.g., Yes / No questions, questions that start with "What?")
- turn "echoes" into spontaneous speech
- turn one-word communication into two-word communication
- initiate the routine on his own and complete parts of it independently

What you can do

- Provide repeated opportunities for your child to practise requesting
- Give verbal models of comments (e.g., "Look! Daddy has new pants.")
- Give verbal models of questions and answers
- Model short, grammatical phrases and sentences for a child who uses single words
- Offer fill-in-the-blanks and then more natural cues to help your child use speech spontaneously
- Use Visual Helpers
- Engineer the situation

Snack at the Early Communicator stage

What you can expect

Different children at the Early Communicator stage will request their snacks in different ways. One child may exchange pictures and say a word after you model it and another child may ask for what he wants all on his own without using pictures.

At this stage, you can expect your child to learn to:

- ask for his snack using a short sentence (printed or spoken)
- respond with words and/or by pointing when you ask him what he wants
- comment about changes in the routine

What you can do

- Turn "echoes" into spontaneous speech
- Help your child communicate for new reasons
  - Give your child a lot of practice using new words
  - Offer a variety of choices
  - Help your child understand when choices are unavailable
  - Be "creatively stupid"
  - Take advantage of when things go wrong
  - Give your child a snack he doesn't like
- Involve your child in snack preparation
- Use Cue Cards

When Tyler has a choice, he always says "yes" to bananas!

Snack: The steps of the routine at the Early Communicator stage

What you do	What you say	Your child's turn
For an Early Communicator who consistently requests by using a single picture: Have cookies ready and pictures of different snacks on a Choice Board where your child can see them.	Nothing. Wait for your child to request with a picture.	He may choose a picture and give it to you.
Take the picture from him and show him how to put the picture of the cookie on a **Cue Card** that says, "I want" before he gives you the picture.	"**I want** a cookie."	He may place the picture of the cookie on the "I want" Cue Card.
For an Early Communicator who requests with a picture and echoes your words: If your child already echoes "cookie," offer a fill-in-the-blank cue. If your child doesn't fill in the blank, hold up the cookie or point to a picture of a cookie.	"**(I) want** ..."	He may say "cookie."
For an Early Communicator who requests using one word: If your child requests with one word ("cookie"), do something to elicit some spontaneous language. Try some creative stupidity (e.g., pretend you want a cookie and that you think that there are no more).	"I want a cookie too. Oh no. There aren't any more cookies."	He may use his own words and come up with a new idea. For example, he may hand you a cookie and say "Here's a cookie, Mommy."

Turn "echoes" into spontaneous speech

If your child echoes your verbal models, say less and less so that he has the chance to say more and more. Instead of giving the entire verbal model, provide a fill-in-the-blank for one word. Gradually increase the number of words you expect your child to say, until eventually he says the whole model without any explicit cues. For example, when your child is echoing, "I want a cookie," say, "I want a . . . .," and then wait for him to fill in the blank with "cookie." Then say "I . . . .," and let him fill in "want a cookie." Finally, simply wait for your child to say the whole sentence on his own. An "I want" Cue Card, placed beside the snack can also remind your child what to say. Remember, however, that your child doesn't have to stick to *your* script. The goal is for him to say things using his own words.

Help your child communicate for new reasons

• **Give your child a lot of practice using new words in different places and for different reasons.** If your child learns to say "milk" to ask for a drink in a snack routine, set up situations in which he can practise saying "milk" for reasons other than requesting. For example, "accidentally" spill some milk, point to it and say, "Look! Mommy spilled . . . ." Wait for your child to fill in the blank. Your child can also practise using his new word if you offer him choices between milk and a drink he doesn't like.

Fill-in-the-blanks helps Jahmal use the word "milk" to comment.

- **Offer a variety of choices.** At this stage, your child's Choice Board can have several foods and drinks on it. You can use the board to ask your child to name his choice (e.g., "Do you want milk or water?") or simply to answer "yes" or "no" questions (e.g., "Do you want an apple?"). When your child doesn't want a certain food, give him a model of how to respond by shaking your head and saying "no."

  For an Early Communicator who is just starting to echo what you say, offer the preferred choice last. Once your child's understanding improves, you can change the order in which you give the choices. At first, keep the choices between very familiar foods, such as juice or milk, using visual cues only if your child needs them. At this point you also can ask choice questions that encourage your child to compare two things and use new vocabulary. For example, you can ask "Do you want a *little* cookie or a *big* cookie?" or "Do you want *hot* pizza or *cold* pizza?" If you are introducing new words, like big, little, hot, cold, and fast and slow, show your child what you mean with real objects, actions or pictures.

It's easier for Jake to make a choice between a big cookie and a little cookie when he sees the cookies.

- **Help your child understand when choices are unavailable.** Once your child realizes the power of his communication, he might not stop asking you for all those treats you have been so willing to give him. If you want to tell your child that he can't have something, use the No Sign described on page 236 in Chapter 7. Place the sign over the picture of the unavailable snack and tell your child that it's not a choice. Then help him to find something else to eat. When you use the No Sign, you can also provide new verbal models for your child, such as "No more cookies" or "I can have an apple."

The No Sign tells Sasha that there are
"No more cookies."

- **Be "creatively stupid."** Your child will have to do or say something if you give him give him his cereal spoon without the handle, his glass without the juice or the raisin box without the raisins. If your child looks surprised but doesn't say anything, provide a verbal model he can copy, such as "Uh oh! No juice!" At mealtimes, serve everyone but "accidentally" forget to serve your child. If he doesn't react, do so for him – "Oh no! Mommy forgot Jake." Put the juice out at snacktime but "forget" to give your child a glass or put out the cereal box but forget to give him the bowl. However, be careful not to overdo it – one "silly" mistake per snack is enough.
- **Take advantage of when things go wrong.** Put out the pizza even if it's too hot and comment in an animated way: "Hot! Ooo! Too hot!" If milk is spilled, look surprised and wait for your child to do or say something. If he doesn't, say it for him – "Oh no! The milk spilled!"
- **Give your child a snack he doesn't like.** By offering a food that is sure to make your child's nose wrinkle up, you are giving him a great chance to shake his head or say "No." Make sure that you offer a favourite snack after suggesting less appetizing ones. Remember, your child might not answer "yes" and "no" on his own, so take his turn by stressing the answers with your voice and exaggerating your head nods and shakes.

When you "forget" to give your child something, he may comment on it.

Involve your child in the snack preparation

Activities that are collaborative and have a clear end product are called **Joint Action Routines**. Making a cake or an ice cream sundae can both be Joint Action Routines if you do them with your child. Joint Action Routines have small steps built into them, and, just like the other daily routines, they have specific turns for you and your child.

Because you are creating something together as partners, two-way interaction can occur naturally. And if you show your child pictures of what the end product will look like, he will be inspired to work towards the routine's finish.

There are many snacks that are easy to prepare, such as chocolate milk, ice cream sundaes, sandwiches, and Jello or pudding. You can make popcorn and then sprinkle salt on it, ice cupcakes and decorate them with candies or fill celery sticks with cream cheese or peanut butter. Prepare a salad with your child – tearing lettuce leaves can be more fun than you think! Even setting the table and cleaning up are two things you can do together.

Here's a step-by-step plan for making chocolate milk with an Early Communicator who is just starting to repeat words that he hears. If your child is ready, use a Picture Board showing each part of the preparation. If needed, use the Helper's Rule: "Ask once and wait. Then ask again, adding help."

You can use pictures to show your child how to make chocolate milk.

Chocolate milk: The steps of the routine at the Early Communicator stage

What you do	What you say	Your child's turn
For an Early Communicator who "echoes":		
Point to the picture of milk.	"First, let's get the (*pause*) **milk**." Eventually leave out "milk" and let your child say it.	He may get milk out of the fridge and may repeat "milk."
Point to the picture of the spoon.	"Then, let's take the (*pause*) **spoon**. Put chocolate on (*pause*) **spoon**." Eventually leave out "spoon" and let your child say it.	He may take the spoon and repeat "spoon."
Point to the picture of chocolate powder.	"Take one spoon of the (*pause*) **chocolate**." Eventually leave out "chocolate" and let your child say it.	He may measure the powder and repeat "chocolate."
Point to the picture of the glass.	"Let's put the chocolate in the (*pause*) **glass**." Eventually leave out "glass" and let your child say it.	He may put chocolate in the glass and repeat "glass."
Point to the picture of milk.	"Let's put the (*pause*) **milk** in the (*pause*) **glass.**" Eventually leave out "milk" and "glass" and let your child say the words.	He may watch you pour the milk into the cup and repeat "milk" and "glass."
Point to the picture of the spoon in the glass.	"Let's stir the milk."	He may stir the milk and repeat "stir."
Hold the glass of chocolate milk and wait.	Say nothing.	He may ask you to give him the glass.
Drink your own glass of milk.	"Yummy! I love chocolate milk"	He may drink the milk and repeat what you said.

Once your child knows exactly how to make the chocolate milk, create more opportunities for him to request, comment, answer and ask questions. Pour the milk in bit by bit, give him sugar instead of the chocolate powder or a fork to stir with instead of a spoon.

The best part of making something together is eating or drinking it!

Here are some other simple snacks that you and your child can make together and pictures of the routines if you want to use them:

• Put icing on cupcakes or a birthday cake

cupcake   icing   icing on   cupcake with icing

• Make ice cream sundaes with ice cream, chocolate sauce and sprinkles

ice cream   chocolate   chocolate on   sprinkles

sprinkles on   ice cream sundae

• Make Kool-aid or another drink using water and crystal powder

water	powder	put in water	put in glass

• Make Jello or pudding

jello	bowl	cup	water

put in bowl, stir	pan	refrigerator	wait
	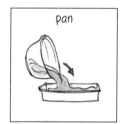		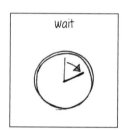

cut	Jello

- Make a fruit-kabob (take turns sticking pieces of apple, orange or watermelon
  on a toothpick or skewer)

- Make a sandwich (filling depends on what your child likes)

Use Cue Cards

Make Cue Cards with reminders of the words and sentences that your child can use in the snack routine, such as "I want," "More please" or "I don't want more." Keep these visual reminders on the table or on the wall next to the place where your child eats, on the cookie cupboard or on the refrigerator door. If your child doesn't say anything on his own, point to the Cue Cards to remind him of the words he can say.

Getting dressed at the Early Communicator stage

What you can expect

At this stage you can expect your child to learn to:

- understand the names of his clothing and directions such as "Come here" and "Put on pants"
- look where you point
- put on most of his clothes by himself
- tell you what the next step in the routine is
- use a Picture Schedule that shows each item of clothing and the order in which he should put the items on
- get dressed independently and follow the schedule on his own

What you can do

As your child relies less on what you say and do to get dressed, you can work on his communication goals.

- Help your child communicate for new reasons
  - Offer choices
  - Try a little "creative stupidity"
  - Help your child initiate the routine

A Self-Help Board helps your child get dressed on his own.

Getting dressed: The steps of the routine at the Early Communicator stage

What you do	What you say	Your child's turn
Lay out your child's clothes. Have a Picture Schedule ready. Use a beckoning gesture when you call your child.	"Adam, come here! Lets get dressed!"	Your child may come to you.
Point to the clothes.	"Let's get dressed."	He may take an item of clothing and give it to you to help him. Or, He may wait for you to start dressing him.
Point to the picture of pants.	"First, let's put on your pants."	He may point to the picture, get his pants, hand you the pants or put on his own pants.
Be a "Cheerleader."	"Good job! You put on your pants."	
Wait for your child to pull up his pants.	Nothing. "Okay, your pants are on".	He may pull up his pants.
Show your child the Picture Schedule and wait.	Nothing. You're waiting for your child to take the next step.	He may point to the next item of clothing he needs to put on. Or, He may pick up the next item of clothing on his own. Or, He may say the name of the next item of clothing.
If your child doesn't indicate what item of clothing he should put on next, point to the picture.	"Now, let's put on . . . ."	Your child may say "shirt" or hand you his shirt.
Pull your child's shirt over his head and wait for him to put his arms in.	"Good job! You're all dressed."	Your child may pull the shirt on all by himself.

Repeat the above steps with each item of clothing, letting your child do as much of the routine as possible on his own. If he needs help, try the most natural cues, like pointing, waiting or just looking at the next item of clothing laid out on the bed or on the Self-Help Board.

Help your child to communicate for new reasons

- **Offer choices.** Does your child want his dinosaur T-shirt or his plain white one, his blue jeans or his jogging pants? Ask him without showing him the clothes unless he needs to see them to make the choice. In this way, you encourage your child to communicate for reasons other than requesting.

- **Try a little "creative stupidity."** All those silly things suggested for the child at the Requester stage can encourage protests and comments from your child too. For example, if you put out Daddy's T-shirt one day instead of your child's, he may tell you about your mistake.

- **Help your child initiate the routine.** Put your "Helper" role away. Don't tell your child that it's time to get dressed. Hint at it, by suggesting an outing to a much-loved park or store, and then get dressed yourself. If you have been consistent in the words that you use to start the routine, your child may use these words to ask you to help him get dressed. Or, he might use his own, different words to ask you, which would be a big step forward in his communication.

This little boy knows what to do and say to get his mother to help him put his jacket on.

Routines for the child at the Partner stage

At this stage, you don't need to help your child as much in self-help routines like dressing and toileting. When "your child can do and say more, you can do and say less." If he does need help, he should rely on **Visual Helpers** rather than on you.

Remember, however, that all routines are ideal times for communication and interaction. Even if your child can do a routine on his own, you can be there with him having **conversations** about other things. In this section, we discuss some of the ways that you and your child can have conversations during routines.

What you can expect

At the Partner stage, you can expect your child to learn to:

- do the routines independently (with or without Visual Helpers)
- have short conversations during routines
- understand a variety of gestures and directions

What you can do

- Decide when to have conversations during routines
- Use Visual Helpers
- Have conversations about what's going on in your child's life
- Have family members give verbal models (e.g, pronouns such as "I" and "you") and physical models (e.g., gestures)
- Balance conversation with questions, verbal models and comments
- Use creative stupidity

Decide when to have conversations during routines

If your child is just learning how to carry out a routine, then your communication will focus on the routine itself as you help him move from one step to the next. However, if your child can do a routine automatically and without thinking about it, then he's probably ready to have a conversation about something unrelated to the routine. For example, if your child doesn't need your help to get dressed, you can use the routine time to talk about other things, such as his plans for the day.

For some children, mealtimes are ideal opportunities for conversations. If you can have all family members at the table, your child will benefit from hearing and seeing their repeated models. But if your child is a picky eater, mealtimes may not be the best time for communication: you can only have successful conversations with your child if you're both feeling comfortable and relaxed. One of your child's favourite times for conversation may be just before bed when he wants to stay up longer. Maybe your child likes having conversations in the bathtub. Whenever your child feels like talking is the best time to work on conversational skills.

Use Visual Helpers in conversation

Conversations can be difficult for your child because they are abstract. He must visualize the topic in his mind as you discuss it, which is not as easy as talking about things he can see. Help your child by letting him "see" what the conversation is about. Put out pictures of possible topics for conversation. For example, make a photo album with pictures of your child's classmates or of trips or activities that your child has recently completed and keep it on the kitchen table or on your child's night stand.

Timmy's father came to his swimming lesson and took a picture of the children playing in the water. Now Timmy and his father have something to talk about at bedtime.

If your child is interested in print, have some key phrases written on Cue Cards to remind him of the expressions he can use in his routines. For example, at mealtime put out some printed cards with starting phrases: "I like the . . . (pictures of the foods being served)," "My favourite food is . . . ," "Today at school, I played with . . . ," "I feel (happy, sad) today because . . . ," "Today I went to . . . (pictures of usual places that your child goes)." Once your child starts a conversation, try to keep him there with a balance of comments and questions.

You can't have all the printed Visual Helpers ready because even the most structured conversations are unpredictable. Keep a pen and paper with you and write down a few key words to help your child stay in the conversation. For example, imagine you and your child went shopping together and you bought new shoes. Later, you might want to encourage your child to tell someone else about what happened. You could draw a picture of the shoes and print the word "shoes" on a piece of paper. Then, start the conversation by saying "Today, we went to the store," and show your child the picture you drew. The drawing might remind him of something he could add to the conversation, such as "We bought shoes."

Have conversations about what's going on in your child's life

Some routines lend themselves better than others to conversations on certain topics. For example, when your child is getting dressed in the morning, use his daily Picture Schedule to talk about what's going to happen to him during the rest of his day. Say something like, "First, we're going to get dressed. Then, we're going to have breakfast. Then what's going to happen?" Once he's able to tell you what he's going to do, try discussing what other familiar people are going to do – e.g., "Daddy's getting dressed too. Where's Daddy going today?" or "It's warm out today. Do I need a coat?"

Try to have conversations when your child comes home from school and has a snack or is being put to bed. Talk about what he did during the day. Use the daily Picture Schedule or the Communication Book to review the day's events.

Have family members give verbal models

Take advantage of those mealtimes when the family is together to let your child learn from everyone else. Go around the dinner table so that your child has an opportunity to hear everyone's verbal model. Have everyone use a repetitive pattern to talk about his or her experiences so it will be easier for your child to take his turn. For example, if everyone names his or her favourite food by starting a sentence with "My favourite food is . . . ," then your child will be more likely to copy this model. Family members can also model ways to talk about what happened during the day. Start with one member of the family who says, "Today, I went to work. I saw Ted." Then the next person can use the same pattern, saying where she went and then naming a person she saw – "Today, I went to school. I saw my friend, Ellen" – and so on until it's your child's turn.

Pick one goal per week and emphasize that word, sentence or concept in a specific routine, such as mealtime. In addition to modelling comments about the food and the day's events, you can also use the family to model the use of confusing vocabulary. For example, Tara's mother wants her to understand how to make comparisons. She gives Tara a big glass, her sister Emily a bigger one and Daddy the biggest. At dinner, her mother says: "Tara's glass is *big*." Then big sister Emily says, "My glass is *bigger*." Finally, Daddy holds up his glass and says, "My glass is the *biggest*."

Mealtimes are ideal for learning more about conversations.

Balance your conversation with questions and comments

Here's an example of how to support your child in a conversation at dinnertime:

You: I like macaroni. It's so cheesy and delicious. Do you like macaroni? *(Make a comment and ask an easy question)*

Child: Yes.

You: Daddy puts ketchup on his macaroni. I think that's yucky (wait and look expectant) *(Make comments and use natural cues)*

Child: I put ketchup on my macaroni, too.

You: Everyone likes different things. I wonder what Austin (friend) likes to eat. *(Make a comment that encourages your child to use his imagination and think about another person's point of view)*

Child: Austin always eats pizza.

Engineer the situation

Try some of the same silly things that have been suggested previously. "Accidentally" drop your fork, give your child his cereal with no bowl or offer him his daddy's tie to wear as a scarf. Give your child a choice between more than two things and ask him to choose between things that aren't always in front of him. At this stage, you want more than a single reaction from your child. Move the interaction beyond one comment into a conversation where you each take some turns.

Look at what Dahlia's mother does.

Dahlia's mother gives Dahlia Mommy's shoes and turns getting dressed into an imaginary game.

Use Joint Action Routines

Your child will probably enjoy Joint Action Routines, activities that require teamwork to create the final product. Besides food preparation, other examples of some daily routines that you can turn into collaborative efforts are making beds, sorting laundry, putting groceries away or tending the garden.

Mommy does the planting and Lynsey
does the watering. That's teamwork!

Making a snack together is usually a favourite Joint Action Routine. Not only does your child have specific things to do in food preparation, but there is often something good to eat after the routine is over. Always show your child a picture of the end result so that he understands what he is doing. Refer to the list of simple snacks in this chapter on pages 283–287.

As you prepare the snacks, challenge your child at his level. For example, ask "*Who* is going to eat the cupcakes?" or "Do you think Grandpa will like the salad?"

If your child is very keen, try some more ambitious recipes – bake a cake from a mix or make some applesauce.

Summary

Daily routines, like dressing, eating and even gardening, can be turned into repetitive and predictable interactions that help your child understand and say new words or phrases. You can adapt many daily events – like feeding a pet or setting the table – into structured routines if you break them into small steps with turns for both you and your child. Just as in People Games, the kinds of turns your child takes in daily routines depend on his stage of communication.

Some routines, like mealtime, depend on you being there. In others, like self-help routines, your role will eventually fade out. In the beginning you'll need to show your child how to carry out routines, but eventually he'll do some of them on his own using a Visual Helper. Some children are more flexible than others and can do routines both with you and independently. Others are more rigid and will want to do routines with you the same way every time. You will have to judge how long to stay in each routine. Your child will become better at routines the more he does them with other people and in different places.

Make the Most of Music

9

Craig is two-and-a-half years old and at the Own Agenda stage of communication. He spends most of his time alone, wandering around the rooms of the house or watching TV. He's usually quiet and rarely responds when someone calls his name, but when he hears music he moves his body and makes babbling sounds that are a lot like singing!

Like so many of us, Craig can't resist the power of music. How many times have you found yourself tapping your foot to the beat of a song or whistling a tune you recently heard? People connect with music in a special way, and that's why many children with ASD respond to music even if they don't react to the sound of your voice.

If your child loves music, it becomes easier for her to learn how to communicate in musical activities, especially **songs**. The songs we sing are like People Games set to music: they have repetitive words, predictable actions and turns for both you and your child to take. Your child will naturally move her body to the rhythm of a song, which makes it easier for her to perform actions like clapping or jumping up and down. And, because you sing songs over and over, your child has a better opportunity to learn the words.

In this chapter, we will see how you can use music and songs to teach your child to communicate. We will decide what songs you can sing with your child and what turns you both can take. By the end of the chapter, it will be your turn to try composing songs to fit your child's interests and stage of communication.

When you sing songs to your child, she learns to pay attention, copy you and communicate because:

- the words in songs have a specific, predictable order
- songs have repetitive actions that your child can do
- songs make it easy for your child to know what her turn is and when to take it

Songs can help your child interact with other children

There are some songs that everyone knows. These "old standbys," such as "Ring-Around-a-Rosy" and "Head and Shoulders," are sung at most preschools and childcare centres. If your child knows these songs, she can sing along with the other children. Many games played at preschools also depend on music, like Freeze, Hot Potato or Follow the Leader. In these games, the music may motivate your child to join in with the other children (see Musical Games, page 331).

Songs help your child understand the meaning of words by pairing words with actions

The actions you perform in songs help your child understand the meaning of words and that there is a connection between words and actions. For example, in the song "If You're Happy and You Know It," when you sing, "If you're sad and you know it, cry 'boo hoo,'" you pretend to wipe away your tears. And, when you sing "The wheels on the bus go round and round," you make a circular movement with your hand that resembles the spinning of the bus wheels.

R.O.C.K. while you sing to make it easier for your child to sing along!

Everything that you have learned so far can help you involve your child in singing songs. If you remember to R.O.C.K. while you sing, you and your child can have a musical conversation with each of you taking a turn at the right time.

Repeat what you sing and do

Repeat what you sing and do when you start the song

The names of most familiar songs are catchy and often start off the song (e.g., "Twinkle, Twinkle," "Old MacDonald"). So begin a song by singing the first few words and, to make it easier for your child to identify the song, add an action or show her an object associated with the song. For example, to begin the "Eensy Weensy Spider," wiggle your fingers or find a furry toy spider and make him crawl up your child's arm as you sing or say the name of the song. Or show your child a toy bus when you sing "The Wheels on the Bus." You can also set out a Choice Board with pictures of her favourite songs on it to help her choose which one she wants to sing. (See Chapter 7 for more on Choice Boards.)

A Choice Board lets your child begin the singing by choosing her favourite song.

Repeat what you sing and do when you sing the song

Since most songs are very repetitive, doing and singing the same things over and over is easy. But you might need to make certain songs more repetitive than they already are. You will need to take on the role of the songwriter (we'll see how later in this chapter).

Repeat what you sing and do when you end the song

End your songs by shouting, "Hooray!" and extending your arms above your head or clapping. Since you and your child might enjoy singing songs more than once, save saying "all done" and making the "all done" or "finished" sign for when all the singing is over. If you're using a Choice Board, your child can put the picture of the song you have sung into a "finished" container or envelope.

Offer opportunities for your child to take a turn

Plan when you will offer your child a turn

Children's songs are naturally broken down into small steps with logical places for your child to take her turn. Many children's songs have recurring words and actions at the end of each line that your child can sing or do. If your child "echoes," it is especially important to plan for her verbal turns to be at the ends of lines. Make sure you offer your child her turn at the same place each time you sing.

Plan what turns your child can take

Your child can take many kinds of turns in songs. Depending on her stage, she can ask for a bounce on your knee when you stop, look at you while you sing, sing a word after you or sing whole lines of the song along with you. Think about working useful words and sentences into your songs so that your child can lift and reuse those words in other situations.

Offer new opportunities for turns

Be prepared to change your plan and offer new turns once your child has mastered the old ones. Expand the song by adding new verses, actions and other singers. Think about doing the unexpected, such as "forgetting" the words so that your child needs to remind you what to sing.

Cue your child to take her turn

Give explicit cues when your child doesn't know how to take her turn

When she is initially learning the words and actions of the songs, you need to give your child cues with a lot of information: **models** and **physical help**. Remember to highlight your models by slowing down before you give them and exaggerating them.

Give natural cues once your child is familiar with the song

After your child has heard the song many times, you can pause, lean forward and look expectant to signal your child to take her turn. If she doesn't take it, give a more explicit cue.

K. Keep it fun! Keep it going!

Keeping songs fun is easy because children naturally enjoy the rhythm, melody and actions. You can make the most of music by picking songs with actions that particularly appeal to your child. For example, if your child loves motion, make sure her songs include large motor movements like rocking or jumping. If she enjoys having her hands squeezed, sing a clapping song or hold her hands tightly during "Row, Row, Row Your Boat." As well, many songs include FUN words that your child will enjoy hearing and singing, such as animal sounds and nonsense words. If a song doesn't have FUN words, you can always add them!

"Skinnamarinky dinky dink" may not mean anything,
but it's sure fun to listen to and say!

Sing Less and Stress, Go Slow and Show!

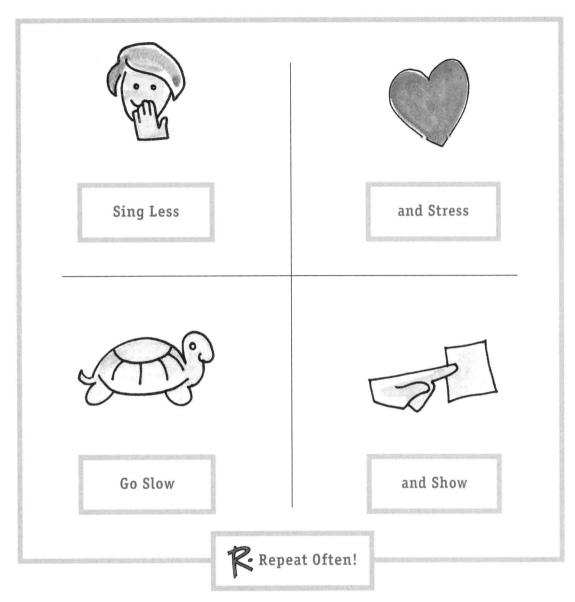

Songs that have words that we remember easily are often simple and are sung slowly. If you stick to those two strategies – "simple" and "slow" – your child will probably learn to recognize and even sing some words. If you stress certain words and show her what you mean with actions or objects, she will begin to understand what she's singing about.

Sing Less

Singing less doesn't mean that you shouldn't sing often. It means that the songs you choose to sing with your child should be short, containing no more than **ten key words**. Songs for children at the Own Agenda and Requester stages should be very, very short (approximately four words). The words in your songs should include familiar vocabulary, names of family members and repetitive phrases.

Stress

Make key words that you want your child to learn stand out by singing them louder, prolonging them and singing them last (e.g., "Head and shoulders, knees and **T – O – O – E – S**").

Go Slow

Sometimes a fast-paced song catches your child's attention, but if the words are sung too quickly she can't make sense of what she hears. We're all familiar with the zippy songs on many commercial CDs and tapes whose lyrics remain a mystery. So, when you sing to your child, make sure that you sing slowly. However, try not to sing *so* slowly that you lose the rhythm of the song.

Show

Most children's songs have actions that show your child the connection between words and what they mean. The best actions are ones that match with a single word. For example, it's easier to understand the words "clap, clap" when the action is clapping. On the other hand, it's harder to know exactly what the phrase "I love you" means when the action is simply a hug. Exaggerate all of your actions to make it easy for your child to notice and copy what you do. You can also use real objects to make clear the meaning of the words, like a toy cow and pig for singing "Old MacDonald's Farm" or a friendly-looking toy spider for singing "The Eensy Weensy Spider."

If objects divert your child's attention from the singing, put them away. Props are meant to help her understand and remember words, not to distract her. However, if at another time you see your child playing with an object or a toy that reminds you of a certain song, sing it. For example, if she picks up a toy bus, sing "The Wheels on the Bus."

A Choice Board shows your child the songs she might sing.

Adapt songs to your child's stage of communication

In this section, we will see how you can fine-tune your singing to your child's stage of communication. Many of the songs you may want to sing are listed on pages 312–322 of this chapter. However, the best songs are often the ones you make up especially for your child. When you're the songwriter, you can make sure that all the necessary elements – the right number of words or the kinds of actions that your child likes – are included in the song. Composing songs for your child is discussed in greater detail on pages 323–328.

As you and your child make music together, keep in mind that nothing goes as planned. You may have the most fun and create the best songs when you follow your child's lead.

♪ Row, row, row your boat, Gently down the stream! ♪

Zachary's mother starts "rowing" in the usual back-and-forth way.

♪ Row, row, row your boat, Go from side to side! ♪

Then she follows Zachary's lead and has a new way of "rowing," as well as a new song to sing!

Songs for the child at the Own Agenda stage

What you can expect

At this stage, your child may not be interested in staying with you while you sing, but don't be discouraged. Even though she may not take any turns at first, she will start to do so once she becomes familiar with the song. You can expect her to learn to:

- move her body
- look at you
- smile, laugh
- come to you when you start singing

What you can do

You do most of the work!

Zachary's mother works hard to keep his attention.

Get your child hooked with large motor movements, gestures and other sensory stimulation

The most important thing is for your child to enjoy singing with you. Choose songs that include large movements and gestures and lots of sensory stimulation – like tosses in the air, bumps on your knee or big, deep hugs. Sometimes silly songs with catchy melodies and nonsense lyrics (e.g., "Doo-wa-ditty") grab your child's attention. Your child may not learn any words in these songs, but she'll learn that it's fun to make music with you.

Choose short songs with fewer than ten familiar words (three-word songs are ideal)

Simply having fun is the first step. Once your child is interested in singing with you, choose one or two short songs to teach her. A few words repeated over and over make the best songs for your child at this stage. You may have to create your own songs. The words you use should be ones your child is familiar with and that are important to her (e.g., "up" and "down" or the names of the people in her family).

Cue your child first with exaggerated models and physical help and then by pausing and looking expectant

Exaggerate what you do so that your child will notice your actions. And, if you make your actions big, it will be easier for her to copy them. For example, if you are acting out "round and round" make a large circle in the air rather than a small one that your child might miss or find difficult to imitate.

Make up songs just for your child

You don't always have to plan ahead – some of the best songs are composed on the spot! You can make up songs to go with your child's **daily routines.** These songs will help her stay focused on what's happening and learn to follow some simple directions. For example, as your child puts on her hat, you can sing a simple four-word song that might go something like this: "Sophie has a hat! What do you think of that? Sophie, Sophie, Sophie has a hat!" Songs can also prepare your child for what's about to happen. For example, if it's bath time, you can sing, "Kelsi's bath, Kelsi's bath. Time for Kelsi's bath," to let your child know what she's going to do next. After a while, your child will start to associate the words and melody with the event.

Songs for the child at the Requester stage

This boy makes the "eensy weensy spider walk up the water spout."

What you can expect

At the Requester stage, your child pays attention to you while you sing, but at first only for a short time. As your child practises the songs, you can expect her to learn to:

- copy a few of your actions
- make some noises that sound like words
- understand some words
- take some turns on her own

What you can do

Choose short songs with fewer than ten familiar words

Sing songs about family members, things your child does during the day or her favourite toys, and use your child's name in the song. Keep the songs short and repetitive with about **three or four** words in each line.

In addition to teaching your child songs with new actions and words, use actions and words that your child has learned in other games and activities too. For example, if you have been playing a People Game in which she has been asking you to put her down, sing a song with the word "down" in it. It's also important for your child to generalize any actions or words that she learns in a song to another situation. For example, if she learns to touch her head in "Head and Shoulders," provide an opportunity for her to touch her head before you put her hat on or when you wash her hair.

Expect your child to take a few action turns on her own after you provide a model and give physical help

Repetition is once again the key to successful turn-taking. Because of the predictability built into songs, many children at the Requester stage make their first word attempts while singing. After you have sung a song over and over and provided repeated exaggerated models of the actions, your child may perform some actions – clap her hands, touch her nose or extend her arms to shout "hooray" – all on her own. Her turns will be large, obvious actions that are easy to see and do. She'll still need some hand-over-hand guidance to make the movements, but quickly try to fade out this kind of help. A touch on her arm or leg may be all she needs to get started.

Pause and look expectant to signal her turn

The most natural cues work best once your child knows what to do.

Make up songs just for your child

Make up some songs in which your child gets practice asking for things in a new way – perhaps by using a gesture. For example, if your child wants a cookie, you can sing the words "Give me a cookie" to the tune of "Twinkle, Twinkle" while making the hand sign for cookie. You can also sing songs to help your child follow directions and do her daily routines. Here's an example of a made-up song about washing hands: "Wash Brian's hands. Wash Brian's hands. Mommy washes Brian's hands." As you can see, you don't have to be Mozart to write a good song for your child. (See pages 323–328 for more examples of made-up songs.)

Songs for the child at the Early Communicator stage

What you can expect

At the Early Communicator stage you can expect your child to take turns throughout the entire song. You can also expect her to learn to:

- choose a song using words, pictures or gestures
- sing some words and perform several actions after you model them or on her own
- start to sing a song
- understand and follow some directions in a song

What you can do

Use props and a Choice Board

Put a few pictures that represent the different songs on a Choice Board and ask your child which one she wants to sing. Once your child is good at making choices between songs, you can give her opportunities to make choices *within* songs. For example, in the song "Old MacDonald," your child can choose whether she wants to sing about the cow or the pig by picking a toy or picture from the board. If you use props when you sing, your child can give you one to tell you what she wants to sing.

Choose songs with words that your child can use in other situations

Since your child may start to talk by echoing whole phrases, sing songs that contain words and phrases that she can lift from the song and use in other situations. If a certain song doesn't have useful words, change the lyrics so that it does!

Here are some phrases you can include in your child's songs: "I want," "I see," "Where is?," "Who is?," "What is?," "Look at (people, things)," "No thank you" and "Yes please."

Work specific communication goals into your made-up songs

Because they are repetitive, you can use songs to teach your child to ask and answer Yes/No questions, as well as questions that begin with "what" and "who." For example, to the tune of Frère Jacques, sing "Do you want a cookie? Do you want a cookie? Yes. Yes. Yes." You can also work comments into your songs by pointing out things or people and singing about them – e.g., "Look at Micky" or "I see Sarah."

Let your child start the songs

If you have consistently done or said the same thing at the beginning of a song, your child should be able to ask you to join her. Most of the time, she'll initiate by starting to sing on her own. Then it's up to you to join in! You can remind her to sing a song by leaving her song Choice Board or props in a noticeable location.

Songs for the child at the Partner stage

What you can expect

At the Partner stage you can expect your child to sing most of the song. She may even make up her own songs as she experiments with sounds and words. You can also expect her to learn to:

- choose songs
- sing words and phrases with you
- sing words and phrases on her own
- perform all the actions on her own
- make up her own songs
- start and end songs
- understand most of the song

What you can do

Sing songs that highlight new words and ideas

You and your child can sing duets!

Songs provide an ideal opportunity to practise pronouns, question words and answers to questions. You can also sing about abstract things that you can't see, like feelings and the future. And if there isn't a song with your child's communication goals in it, you can make one up. You can sing a fast or slow song, a loud or soft song. Then you can give your child a choice: "Do you want to sing a loud song or a soft song?"

Introduce pretending into your child's songs

You can introduce props to help your child pretend in songs or have her act out the actions with imaginary objects. For example, in the song "This is the Way You Wash Your Face" your child can use a real or an imaginary washcloth to wash her face, hands, etc. Songs that tell simple stories give your child a lot of opportunities to pretend. For example, in the song "Miss Polly Had a Dolly Who was Sick, Sick, Sick," your child can pretend to call the doctor on a telephone and put the sick dolly to bed.

Practise having conversations in songs

Your child may know all the words to some songs and enjoy singing solos. However, make sure that you have your own part in some songs so that your child can practise having musical conversations with you. Songs in which one person sings a question and the other sings the answer or one person begins a line and the other finishes it teach your child an important rule about conversation – when one person talks (or sings) the other listens and then responds.

Some popular songs and chants you can sing with your child

Songs that use familiar vocabulary are best for all children. The "old standbys" listed below contain many of the words – such as names of body parts, "up-and-down" and FUN words – that your child may already be familiar with.

Short songs with only a few words are more suitable for a child at the Own Agenda or Requester stages, while some of the longer ones are better for children at the Early Communicator or Partner stages. Your child has her own musical tastes as well. By trying out different songs with your child, you'll find out what those tastes are.

Head and Shoulders
(sung to the tune of "London Bridge")

> Head and shoulders
> Knees and toes, knees and toes, knees and toes
> Head and shoulders, knees and toes
> Eyes, ears, mouth and nose!

Point to the part of your body as you sing the word. Give your child physical help if she needs it so that she can learn her turns. Eventually, just pause and wait for your child to do the action on her own.

If You're Happy and You Know It

> If you're happy and you know it, clap your hands *(clap, clap)*
> If you're happy and you know it, clap your hands *(clap, clap)*
> If you're happy and you know it
> And you really want to show it
> If you're happy and you know it, clap your hands! *(clap, clap)*

Repeat with: "stamp your feet," "touch your nose," and "shout 'hooray'" *(arms over head)*
Later, add: "If you're sad and you know it, cry boo-hoo" *(pretend to dry your tears)*

For Early Communicators and Partners:
- If you're mad and you know it, say, "Oh no!"
- If you're tired and you know it, give a yawn *(stretch arms, sigh)*
- If you're hungry and you know it, rub your tummy *(rub your tummy)*

If your child echoes much of what you say, sing the song "as she would if she could." Change "If you're happy and you know it, clap your hands" to "If I'm happy and I know it, clap my hands."

The Wheels on the Bus

The wheels on the bus
Go round and round *(rotate hands)*
Round and round
Round and round
The wheels on the bus
Go round and round
All through the town.

For children who can pay attention longer, add the following verses:

- The people on the bus go up and down *(bump your child up and down on your knees)*
- The door on the bus goes open and shut *(start with palms of hands together and then open hands away from each other)*
- The horn on the bus goes "beep, beep, beep" *(pretend you are honking a horn)*
- The babies on the bus go "Wah, wah, wah" *(pretend you are drying tears from your eyes)*
- The mommies on the bus go "Sh, sh, sh" *(bring your finger to your lips in the "be quiet" action)*
- The wipers on the bus go "swish, swish, swish" *(raise your index finger and move your forearm back and forth like a window wiper)*
- The driver on the bus says "Move on back" *(make the "come" gesture above your shoulder)*
- The money on the bus goes "clink, clink, clink" *(wiggle your fingers)*

This is the Way We Wash Our Face

(sung to the tune of "Here We Go Round the Mulberry Bush")

This is the way we (I) wash our (my) face
(pretend you are washing your face)
Wash our (my) face, wash our (my) face
This is the way we (I) wash our (my) face
Early in the morning *(or repeat "Wash our (my) face")*.

(Other verses can include: "comb my hair," "brush my teeth," "put on my hat" etc.)

Use actions or real props (e.g., washcloth, bar of soap, hairbrush and toothbrush) depending on your child's stage. You can also change the "we" to "I" and "our" to "my" if your child needs practice using those pronouns.

The Eensy Weensy Spider

The eesnsy weensy spider went up the water spout (Jakey's arm)
(use both hands to pretend spider is crawling up)
Down came the rain and washed the spider out (down)
(use both hands to pretend rain is falling)
Out came the sun and dried up all the rain
(arms above head to show sun)
And the eensy weensy spider went up the spout (Jakey's arm) again.
(repeat crawling gesture)

Hokey Pokey

You put your one leg in
You put your one leg out
You put your one leg in
And you shake it all about
You do the Hokey Pokey
And you turn yourself around
That's what it's all about!
Yeah!

(Repeat with "other leg," "arms," "head," "yourself")

Change the words to "*I* put my one leg in, *I* put my one leg out" for all except those at the Partner stage.

Round and Round the Garden

Round
and round
the garden

Round and round the garden
(take your child's hand and make a circle on it)
Goes the teddy bear
One step... *(start walking fingers up your child's arm)*
Two steps...
Tickle under there! *(tickle your child under her arms or chin)*

Ring-Around-a-Rosy

Ring around a rosy,
(join hands and go around in a circle)
A pocket full of posies,
Husha-husha
We all fall *(pause)* down!

Run around a rosy *(run in your circle)*
A pocket full of posies
Husha-husha
We all fall *(pause)* down!

For children at the Own Agenda and Requester stage, "sing less":
Round and round
And round and round
We fall down!

For children at the Partner stage there's a second verse you can add:
Pulling up the daisies *(pretend you're picking flowers)*
Pulling up the daisies
Husha-husha
We all stand *(pause)* up!

Humpty Dumpty

Humpty Dumpty sat on a wall *(sit your child on your knees)*
Humpty Dumpty had a great fa-a-a-all *(your knees come down)*
All the king's horses and all the king's men
(*or* "all the mommies and all the men")
Couldn't put Humpty together again!

For children at the Own Agenda and Requester stages, simplify:
Tommy, Tommy (*substitute your child's name*) sits on a ball *(use a big ball)*
Tommy, Tommy has a great fa-a-a-all!

The Grand Old Duke of York

The Grand Old Duke of York *(bounce your child facing you on your knees)*
He had ten thousand men
He marched them *(pause)* up
(push your knees up so that your child goes up) to the top of the hill
And he marched them *(pause)* down
(bring your knees down so that your child goes down) again
And when they're *(pause)* up *(knees up)*, they're up!
And when they're *(pause)* down *(knees down)*, they're down!
And when they're only half-way up *(knees halfway up)*
They're neither up *(knees up)* nor down! *(knees down)*

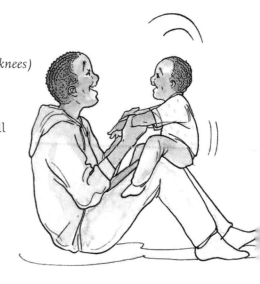

Here's an adaptation that your child will understand better:
Mommy bounces Zachary *(bounce child facing you on your knees)*
She bounces again and again
She bounces him *(pause)* up on her legs
And bounces him *(pause)* down again!

A Little Bit Up

A little bit up *(stand up on toes with arms above head)*
and a little bit down *(crouch down on the ground)*
A little bit up and a little bit down
A little bit up and a little bit down
That's what makes the world
(you can change "world" to your child's name)
go round! *(turn around on the spot)*

I've got two hands and I can make them clap *(clap hands)*
I've got two hands and I can make them clap
I've got two hands and I can make them clap
That's what makes *(your child's name)* go round! *(turn around on the spot)*

Repeat with:
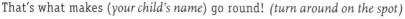
- I've got two feet and I can make them stamp *(stamp feet on the spot)*
- I've got a mouth and I can make it kiss *(air kisses)*
- I've got a nose and I can make it sniff *(smell the air)*
- I've got two arms and I can make them wave *(wave arms over head)*

Row, Row, Row Your Boat

Sit on the floor face-to-face with your child, legs apart in a straddle position, with your child between your legs. Hold your child's hands and rock back and forth.

Row, row, row your boat
Gently down the stream
Merrily, merrily, merrily, merrily
Life is but a dream!

Adaptation:
Go, go, go (*your child's name*)
Go fast if you can,
Faster, faster, faster, faster
As fast as you can!

Sleeping Bunnies

See the sleeping bunnies (*lie on floor with eyes closed*)
Sleeping 'til it's noon
Come and help us wake them
With this happy tune
Oh, so still. Are they ill?

Wake up, little bunnies, and hop, hop, hop
(*Jump up and hop. You can change "hop, hop, hop" to "jump, jump, jump"*)
Wake up, little bunnies, and hop, hop, hop!

Adaptation:
See the sleeping bunnies
Sleeping on the floor
Wake up, little bunnies, and hop, hop, hop
Wake up, little bunnies, and hop, hop, hop!

Here We Are Together

Here we are together, together, together
Here we are together all sitting on the floor (at the table) (on the chair)
There's Mommy *(help your child to point if he needs it)* and Daddy
And Grandma and *(your child's name)*
Here we are together
Sitting on the floor.

The "Bye-bye" Song

Bye bye, Mommy, *(wave to Mommy)*
Bye bye, Mommy,
Bye bye, Mommy
Bye bye, bye bye, bye bye!

Repeat using everyone's names.

Jack in the Box

Jack in the box
(hide your child under a blanket, or have him crouch down on the ground)
Sits so still
Won't you come out?
Yes! I will!
(you and your child jump up)

Adaptation:
(Your child's name) on the floor
Sits so still!
Won't you jump up?
Yes! I will!

Zachy on the floor sits so still!

Old MacDonald Had a Farm

(good for Early Communicators and Partners)

Old Macdonald had a farm
Ee-eye-ee-eye-o!
And on this farm he had a cow,
Ee-eye-ee-eye-o!
With a moo, moo here
And a moo, moo there
Here a moo, there a moo
Everywhere a moo moo
Old MacDonald had a farm,
Ee-eye-ee-eye-o!

Some other animal sounds you can use are:

pig – *oink*; dog – *woof*; cat – *meow*; duck – *quack*; lion – *rrrr*; chicken – *cluck*

More advanced songs

The next two songs, "I Love You" and "Skinnamarinky Dinky Dink," will help a child at the Partner stage learn how to use the pronouns "I," "me" and "you."

To learn these songs, enlist the help of a third person. Sit in front of your child and do the actions while the other person sits behind your child to help him do the actions too. If another person is not available, try to sing in front of a mirror, so your child can see who the "I," "you" and "me" are.

I Love You (The Barney Song)*

I love you *(person helps your child to point to himself for "I")*
You love me *(person helps your child to point to you)*
We're a happy family
With a great big hug *(hug your child)*
And a kiss from me to you *(kiss your child)*
Won't you say you love me too.
(person helps your child to point to you for "you" and himself for "me")

Skinnamarinky Dinky Dink

(Sharon, Lois & Bram's signature song)

Skinnamarinky dinky dink *(hold right elbow in left hand, wave fingers)*
Skinnamarinky doo *(hold left elbow in right hand, wave fingers)*
I *(help your child to point to himself)* love *(hand on heart)*
you *(child points to parent)*
(Repeat first four lines)
I love you in the morning *(raise arms over head in circle)*
And in the afternoon *(lower circled arms to waist)*
I love you in the evening *(lower circled arms to knee level)*
Underneath the moon *(swing arms to one side and make a moon)*
Skinnamarinky dinky dink *(hold right elbow in left hand, wave fingers)*
Skinnamarinky doo, *(hold left elbow in right hand, wave fingers)*
I love you, you, *(point)* boo-boo-be-do
Yeah . . . *(whispered or a cheer)*

You can hold up pictures or use props to help your child understand "morning," "afternoon" and "moon."

The Tiger or Bear Hunt

(for a child at the Partner stage)

Going on a tiger hunt *(show a picture of a tiger or a toy tiger)*
I'm not scared *(help your child point to himself as you shake your head "no" for "not scared")*
Oh, look! *(shade eyes with hand, peering off in distance)*
There's some ooey, gooey mud *(make squishy sounds)*
Let's go through
(pretend you are walking with your knees raised high)
Squish! Squish! Squish! *(or other FUN sounds)*
There's some lo-o-o-o-ng grass *(show a picture)*
Let's go through *(part grass with hands)*
There's a river
Let's swim across *(make swimming motions)*
There's a big tree
Let's climb up and look
(make climbing motions, hand over hand)
Oh, look, a great big cave
Let's climb down *(point down)*
We're in the cave *(use spooky voice)*
Everybody light a match
Oh, look! *(point, act surprised)*
A tiger! *(show a picture or use a toy)*
Let's run! *(run with your child)*

In a Cottage

(for a child at the Partner stage)

In a cottage in the woods *(make roof over your head)*
A little man by the window stood *(use your hands as eyeglasses)*
He saw a rabbit hopping by *(hold two fingers up and hop them along)*
Knocking at his door *(knock on table)*
"Help me, help me" the rabbit said *(throw hands back over shoulders)*
"There are rain clouds overhead" *(make rain fall with fingers)*
Come *(use beckoning hand gesture)* little rabbit
Come with me *(point to self)*
Happy we will be. *(smile and point to sides of mouth)*

One, Two, Three, Four, Five, I Caught a Fish Alive

One, two, three, four, five
(help your child count on his fingers)
I caught a fish alive
(pretend to catch a fish in your hands)
Six, seven, eight, nine, ten
Then I let him go again.
(pretend to release fish from your hands)

Miss Polly

Miss Polly had a dolly *(rock doll in arms)*
Who was sick, sick, sick
So she called for the doctor *(pretend to telephone)*
To come quick, quick, quick
The doctor came with his bag *(pretend to hold bag)* and hat *(point to head)*
And he knocked on the door with a rat-tat-tat *(knock on table)*
He looked at the dolly
And he shook his head
He said, "Miss Polly, put her right to bed!"
Then he wrote on a paper for a pill, pill, pill *(pretend to write)*
"I'll be back in the morning with the bill, bill, bill." *(sing in doctor's voice)*

Make up songs especially for your child

Now it's your turn. Follow the guidelines and compose a song just for your child. It doesn't have to rhyme and it may simply be the same three words sung over and over. But if you put excitement into your voice and animation into your gestures, your child will think it's the best song she's ever heard.

> **Guidelines for writing a song:**
> - Choose a simple, familiar tune or make up your own
> - Make sure there are between three and ten different key words or phrases in the song
> - Place the key words and phrases at the ends of lines
> - Use carrier phrases in some songs (e.g., "I want," "I see")
> - Be repetitive
> - Sing about things and activities that your child is familiar with
> - Add simple actions to the song

Use songs to help your child learn names

The Breakfast Song
(To the tune of "Jingle Bells")

Cheerios, Cheerios
Cheerios for me
Toast or eggs or pancakes
For my daddy and mommy!

(Use the names of foods that family members like. You can use this same song to sing about favourite TV shows or activities).

Use songs during daily routines

The "Drink, Drink, Drink" Song
(to the tune of "Row, Row, Row Your Boat")

> Drink, drink, drink your juice
> Drink up all your juice
> Drink your juice, drink your juice
> Drink up all your juice!

Also: "Eat, eat, eat your cheese," or "Brush, brush, brush your teeth"

A Potty Song
(to the tune of "London Bridge is Falling Down")

> Brian's pants are coming down
> Coming down
> Coming down
> Brian's pants are coming down
> Pants are down (*or* Let's make poo poo!).

I Like Trains
(to the tune from "This Old Man" – same tune as Barney's "I Love You")

> I like trains (*hold up a toy train*)
> I like trains
> I like trains and aeroplanes
> With a choo choo choo
> Choo, choo, choo
> Choo, choo, choo, choo
> And a big kiss (*kiss your child*)
> From me to you! (*point to yourself and your child*)

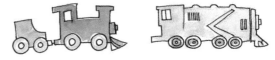

(Name of Child) Has a Hat
(to the tune of the Mexican Hat Dance)

Sophie has a hat
What do you think of that?
Sophie, Sophie, Sophie, Sophie
Sophie has a hat!

You can put the hat on someone else's head and sing the same song using that person's name.

Use songs to help your child ask or answer Yes/No questions and practise important words and phrases

Do you Want an Apple?
(to the tune of "Frère Jacques")

Do you want an apple? *(hold up a real apple or something that your child likes)*
Do you want an apple?
Yes, yes, yes! *(nod head "yes" three times)*
Yes, yes, yes!
(nod head "yes" three times and give your child a piece of an apple)
I want an apple
(or use your child's name,
e.g., Kenny wants an apple)
I want an apple
Yes, yes, yes!
Yes, yes, yes!

Do you want a carrot?
(hold up a real carrot
or something that your child doesn't like)
Do you want a carrot?
No, no, no! *(shake head "no" three times)*
No, no, no!
I don't want a carrot
I don't want a carrot
No, no, no!
No, no, no!

Adapt with any object – e.g., "Do you see a train?" or "Do you like TV?"

Use songs to help your child learn to greet "Hi" and ask and answer questions

The "Where Is?" Song
(to the tune of "Frère Jacques")

Where is Adam? Where is Adam?
(hide your child under blanket or behind a cushion)
There he is! There he is! *(child comes out from hiding)*
Say hi to Adam *(wave to child)*
Say hi to Adam *(wave to child)*
Hi, hi, hi,
Hi, hi, hi! *(help child to wave for each "hi")*

The "How are you today?" Song
(to the tune of "Happy Birthday")

How are you today?
How are you today?
How are you today?
I'm fine, thank you.

How old are you?
How old are you?
How old are you?
I'm four *(hold up four fingers)* thank you.

Use songs to describe what your child is doing

The "Holding Something" Song
(to the tune of "Mary Had a Little Lamb")

Tyler has a banana
Banana, banana
Tyler has a banana
In his hand.

Replace "banana" with the name of whatever your child holds.

Use songs to help your child understand some simple directions

The "Look At" Song

(to the tune of 1–Twinkle, Twinkle or 2–Happy Birthday)

1– Look at Micky	2– Look at Daddy drink his juice
Look at Micky	Look at Daddy drink his juice
Look at Micky	Look at Daddy, look at Daddy
In his chair.	Look at daddy drink his juice

Remember to point when you sing "look at." You can sing the same song using names of other people and objects: e.g., "Look at kitty."

The "Give me" Song

(to the tune of Twinkle, Twinkle)

Give me, Give me
Give me the ball
Give me the ball
Give me the ball.

Use songs to help your child learn prepositions

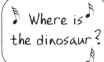

The "Where Is" Song #2

(to the tune of "Frère Jacques")

Where is the dinosaur? Where is the dinosaur?
Under the table. Under the table.
(put toy dinosaur under the table)
Where is the dinosaur? Where is the dinosaur?
Under the table. Under the table.

You can replace "under" with "in," "on" or "behind."
You can replace, "Where is" with:
• What is this? *(hold up real objects or pictures of objects)*
• Who is this? *(point to different people or hold up photographs of them)*

The Jumping (or Swinging or Eating) Song

(to the tune of "Frère Jacques")

Kelsi is jumping, Kelsi is jumping
Up and down
Up and down
Kelsi is jumping, Kelsi is jumping
Up and down
Up and down.

You can make up a song for your child anywhere, anytime and about anything. Give it a try. Just remember to use meaningful words and phrases, add actions and cues, and don't worry about how you sound or if it rhymes.

Here is a list of familiar tunes that you can use to write a song for your child.

- Here We Go Round the Mulberry Bush (This is the Way We Brush Our Hair)
- Twinkle, Twinkle Little Star
- Jingle Bells
- The Farmer in the Dell
- Head and Shoulders
- If You're Happy and You Know It
- Old MacDonald Had a Farm
- Happy Birthday to You
- Mary Had a Little Lamb
- Row, Row, Row Your Boat
- Yankee Doodle
- This Old Man (Barney's "I Love You" Song)
- He's Got the Whole World in His Hands
- London Bridge
- Hokey Pokey
- Frère Jacques (Are You Sleeping?)
- When the Saints Go Marching In
- When Johnny Comes Marching Home Again (The Ants Go Marching One by One)

Some other musical tips

Listen to recorded music

Some children would rather listen to a recording than have someone sing to them. Listening to recorded music can help your child learn new words, but only if you listen to the right kind of music. In recorded children's music, many of the words are sung so quickly that all your child may hear are meaningless sounds. Pick recordings by singers who sing slowly and clearly. (Raffi is an excellent choice.)

Listening to music, though, isn't always about learning new words. When your child is upset she may want to listen to some slow, calming music to relax herself. At other times, you may put on a lively song and get up and dance together for no other reason than to have a good time!

Use musical instruments

Sometimes a silent child may respond to certain sounds by babbling, humming or grunting. Experiment with different instruments to see which ones have an effect on your child. One parent found that his child loved to sing along with an electric keyboard and learned to sing sounds and then words when accompanied by this instrument. If you find an instrument that motivates your child to use her voice, you can take advantage of the tones of the instrument to help her learn to say words. For example, if your child responds to a certain note on the piano, sing a sound along with the note. She may replace her noise with your sound. Eventually you can model a word instead of a sound.

You can also use musical instruments to play copycat games. Keep duplicates of some instruments: for example, a toy drum, a tambourine or an xylophone. Give your child one instrument and let her play on it. Then follow her lead by imitating what she does on your own instrument. If you can't get an interaction going by imitating your child, try to get her to imitate you. For example, if you're using a drum, bang on it first and then give it to your child and say, "Bang drum." Be a "Helper," gently guiding your child to copy you if she doesn't do it on her own. Remember to be a "Cheerleader" as well when your child finally makes her music. Add some FUN words to describe your music, like "Brum, brum!" or "La, la!" When your child can play after you, get out your own instrument and keep the music going for as long as your child wants.

Don't just say it, sing it!

Some children at the Own Agenda and Requester stages sing before they speak. If you find that your child responds well to the words in songs, try singing the same words when you talk to her. For example, say "Let's go," and then sing "a little bit up" (a phrase from a song) as you walk up the stairs together.

Even if your child hasn't heard a certain word used in a song, try singing some everyday words, like her name or the name of a book. You can even turn "hello" into a little one-word melody.

Sing songs in both the standard and simplified ways

As a parent you want your child to practise songs that have useful words. However, the words to some of the old standards will often be meaningless to your child. For example, what child knows who the Grand Old Duke of York is or what the "king's horses and king's men" are? You will probably want to change some of these difficult lyrics. If you teach your child a simplified version, make sure to tell her teacher how you sing it at home. Maybe she can sing it both ways with the children at school.

It's also important that your child be able to sing songs in the same way as the other children. Ask the teacher for permission to videotape the children at song time so that your child can spend time learning the songs at home. Watch the tape with your child and use the pause button to offer your child an opportunity to perform an action or sing a word.

If your child doesn't attend a preschool, try enlisting some cousins or your friend's children to sing on a videotape. Then your child can watch and listen to them singing the songs and maybe sing along too.

Play musical games

If your child enjoys music, playing musical games may provide her with a stress-free way to begin playing with other children. The beauty of musical games is that your child can still play even if she doesn't talk. Here are a few examples of musical games.

Freeze

Find a tape or CD that your child likes and encourage her to dance or move with the music. Then stop the music and help your child to stop dancing at the same time. Saying "stop" may be enough, or you might need to give some physical help. Use the Helper's Rule, giving less and less help each time you play. Turn on the music and start dancing again. You can repeat the game as many times as your child wants!

Hot Potato

You'll need to include siblings, grandparents or babysitters in this one. Everyone sits in a circle. Play the music and encourage the players to pass a ball around the circle. Stopping the music tells everyone to stop passing the ball. Whoever is holding the ball gets a hug. You can play this game over and over, too!

Follow the Leader

Players march in a line behind the leader while the music plays. The leader can make up actions that the other players copy. As soon as the music stops, choose a new leader.

Summary

Many children enjoy music and are more responsive than usual when they sing or listen to it. Songs are often the first place where children with ASD use words and the first activity where they join in with other children. In this chapter, we looked at how you can make the most of music for your child by singing songs at her level of ability. We saw how easy it is to make up songs that include some of your child's communication goals, such as using new words or practising old ones. Children usually aren't fussy about what you sing – your child may like it when you simply sing the same one or two words over and over, especially if one of those words is her name. Or, your child may enjoy acting out the song's story. Some children find the sounds of musical instruments, such as the piano or xylophone, so irresistable that they join in all on their own. Music is a powerful way for your child to learn more about communication.

Bring On
the Books

Some children can pore over a book for hours while others may only glance at the cover. However, all children who like to look at pictures or printed words tend to enjoy books. Unlike the spoken word, the pictures and print do not disappear after they're read. They remain on the page so that your child can make sense of what he is seeing *and* hearing. A good book can also be read many times over. Each time your child hears a story, he understands more and more as the book's language becomes familiar.

Some children with ASD have a precocious ability to read and are often more interested in looking at words than at pictures. Yet even though they can recognize long and difficult words, they don't always understand what these words mean.

In this chapter we will look at how books help your child understand his world and encourage him to communicate. We will also see how you can use the printed word to give your child information and a new way to express himself.

When you read a book with your child, a lot of learning happens:

- Your child discovers the pleasure of sharing a book with you. Book reading offers you and your child the opportunity to make a connection and find enjoyment in two-way communication.
- Your child learns new words and sees words that he already knows used in a new context.
- Books encourage your child to think beyond the words written on the page, as you help him imagine how characters feel or what might happen next.
- Your child may discover another way to communicate through the printed word.

Alexander loves to read words, but he doesn't always understand what they mean.

Reading together

Choose the right books

(See the reference section for a short list of recommended books.)

Take into consideration what your child does with a book, his understanding, his interests and the kinds of pictures that are meaningful for him. You may find that the best books have colourful pictures and text that relates directly to the picture under which it appears. Books for preschoolers usually have a couple of large pictures of familiar objects on each page, but your child may like more detailed pictures as well. Some children enjoy books with pictures of their special interests, such as animals or characters from favourite TV shows.

Remember that even books written for older children have wonderful illustrations. With a little reworking on your part, these books can be transformed into the right book for your child. (See "Read the Right Way" for guidelines on how to modify books for your child's stage.)

Cardboard, cloth and soft vinyl books

If your child prefers to chew on books or tear pages, choose books made from durable materials that will last while he learns how to use books the way he's supposed to.

Books that are good for pointing to and naming things

Books that encourage pointing and labelling usually have one or two brightly coloured pictures or photographs of things that your child is familiar with on each page. These books can be about the **alphabet, numbers, animals, everyday items**, like food and toys, and **daily routines**. Your child may like books with **hidden objects** in the pictures. It can be fun to search for the tiny mouse or little ducky hiding on the page! And don't forget about store catalogues. If your child is fascinated by trains, he may appreciate a train catalogue (available at hobby stores) more than any other book.

Your child may like books with one or two realistic pictures on each page.

It can be fun to search for the hidden ducky together.

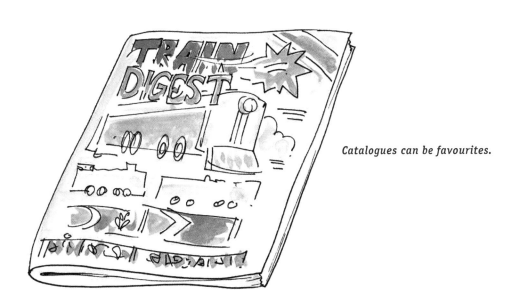

Catalogues can be favourites.

Interactive books

These books provide things for your child to do even if he isn't yet talking or pointing to pictures. Children like books with flaps to lift, buttons to push and fuzzy fabrics to touch. Long before they recognize the meaning of the pictures under the flaps or the sounds that the buttons create, they learn that books can be fun.

Predictable books

Predictable books have repetitive words and phrases. It's much easier to recall something said ten times than something said once. Books that repeat key phrases, such as "I see," "I like" or "Who is that?" are especially useful for your child. Predictable books are also ideal for a child who enjoys music because they have their own rhythms and rhymes. A good example of a repetitive and predictable rhyming book is *Brown Bear, Brown Bear, What Do You See?* by Bill Martin Jr.

Simple story books

As your child's understanding increases, choose books that have a simple plot with a beginning, middle and end. At first, the stories should be about things your child is familiar with, such as a visit to a friend's house, a familiar daily routine or a problem he is likely to encounter. Later, introduce story books that encourage your child to use his imagination and think about unfamiliar things, like scary monsters or life on a farm.

Choose books to help your child generalize words he knows

Once your child learns a new word in one situation, it is often difficult for him to transfer it to another place. To help your child generalize, choose books that emphasize words he's already learned in People Games, songs and daily routines.

First, Kelsi learns the word "up" in a People Game with her father.

Then she sees that not only little girls but also balloons can go "up."

Create a book just for your child

Homemade books appeal to children at all stages. You can make scrapbooks with photos of family, friends and pets or with pictures cut out from magazines or toy catalogues. If your child understands much of what you say to him, you can write a special "Personal Story" just for him. A Personal Story gives your child information that will help him understand confusing or new situations, such as a visit to the Doctor's. (For more about Personal Stories see Chapter 7, page 239.)

Most children like to look at realistic pictures of themselves, their family and other familiar things.

Read the right way

Get your child hooked on books by creating interest and excitement

Think of yourself as an entertainer, and your reading as an award-winning performance. You have to be more interesting to your child than the things that might distract him.

Follow your child's lead

Sometimes the part of the book that interests your child most is not the part that you're reading to him. When this happens, it's best to abandon your plan and follow his lead. Once you notice what your child's looking at, include his interest by labelling the picture that captures his attention and making this picture a part of the story you're reading.

Molly is more interested in the dog than the snowman...

...so her mother follows her lead and tells the story a different way.

Say Less and Stress, Go Slow and Show!

All the communication strategies that you have read about in this book come into play when you read to your child. The rhyme you learned in Chapter 6 – say less, and stress, go slow and show – tells you exactly how to read to your child so that he will learn to love books, understand what you are reading and participate in the book at his level.

Say Less

Simplify and shorten what is written

If the text is too long and complicated for your child to understand, don't read it exactly as it is written. Depending on your child's stage, reduce three-word sentences to one clear label or fifteen-word sentences to three words. For example, if the book reads, "Once upon a time, long ago, there was a little girl named Goldilocks," change it to, "That's a girl. The girl's name is Goldilocks. That's Goldilocks."

You can actually rewrite the text on a piece of paper, either by hand or on the computer, and then paste the new, simplified version right over the original, more complicated one. This not only gives your child the visual cues that match your words, but also helps you to "read" the book the same way each time.

If the pictures are right but the words aren't, simply change the words.

Stress

Be animated and expressive

Use your voice and facial expressions to create excitement. Be an actor. Use sound effects – moo like a cow or take on the scary voice of a monster. Use the book as an excuse to let the "kid" in you come out.

This father captures his child's attention with animation and lots of expression.

Exaggerate key words

Make the important words stand out by using a loud or soft voice, depending on the word you are saying. For example, in the children's classic, *Goodnight Moon*, the word "hush" occurs frequently. If you say it in a whisper each time, the word becomes much more meaningful and memorable to your child.

This mother uses the same voice and intonation whenever she says the word, "hush."

Put the key word at the end of your sentence

Most good children's books put the important words in just the right place – at the ends of sentences. When words come at the end of a line, they are easy for your child to remember and provide a consistent place for him to fill in the blanks. If the words aren't in the right place, you can always rewrite the book so that they are.

 ### Go Slow

Give your child an opportunity to take in what he is seeing and hearing. Your child's attention may move from one thing on the page to another. Give him time to take in the information and to match what you say to what he sees.

Pause between words and phrases

Your pauses are very important. They highlight your child's expected turn and let him know when he should take it.

Be natural

It's important to read slowly, but never so slowly that the meaning or rhythm of the book is unclear.

Show

Show with pictures

Don't expect your child to look at the pictures in a book just because they are in front of him. You need to help him focus on the pictures by pointing to them as you talk about them. Some children start to point to the pictures on their own or will guide your finger to do the pointing for them. For those who don't, give some physical assistance to get the pointing going. You may need to shape your child's finger into a point, or simply support his wrist. But remember to fade out your help as quickly as possible so that your child doesn't become dependent on it.

One, two ....

Three!

David's father helps David concentrate on the numbers by shaping his finger into a point.

Show with the printed word

Not all children are ready to look at the printed word. But if your child shows an interest in print, draw his attention to it by running either his or your finger under the words as you read them.

Show with actions and gestures

Make the words come alive for your child by acting out their meanings with actions and gestures. For example, if a character in the book is swimming, make large swimming motions with your arms; if a character is cold, hug yourself as if you are trying to keep warm.

Show with real objects

If you can match some of the pictures in the book to real objects, your child has another way to understand what you're talking about. Whether real objects are helpful to your child depends on his understanding and interest in objects.

R.O.C.K. when you read

Be careful that you don't become the only performer in the show. Book reading ought to be a two-way experience. Use the **R.O.C.K.** guidelines as you did in People Games, songs and daily routines.

R.O.C.K. with books!

 ## Repeat what you say and do

Repeat what you say whenever you invite your child to share a book. Call his name, hold up the book and say, "Book," "Let's read a book" or the name of the book, depending on his stage.

Some children like books so much that they will read one any time, anywhere. It takes other children longer to discover the pleasure of reading. If you pick a special time for reading, like bedtime, your child will start to anticipate and look forward to the reading routine. When the story is finished, you can end the routine by putting the book away, saying "all done" or "finished" and giving your child a goodnight kiss.

Read the same book over and over so that your child becomes more comfortable and familiar with the pictures and the words. Repetition will make it easier for him to participate when you read. However, sometimes your child might get attached to one particular book and insist on reading that same book *all* of the time. If your child gets *too* attached to a book, help him read other books by using a Picture Schedule. Put two pictures of books on your Picture Schedule: first a new book and then the old one. Make the new book short so that your child won't have to wait long before he can read his favourite. Then read the old book as a reward for trying something new! Try to find new books with the same characters that appear in the old book to make the transition easier for your child. Eventually, your child will find another book or two that he enjoys and forget all about the old one.

O. Offer opportunities for your child to take a turn

Offer opportunities for your child to lift a flap, turn a page, point to a picture, say words or answer questions. Many children's books are written to make it easy for your child to participate.

That one again?

Don't worry if your child wants to read the same book over and over. He won't get bored, he'll only get better at taking his turn.

 Cue your child to take his turn

Cue your child in the same way you have been doing in songs and People Games. Provide lots of verbal models and physical help for the inexperienced reader and less obvious cues for the child who finds it easier to take turns in book reading.

K. Keep it fun! Keep it going!

Now's the time to be a ham! Make reading a pleasurable experience by being lively and animated. If you "say less, and stress, go slow and show," and remember that sometimes it's all right to abandon your plan and follow your child's lead, your child will discover the joy of reading with you. For those children who can't focus on a book for too long, do something that will help them take one more turn each time you read.

Adapt reading to your child's stage of communication

Your child's interest in books usually corresponds to his stage of communication: the more he understands speech and the world around him, the more he will understand pictures and print. However, because many children with ASD are visual learners, it is not uncommon to see a child at the Own Agenda or Requester stage carefully studying books of all kinds.

Your child's stage of communication will determine what you read and how you read to him. If your child thinks books are for eating, your approach to reading will be very different than if he enjoys sitting and listening to a story.

Your child's communication stage can also help you decide what he can learn from the books you read together. For some children, the goal may be simply to interest them in looking at books and to help them understand what the words mean. For others, the goal may be to participate in the story by labelling pictures or talking about the book.

The following section looks at how you can read books with a child at each stage of communication. Children can surprise you with their tastes, so keep in mind that the following are meant only as guidelines and that strategies and books suggested for a child at one stage may work well at another.

Reading books for the child at the Own Agenda stage

Rebecca tends to prefer chewing the book instead of looking at the pictures. When her parents try to read the book to her, she pulls it away and crumples the pages or puts the book into her mouth.

What you can expect

At this stage, your child isn't very interested in books and may rarely pick one up. If he does show an interest, it may be in how the book tastes and feels in his mouth. He may also chew, throw or tear books, or use them for visual stimulation by flipping the pages or lining them up. A child at the Own Agenda stage doesn't yet understand that the pictures in the book represent real objects.

You can expect your child to learn to:

- hold the book the right way
- open and close the book
- look at one or two pictures
- understand that pictures represent real things

A child at the Own Agenda stage explores books by chewing them.

Choose the right books

Choose cardboard, cloth or soft vinyl books

If your child is exploring books with his mouth or tearing pages, it's important to choose books made out of durable materials. Board books made of heavy laminated cardboard are ideal for this stage. Most board books are written especially for very young children and have large, colourful pictures of familiar people and objects.

Choose books with realistic or eye-catching drawings

You're trying to grab your child's attention. The first book your child likes might be a photo album with pictures of his favourite people or toys.

Choose picture books with familiar words

You want your child to understand how the pictures relate to the real objects in his life. Look for books with pictures of food, clothing, toys and activities that are familiar to your child.

Choose books that lend themselves to making FUN sounds and words

Books about animals give you an opportunity to "moo" like a cow or "meow" like a kitty. Your child may not know why you're making these silly noises, but if he associates them with certain pictures, he may become more interested in looking at them.

Choose interactive books

Your child may enjoy books that make sounds when you push buttons, "scratch and sniff" books or "feely" books, where he can touch something soft, like fur. If your child likes watching videos, you can try showing him a book that corresponds to his favourite video. Make sure you look at the book right after the video ends.

If you show your child a book with the characters from his favourite video, he might get interested in the book.

Make a book that will interest your child

Stick something that might interest your child in a scrapbook to tempt him into opening the book. For example, put a small bear, a candy or labels from a favourite video in the scrapbook.

Read the right way

You will be following your child's lead often at this stage, watching to see which part of the book catches his interest. It may not be a picture, but perhaps a rip in a page or the tape that binds the book. That's a good start! Here are some ideas on how to interest your child in the book itself:

Create excitement about the book

If your child isn't interested at all in looking at the book, use your voice to engage him. Add sound effects, like animal noises, or exaggerate "open" and "shut" as you open and close the book.

Make it a short read!

At this stage, reading a book with your child may only consist of showing him how to open and close the book.

Don't expect to read the text as it is written

Unless there is only one word per page, you will need to simplify what is written to a single word.

Find the one picture that your child seems to be the most interested in

Quickly guide his finger to point to that picture while saying what it is.

Attach real objects over their matching pictures on the page

Use Velcro or tape. As soon as your child shows an interest in the objects, show him how to pull the object from the page. In this way, your child may begin to see how the picture represents the real thing.

Reading books for the child at the Requester stage

Kevin only looks at the covers and a few pages of most of his books. But, he can spend a longer time with his favourite book – one that plays children's songs when he pushes the buttons. Whenever Kevin's mother tries to point out the pictures, he pushes her hand away. If his mother persists, Kevin usually gets up and takes his book into his bedroom.

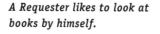
A Requester likes to look at books by himself.

What you can expect

At this stage, your child starts to show some interest in books. He may pick one up and look at it briefly, or he may look at one or two of his favourites for a longer time. But he probably doesn't want to share the book with you. More likely, he prefers to look at it by himself because it's easier for him to focus on one thing at a time.

At this stage, you can expect your child to learn to:

• spend a longer time looking at books
• point to pictures you label
• turn the pages, lift flaps or push buttons
• start to include you in reading the book

Choose the right books

Choose cardboard or vinyl books with simple pictures of familiar things

These books are strong and durable and your child will find it easier to turn the pages. Most of these books have one or two large, bright pictures of familiar objects, people and activities on each page.

Choose books with hidden objects

At this stage, your child may like looking at books with more detailed pictures, in which there is a hidden object, like an animal or a toy, on each page. Try one of the *Find It Board Books* by S. Cartwright.

Choose books with pictures of your child's favourite interests

Books about dinosaurs, TV characters or trains are often a child's first choice. In addition, your child may like family photo albums and store catalogues. Some children show a particular interest in number and alphabet books. If your child likes music but not books, find a book that illustrates some familiar songs or one that has a companion audio recording.

Choose interactive books with flaps, "scratch and sniff" books, "feely" books and books that make sounds when you push buttons

The beauty of these books is that a hands-on learner has something to do and they lend themselves easily to the use of FUN words.

Corey loves alphabet books!

Read the right way

Talk about the picture so that your child will understand

"Say less and stress" are the rules when reading to your child. You may have to reduce the text to one or two key words. Make the words stand out by exaggerating them and saying them the same way every time you repeat them. Use FUN words to keep your child's interest and to give him something easy to say. For example, if you are looking at a book that makes sounds when you push buttons, add your own sound effects, like "vroom, vroom" or "beep, beep."

Show your child what you mean with pointing, actions and real objects

When your child looks at a picture, help him focus on it by pointing to the picture or guiding your child to point to the picture as you say its name. Include gestures to help your child understand the words. You'll have to experiment with props to find out if they help or hinder your child's understanding of the book. If your child pays more attention to the object or toy than the book, put the props away.

Give your child an opportunity to show you he understands by pointing to pictures, turning a page or responding to simple directions

While your child may not label the pictures in the book, he might be able to point to one or two pictures when you ask him to. You can also ask your child to turn the page, push a button or lift a flap. At first, you need to use the Helper's Rule to help your child respond to your directions. For example, if you tell your child to point to a certain picture, ask simple questions like "Where's the ball?" and then wait. Repeat the question and if your child doesn't respond, help him to point to the picture of the ball in the book.

When her mother asks, Cara can
point to a few pictures on her own.

Reading books for the child at the Early Communicator stage

Jake will look at many books with his father, but he prefers to look at one or two books over and over again. He especially loves books about Spot the dog, maybe because he watches videos about Spot. Jake's had a lot of practice answering "no" to the questions the book asks, like "Is Spot under the bed?" and "Is Spot in the closet?" Now, Jake has become so good at saying "no" that his father wants to find a book with opportunities for Jake to say "yes!"

**An Early Communicator enjoys
sharing books with you.**

What you can expect

At this stage, your child probably likes books and can look at a book from beginning to end. He may still like to look at books alone, but you can look at books together too. When you and your child read familiar books, he may expect you to ask him to point out or name some things. Sometimes he might even bring you a book to read with him. Your child may also copy some words and phrases after you say them.

You can expect your child to learn to:

- repeat more of what you say
- point to or label pictures
- fill in the blanks with words and short sentences
- look at you and then back at the book
- answer Yes/No and "What's this?" questions about pictures in the book
- follow a story with a simple plot
- ask for the book he wants to read

Carl likes to fill in the blanks.

Choose the right books

Your child may enjoy all the books listed for children in the previous stages: alphabet and counting books, animal books, books with pictures of familiar words and daily routines, detailed picture books with hidden objects, photo albums and interactive books.

In addition:

Choose predictable books with repetitive words and phrases

Books that repeat key phrases are perfect for your child because they have words and sentences that he can use in other situations and make filling in the blanks easier. For example, the book *Brown Bear, Brown Bear, What Do You See?* uses a recurring pattern in which the author always asks the question "What do you see?" and the answer always begins with "I see a (name of animal) looking at me." There is a short list of predictable and repetitive books in the reference section at the end of this book.

Choose rhyming books

Books with silly rhyming words, like Dr. Seuss's *Mr. Cow Can Moo, Can You?* and *Green Eggs and Ham,* have the same kind of rhythm found in songs. They are fun to read and increase your child's awareness of sounds. If your child likes the way something sounds, he may try saying it himself.

Choose stories with simple plots

Once your child understands what you're saying, tell him stories that have a beginning, middle and end. You can start with:

- homemade books about an outing/experience your child has had (e.g., going to school or visiting grandparents)
- homemade books about a familiar routine (e.g., taking a bath, talking on the phone)
- Personal Stories. These are stories written especially for your child to help him learn what to say and do in different situations. (See Chapter 7, page 239 for guidelines for writing Personal Stories.)
- books in which the character has a simple problem to solve, learns a lesson or changes in some way (e.g., *Max's New Suit* by Rosemary Wells and *The Very Hungry Caterpillar* by Eric Carle)

Read the right way

Change the text if necessary

Change the text so that your child can understand the book and have an opportunity to hear appropriate verbal models. One way to change the text is to insert carrier phrases, even if they do not appear in the book. For example, if the pictures in the book are of different kinds of vehicles, create a script like this: "Here's a train. Choo, choo! Here's a car. Beep, beep!" The carrier phrase "Here's a . . . " will make it easier for your child to fill in the blank.

Another way to change the text is to take out all the confusing words, put the subject of the sentence first and use buildups and breakdowns (see Chapter 6, pages 207–208). Look at how you might adjust this line from *The Very Hungry Caterpillar*. Instead of "One Sunday morning the warm sun came up and pop! out of the egg came a tiny and very hungry caterpillar," try "Pop! A caterpillar comes out. He comes out of the egg. He's hungry."

Use props and real objects

You can usually add props and objects to book reading when your child is at the Early Communicator stage because he is able to focus on the book and the toy at the same time. Help your child understand that the pictures in the book represent real life by showing him toys that resemble the things in the story. Use the objects to act out parts of the story. Let your child hold some objects as well and encourage him to act things out too.

Reading books for the child at the Partner stage

Jerry enjoys all kinds of stories and likes to pretend he is reading a book by running his finger under the printed words and reciting the lines that have been read to him. Jerry can actually read some words too. When Jerry's father asks questions like "What is the man doing?" or "Who do you see?" Jerry has no problem answering and even offers some comments and opinions of his own. But sometimes his father asks Jerry a question that goes beyond the book, like "What do you think will happen next?" This question is hard for Jerry so he answers by telling his dad something else about the book.

A Partner is an active participant in the book reading.

What you can expect

At this stage, your child enjoys a variety of books and will include you in his reading. He understands that the book reflects real life and he can act out situations from the book. He can also answer questions about what's happening, ask a few questions of his own, and he will probably let you know if you tell the story in a way that's different from what he's used to. He might still repeat the things you say when he has trouble coming up with his own answers.

You can expect your child to learn to:

- think beyond what's happening on the page: to imagine, predict what might happen and consider how the characters feel
- learn more advanced ways to express himself (e.g., to ask and answer "what," "who," "where," "when," "why" and "how" questions)
- use the words and sentences he's learned in books in other places
- read a few words

Choose the right books

Your child may enjoy all the books listed for children at the previous stages – word books, alphabet and number books, catalogues, photo albums, interactive books, predictable books and books with simple stories – if you adapt them to his level. In addition:

Choose books that target your child's communication goals

There is probably a book that can help your child learn any aspect of language. For example, a book that repeatedly asks and answers questions beginning with "who," such as "Who is in the tunnel?" and "Who is in the engine shed?" (in *Meet Thomas and His Friends*) gives your child models of how he can ask and answer these questions himself.

Choose books with simple plots

Choose stories that have a logical progression from beginning to middle to end. Books with simple plot lines make it easier for your child to predict what's going to happen. Simple stories are also ideal for you, your child and a brother, sister or friend to act out (e.g., *The Very Hungry Caterpillar* by Eric Carle and *Max's New Suit* by Rosemary Wells).

Choose some books with unfamiliar themes

You want to help your child use his imagination and learn about new things by introducing him to a few books that talk about unfamiliar situations, such as a trip to the moon or a faraway land.

Introduce books where the pictures don't always match the text

If the answers to your questions aren't always in the pictures on the page your child will be forced to listen more carefully to make sense of what you say.

Use homemade books

- Make a book about an outing/experience your child has had so you can talk about what happened. Picture Diaries and Communication Books, described in Chapter 7, help you talk about things that your child did when you weren't with him.
- Write Personal Stories especially for your child to help him understand what he might say and do in different situations (see Chapter 7, pages 239–240).
- Make books to explain abstract concepts, like feelings, in a concrete way. (See Chapter 7, pages 247–248 for examples of these stories.)

Read the right way

In addition to reading as you would with a child at the Early Communicator stage, you can now begin to encourage your child to think about books in new ways.

Encourage your child to think by asking questions and making comments about things that are not told in the story

Here are some examples of ways to encourage your child's thinking:

- Read the title of the book and ask your child what he thinks the story is about. If you are reading a story about dogs, encourage your child to think about other places he has seen dogs. Refer to the past. For example, "Betsy has a dog. His name is Andy. We saw Andy at Betsy's house."
- Point out details in the pictures that will help your child understand feelings. For example, "I think that Max's mommy is mad. Look at her face."
- Make reference to the ideas and characters in the books at other times: "That dog looks just like the one in *101 Dalmations.*"

Help your child retell the story

Choose one of the storybooks with a simple plot that your child especially likes. Read the book several times and encourage your child to complete parts of the story by filling in the blanks. Once your child knows the story well, ask questions that will help him retell it. For example, for the story of *The Three Little Pigs* you could ask, "What does the wolf do then?"

Help your child act out the story

Some stories lend themselves to acting out. If you have props that resemble things from the story, it will be even easier for your child to act out the story. For example, in *The Three Little Pigs,* you can let your child hold a toy pig or a pig puppet and encourage him to say the things that the pig says in the story. This will be easier for him if he has heard you model the little pig's part many times before.

It's easy to turn some stories, like **The Three Little Pigs,** *into pretend play.*

Say it with print

Once your child is very familiar with books, usually at the **Partner** stage, he may start to recognize a few printed words. Learning to read these **sight words** is the first step towards becoming a reader. The other way to learn to read is through phonics – blending together the sounds that letters make to form words – and happens much later.

Some children with ASD recognize words by sight before they are five years old. They are also fascinated by the printed word: the credits at the end of videos and television programs, street signs or the text in books. Most of the time, however, they don't understand what they are reading.

Understanding the meaning of printed words can open the door to a better comprehension of the world. For some children, print offers another way to communicate. In this next section, we will look at how you can help your child learn to see that the printed word performs the same job as the spoken word.

Osteoporosis.

Alexander doesn't understand what he's reading, but with some help he can use his reading ability to get information about the world around him.

How to use print with your child

It's not enough to expose your child to the printed word; you have to encourage him to notice the print that is around him and show him the value of what is written. Draw your child's attention to the print in books, on signs or in magazines. Read words slowly and clearly, pointing or helping your child to point to the words as you say them. Then demonstrate the meaning of what you say by holding up the real objects if they are available and repeating the words. Below, we discuss some of the many ways in which you can show your child how print "talks."

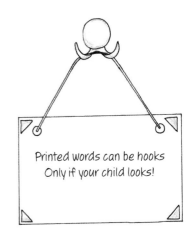

Printed words can be hooks
Only if your child looks!

Use labels to help your child understand the power of the printed word

Print labels by hand or use a computer. Print and type labels in lower-case letters, since this is how words most often appear in books. Put a picture under your label to help your child understand what the word means.

Put labels where your child will notice them

Put some labels directly on objects and others near the spot where the object is most likely to be found. Then draw attention to your labels as you talk about them. For instance, put a "coat" label next to the hook where your child should hang his coat. Before you help him put his coat away, point to the label and run your finger under the print as you say "coat" slowly and clearly. Then hold up his coat, say something like "Let's hang up your coat." Let your child hang up his coat. In this way, labels will become meaningful to your child: not only do they tell him where to put things, but they also help teach him to recognize a few words. To help your child notice labels, put them where he can see them best – at his eye level.

Labels can tell your child where to put his shoes.

Use labels to give your child information

Put labels on opaque containers so that the only way your child will know what's inside is by reading the label. You can also make placemats (include your child in the preparation) with every family member's name and picture on them. As soon as your child is able to recognize the pictures or names on the mats, encourage him to set the mats on the table for each family member.

Reading the box can be just as much fun as playing the game.

Point out labels that will be meaningful to your child

- At meal and snacktime, draw your child's attention to the labels on his cookie bags and cereal boxes.
- Read and show your child the labels on the toothpaste, soap wrapper and other products during his tooth-brushing, hand-washing and bathtime routines.
- Keep some of your child's favourite toys in their boxes and read the name of the toy with your child before you take it out of the box.
- Print your child's name or have your child print his own name on his scribbles or drawings and hang them up where he can see them. Show everyone his masterpiece and his signature.

At first Jerry's mother printed his name on his paintings, but now Jerry signs all of them himself.

Use labels in Joint Action Routines

With your child, prepare a shopping list of ingredients that you will use in a cooking or baking recipe. Then match the words on the list to the items at the store. When you and your child follow the recipe at home, once again point out to him the labels on the food items and ingredients you use. You may have to print the recipe out yourself, using simple steps and pictures.

The recipe for applesauce is easy to follow – all you need are some apples and water.

Use the TV and videos to help your child understand the printed word

- Look at the TV guide with your child. Point out his favourite shows to him before switching on the television.
- If your child looks at the credits after the TV show is over, follow his lead and read some of the names to him.
- Show and label the name on the video cover before putting the video in the VCR. Show two video labels and let your child choose the video he wants to see. Guide his finger underneath the word as one of you reads the name of the video.
- Watch TV shows with your child that encourage letter, sound and number experiences. "Sesame Street" and "Wheel of Fortune" are favourites with children who are fascinated by letters.

Use cards and letters to help your child communicate with the printed word

- Write little notes to your child and help him read them: "Mommy loves Ben."
- Let your child watch and participate in writing birthday cards, Mother's and Father's Day cards and holiday cards.
- Encourage friends and family to send letters to your child. Open and read the mail together.
- Display cards, letters, to-do lists and schedules on the refrigerator at your child's eye level so that he can look at them as often as he wants.

If your child sees you giving and getting information from printed words, he's more likely to show an interest in reading.

Other ways to show your child that print "talks"

- Point out advertisements in magazines, newspapers and flyers that may interest your child. Show your child the movie section of the newspaper, pointing out the movie that you plan to take him to.

- Read and point out signs and billboards while driving in the car. You can get a book of road signs from a driver's education facility.

Henry's mother always pointed out the stop signs to him. Now he shows them to her!

- Ask for and use children's menus with pictures of your child's favourite foods on them. (Ask if you can have one to take home.) McDonald's has picture menus for breakfast and dinner, which you can get if you make a special request. Show your child the names of the foods he likes on the menu. Read the menu with your child and help him to choose what he wants.

- Use instruction sheets with your child. Toys that require assembly often have diagrams that break the task into small steps.

A word about ABC's

If your child has a good rote memory, he may start to say the names of the letters of the alphabet whenever he sees them. You should also encourage your child to say the *sounds* that the letters make and to understand that these sounds blend together to form a whole word. For example, if you are spelling out your child's name for him, run your finger under each letter and say the sound that the letter makes instead of just the letter's name – "This says 'Je-ai-er-ee'" instead of "This says, 'J E R R-Y.'" If your child practises saying the letter names only, it will be more difficult for him to see how the letters go together to make words.

Give your child an opportunity to scribble and write

Once your child sees the value of the printed word, he may want to try some printing himself. Put out paper, crayons and markers in a special "writing" place – perhaps near a desk or a table where other family members write letters, pay bills or do homework. At this point, your role is not to formally teach your child how to print, but to get him interested in the written word and respond enthusiastically to his efforts. His first attempts will be scribbles, but treat what he does as if he has actually printed a real word.

Encourage your child to "write" his name on things like his art work and birthday cards, and give him an opportunity to participate in writing letters and making lists. If your child shows an interest, let him trace letters or copy words but always pair the word with a picture or a real object so that he understands what he's writing. The computer is a great place to learn more about communicating with the printed word – you and your child can have conversations by typing questions and answers to each other.

Summary

Books are an ideal place for your child to learn more about the meaning of words and the pleasure of sharing a story. Turning reading into an interactive experience requires many of the strategies that you already know, like simplifying what you say, emphasizing and exaggerating your words and making sure that your child has opportunities to participate at his level. Some children learn to recognize and read some words on their own. You will find that print can be a valuable way for your child to give and receive information.

Take Out the Toys

11

Play is children's work. Every time your child picks up a toy and plays with you, he "works" at improving his motor, speech and social skills. But playing with toys is often harder than it looks, and all children vary in their ablity to do their "work."

Playing with toys is especially challenging for a child who has motor-planning difficulties. For example, you may have noticed that your child doesn't always play with his toys in the way you'd expect. Instead of filling his toy dump truck with sand and driving it around, he may repeatedly make the "dumper" go up and down. This is because it's far easier to perform one simple action over and over than it is to use toys in more complex ways. Your child's sensory needs may also influence the way he plays with toys. Instead of moving his toy trucks along the floor, your child may like to line them up because he enjoys looking at the pattern.

Once your child learns how to play with toys, it can be difficult for him to include you in the play. He probably finds it hard to concentrate on both you and the toy at the same time. For play to be successful, your child needs to know how to play with *you* first, then with toys and finally with you *and* toys together.

Kelsi isn't ready to play with her piano and her father.

In this chapter we will look at what you can do to help your child learn to play with toys. Then we will see how you can use toys to encourage your child to think and communicate in new ways.

Know your child's "play stage"

The way your child plays with toys and the way he communicates during play depend on his stage of communication. You can know what to expect at each stage by answering the following two questions:

1. How does your child play with toys?
2. How does your child communicate during play with toys?

How does your child play with toys?

No play with toys

Especially at the **Own Agenda** stage, your child may not play with toys at all. He may be more interested in exploring toys by chewing them or rubbing them against his face.

Rebecca is only interested in the way toys taste and feel in her mouth.

Unconventional play

Your child may not play with toys in the way you'd expect. For example, he may line up his trains instead of moving them along a track or bang his blocks instead of building a tower. Unconventional play can usually be explained by your child's sensory preferences – he may like the pattern that his trains form or the sounds of the banging blocks. This kind of play may occur at all stages, but most often at the **Own Agenda** and **Requester** stages.

Instead of moving his trucks along the floor, Carl likes to line them up and look at them.

Functional play

Your child can play with toys the "right" way. Placing a peg in a pegboard, shovelling sand into a pail or fitting a puzzle piece into the puzzle board are all examples of appropriate, or "functional" play.

Functional play can begin at the **Requester** stage when your child performs one action on a toy, such as pushing a lever or taking objects out of a container. Towards the end of the **Early Communicator** stage, your child may learn how to perform many more actions on a variety of toys, but he may still prefer certain kinds of toys, like puzzles or shape sorters.

Jake can do his puzzles in record-breaking time.

Constructive play

In constructive play, your child uses materials to create something. For example, he builds a tower with blocks or uses paint to make a picture. Constructive play is different from functional play because it involves planning ahead and working towards a goal. A child at the **Early Communicator** or **Partner** stage who's very interested in building things may work on making something out of blocks or Lego.

Symbolic or pretend play

In symbolic play, your child pretends to do or be something imaginary. He might drink from an empty teacup or get down on all fours to act like a puppy. This kind of play is linked to **language**, because both words and pretend actions symbolize or stand for real things. Some children develop pretend play on their own; many others can be taught how to pretend. Pretend play helps your child develop his imagination, understand how others feel, learn to solve problems and practise communicating.

At the **Requester** stage, your child may perform one pretend action on himself, using real objects or realistic-looking toys. This is called **self-pretend play**. Your child may pretend to drink from an empty cup or hold a toy telephone to his ear.

Your child may start to pretend on himself.

At the **Early Communicator** stage, your child may perform one pretend action on toys or other people, copying something that he has seen you do. He may pretend to cook with a pot on a toy stove or give his teddy bear a drink from his cup. To play this way, your child needs to use objects that look like the real things.

At the **Partner stage,** your child may act out a short sequence of pretend actions, copying his everyday experiences or scenes he has seen on television. For example, he may feed his bear with a spoon, give it a drink and then put it to bed. Or, like Darren in the picture below, he may cook a pretend soup and then set the table for a pretend dinner. In pretend play, a Partner can use objects that look similar to but not exactly like the things they represent: for example, a big red ball can stand for an apple, or a piece of string can represent spaghetti.

In the final stage of symbolic play, your child makes up stories from his imagination and acts them out, sometimes pretending to be someone else. This type of play is challenging because it relies on talking and the ability to plan and carry out many pretend actions.

At preschool, Darren likes to play in the drama centre. He pretends to stir soup on top of the stove, just as he has seen his mother and father do at home.

Games with rules

Children at the **Early Communicator** and **Partner** stages may start to play games with rules, like Hide-and-Go-Seek, as well as different board games. These games require players to take turns and do or say different things in order for the game to progress. Unlike most play, games with rules cannot be improvised as you go along, but must always be played in a specific way. For this reason, many children with ASD enjoy games with rules. After they have learned how to play the game, they know exactly what to do every time they play.

How does your child communicate during play?

Almost no communication

At the **Own Agenda** and **Requester** stages, your child is just learning how to play with toys and how to send messages directly to you. But he has a long way to go before he can do both of those things at the same time. Yet even though your child isn't communicating intentionally, he may do something, like reaching for or pushing your hand away from a toy, that you can interpret as communication.

Through actions and body language, Benjamin lets his father know that it's hard to concentrate on both him and his train at the same time.

Nonverbal communication

At first, your child communicates only to get what he needs. For example, if you are holding a puzzle piece that he wants, he may pull your hand to ask you to give him the piece. Nonverbal requests start at the **Requester** stage and continue into the **Early Communicator** stage.

Verbal communication

Verbal communication during toy play may start when your child is an **Early Communicator** or **Partner**. At first, your child may communicate with a single word to request toys that he needs or to ask you to help him. Then, he may be able to answer simple questions, such as "What is the name of that toy?" Later, he can make comments, ask questions or let you know when he doesn't want to play. Some children communicate verbally all on their own while others need to be taught scripts to use during play.

Choose the right toys

The kinds of toys that you offer your child depend on his interests and on what you want him to learn. Hard-to-operate toys, like music boxes and other People Toys (see Chapter 2, pages 71–73), lend themselves quite naturally to interaction and communication, while others, like puzzles, games with rules and computer games, develop different skills and need more adaptations to make the play interactive.

Kinds of toys

The toys discussed below are useful for children at all stages.

Cause-and-effect toys

The easiest toys for your child to use are cause-and-effect toys. These toys require your child to push a button or pull a lever in order to produce a sound or make a pop-up toy appear. Some examples are See and Say Wheels, a toy that lets your child pull a lever to hear animal or musical sounds; Busy Boxes, toys that have balls to spin or bells to ring; and Jack-in-the-boxes. Lots of things can be used as cause-and-effect toys – flashlights, tape recorders, computers, light switches and even the VCR!

Visual-spatial toys

Visual-spatial toys have a built-in structure that is easy for your child to figure out. These toys, like puzzles, nesting cups, stacking rings, shape-sorters, pegboards and marble works (marbles speed down a ramp), are toys that your child may understand just by looking at them.

Construction toys

Lego, building blocks and connecting toys, like
beads for stringing or pop-it beads, appeal to
the hands-on-learner. Make sure you keep the
containers for children who like taking
things out and putting them back in.

Exchange toys

One of the ways that your child first learns to include
you in his play with toys is by giving you an object
and then taking it back. This is called an exchange.
Small hand-held objects, like beanbags, plastic
keys, Koosh balls, Nerf balls, hand stress relievers,
blown-up balloons or silly putty, make good
exchange toys that you and your child can pass back
and forth. When your child is ready, you can turn the
exchange into a game of catch.

People Toys

Toys that are easy to operate are the best ones to use when
teaching your child how to play. However, when your
goal is to set the stage for interaction, you need to create a problem that your child can't solve on his own.

People Toys, like wind-ups, music boxes, bubbles, balloons, hand-held air pump toys, pinwheels
and spinning tops are lots of fun to watch but hard
to work. Your child will have to ask you to help
make them go. You can create your own People Toy
by putting something that your child likes in a hard-
to-open clear container or simply turning the water
tap on and off. (See Chapter 2, pages 71–73 for a list of
People Toys.)

Sensory/creative toys

Sand, water, cotton balls and even a bowl full of uncooked rice, pasta, beans or lentils can appeal to your child. If he likes the feeling of pressure on his hands, he may enjoy squeezing glue out of a plastic container or play-dough between his fingers. A young artist may enjoy making crayon marks on a piece of paper. Sometimes, the best toys are right in your own cupboards!

Pretend play toys

The best toys for early pretend play are usually ones that resemble real objects: toy telephones (one for your child and one for you); toy cars, trains and trucks; dolls; doll brushes; doll clothes; a toy cash register with big coloured toy coins; a house centre with realistic-looking toys (like a toy stove or refrigerator); toy dishes; pretend food and some costumes (e.g., an apron, daddy's tie, or mommy's shoes and purse). Puppets appeal to children at all stages.

Large play equipment

Slides, swings, jungle gyms, teeter-totters, rocking chairs, trampolines, rocking horses, wagons and bicycles provide movement and a natural place to interact with other children.

If your child likes looking at pictures, he may enjoy some kind of matching game.

Games with rules

For **Early Communicators** and **Partners** you can make up your own games – e.g., hiding toys or throwing beanbags into baskets – or buy commercial games that are designed for preschoolers. Most board games have turns built into them, and ones that require the players to move a "man" along a board provide visual cues on how to play.

Some recommended games you can buy or make are:

Hi Ho! Cherry-O (Golden)

In this counting game, your child fills a tree with a number of plastic cherries indicated by his spin on the number wheel. (Be careful – this game has small parts!)

Bingo

You can make a Bingo game for your child by putting pictures of familiar people or objects on cardboard squares and then making Bingo-style playing cards with matching pictures (three pictures on a card). Your child takes the "picture" squares from a bag and matches them to the ones on his card.

Barnyard Bingo (Fisher-Price)

In this game, based on traditional bingo, your child matches pictures of farm animals to the same pictures on his Bingo card.

Memory games

You can make these yourself. Put two identical pictures of people, objects, letters or numbers on a pair of cards. Start with three pairs of such cards. Turn them upside down, mix them up and try to find a match.

Thomas the Tank Engine & Friends – Math Game (Briarpatch)

In this game, your child spins a number and then finds a puzzle piece with that number on it. He places the puzzle piece in one of the train puzzle boards.

Boggle Jr Letters (Parker Bros.)

Your child is given a card with a picture and a word on it. His job is to search for the plastic letters that match the ones on the card.

Peanut Butter and Jelly Sandwiches (Parker Preschool)

The object of this game is to create an entire peanut butter and jelly sandwich by collecting all of the "parts" of the sandwich (made from cardboard). A spinner tells your child what part of the sandwich to take.

Sesame Street Gigantik (Canada Games)

This game is played on a plastic mat on the floor. Players copy the actions of the Sesame Street characters that are pictured on the game mat.

R.O.C.K. while you play

Use the R.O.C.K. guidelines when you and your child play together with toys to create repetitive, structured routines in which your child knows what turns he can take and when to take them.

Repeat what you say and do at the beginning, middle and end of the game

Hold up the toy or the toy package and say the name of the game the same way every time you play. Even if your child initiates the play, try to label the play consistently by saying something like "Lego" or "Play puzzle."

Offer opportunities for your child to take a turn

Plan when you will offer your child a turn by breaking the play into parts. There should be things for your child to do and say when the play begins, during the play and when the play ends. The number and kinds of turns your child takes will vary according to his stage and whether he is learning how to play or working on communication goals.

Cue your child to take his turn

Use the cues that your child needs (explicit and natural), fading them out as quickly as possible. When you teach your child how to play with toys, your most frequently used cue will be to give physical help.

Keep it fun! Keep it going!

If you approach play as a child would, being lively and animated, your child will be more likely to approach play in the same way. Your child's willingness to become involved in the play will determine how much he will learn.

Playing together at all stages

In this section we'll look at what you can expect and what you can do with your child at his stage of communication. But you might want to read about the other stages too, since your child's "play stage" may not always correspond exactly to his communication stage. For example, a child at the Partner stage who communicates during People Games may not communicate when he plays with toys (in this case, you should look at the Early Communicator play stage). Each stage requires that you do things a little differently. Let's consider the adaptations.

Play with the child at the Own Agenda stage

What you can expect

No play with toys
At the Own Agenda stage, your child plays with you in motivating People Games but he doesn't play with any toys. He explores toys with his mouth or in other ways, such as by throwing them on the floor.

No intentional communication
If you try to interest your child in a toy, he'll probably push your hand away or reach for what he wants.

At this stage, you can expect your child to learn to:
• play with simple toys
• include you in his play with toys once in a while
• send some messages directly to you
• understand some of your directions

Rebecca is only interested in the way toys taste and feel in her mouth.

Choose the right toys

- **Cause-and-effect toys**

  Look for cause-and-effect toys that require only one simple action, like pushing a button or pulling a lever to produce a sound. Take into account your child's strength and co-ordination when you choose toys.

- **Visual-spatial toys**

  Use very simple toys with just a few pieces. At most stores, you can buy wooden puzzle boards that have places for one or two wooden pieces shaped like letters of the alphabet, numbers or animals.

Start with the toys that your child will find easiest to play with.

- **Construction toys**

  Your child isn't ready for building towers, but he may enjoy knocking them down! He may also like taking or pulling things apart – e.g., pulling beads off a string or separating pieces of Lego.

- **Exchange toys**

  Use big, soft balls that are easy to grasp, like foam or rubber balls. Any toy that fits in your child's hand, such as beanbags or plastic keys, can be used for giving and taking.

- **People Toys**

  Music boxes, bubbles, balloons, hand-held air pump toys, larger wind-up toys, jack-in-the-boxes, pinwheels and spinning tops may interest your child. At this stage, some children are very motivated by clear containers with tempting objects in them. You'll need to experiment to find out which toys will keep your child asking for more.

Bubbles are everyone's favourite!

- **Sensory/creative toys**

  At the Own Agenda stage, your child will probably like sensory toys better than creative ones. Fill up a container with uncooked rice, chickpeas or lentils and add some shovels (one for your child and one for you) and some plastic containers. Put out a bowl of sudsy water, sand, cotton balls or sticky playdough. Your child may not be ready to glue pictures on paper, but he may like squeezing the glue container.

- **Pretend play toys**

  There's very little pretend play at this stage, but you can introduce it to your child with puppets, stuffed animals, a doll, a toy telephone and toy trains and trucks.

- **Large play equipment**

  Slides, swings, jungle gyms, trampolines, teeter-totters and wagons provide opportunities for your child to be near other children, even if he's not yet ready to play with them. Swings and teeter-totters are also ideal for offering your child opportunities to ask for "more."

Do you want another push?

Join in and play

It's hard to join in if your child isn't interested in playing with toys. At this stage, joining in means showing your child the joy of play by helping him use his toys the right way, and creating fun-filled interactions even when the way your child plays with the toys isn't what you'd expect.

Help your child learn how to play with simple toys

Your goal is to teach your child to perform one action on a simple toy. Try imitating what your child is already doing and then add a new action with the toy. If your child doesn't imitate you, step into the role of the Helper/Teacher. At first, give your child physical help by guiding his hand to push the button, pull the lever, lift the sand or pull a bead from a string. Use a short, simple sentence to describe what he's doing while he does it – e.g., "Push the button" or "The car goes on top." Gently insist that he complete the action. Then become the Cheerleader and get excited about his accomplishment. Once your child understands that he can make the toy work, he may want to do it again. Stop giving him physical help when he can make it work on his own. If he has some trouble getting started, touch or partially lift his elbow or hand.

Don't worry if there is no two-way communication when your child is simply learning *how* to play with toys. Your child must first master some basic skills and understand how toys work before you can introduce communication goals.

Help your child play with both you and a toy by playing exchange games

Giving and taking objects is a fun way to help your child include you in his play before he can play "catch." You'll be doing all of the giving and taking until your child learns what to do.

A ball exchange game for a child at the Own Agenda stage is very simple and looks something like this:

Ball exchange

What you do	What you say	Your child's turn
Sit face-to-face and close to your child. Hold up the ball so your child can see it and show lots of excitement.	"Here's Rebecca's ball!"	She may look at the ball.
Put the ball in your child's hand.	"Rebecca's got the **ball**."	She may take the ball.
Gently retake the ball.	"Mommy's got the **ball**."	She may look at the ball.
Put the ball in your child's hand.	"Rebecca's got the **ball**."	She may take the ball.
Cue your child to give you the ball by opening your hand.	"Give Mommy the **ball**."	She may put the ball in your hand.

Rebecca's mother will have to repeat the first two steps of the exchange game many times before Rebecca can give and take the ball on her own.

As you play this way with your child, keep moving a little farther away. Your child may start to throw the ball, but not necessarily to you. Treat what he does as if he meant to throw the ball to you by catching it wherever it lands, saying "Mommy's got the **ball**," and returning it to him. Now you're on your way to playing "catch!"

Rebecca's ball.

Giving and taking a ball is Rebecca's first step towards playing with both her mother and a toy at the same time.

Help your child send messages directly to you by using People Toys

A child at the Own Agenda Stage often responds positively to bubbles and balloons. If you wait after making some bubbles, he may make his first requests for "more" by reaching for your hand or moving closer to you. This is a good opportunity to teach him the sign for "more" (see Chapter 6, page 203) or to teach Object Exchange – have your child give you the bubble wand to ask for more bubbles.

Large moving play equipment like swings or wagons can easily be turned into People Toys. For example, if your child likes swings, push him a few times. Then stop the swing and wait, saying, "Push?" or "More?" Try pushing your child from the front so that you can see each other.

Rebecca asks her mother to open the container so she can get the toy inside.

This mother turns the swing into a People Toy by stopping the swinging so that her little girl has an opportunity to ask for "more."

Once your child makes requests when playing with a People Toy, create a structured, predictable routine that looks similar to the one that follows.

A balloon play routine

What you do	What you say	Your child's turn
Show your child the balloon.	"Look at the balloon!"	He may pay attention.
Start blowing up the balloon.	"Blow! Blow the balloon. Blow!"	He may watch.
Stop blowing and wait.		He may move, make a sound or look at the balloon.
Put the balloon to your mouth.	Say nothing	He may push your hand or imitate your blowing.
Or, Give him the deflated balloon. Then, offer your open hand.	Say nothing	He may put the deflated balloon in your hand.

You may have to repeat the routine many times before your child pushes your hand, hands you the balloon or asks you to blow by acting out blowing movements with his mouth.

Austin's mother blows up the balloon bit by bit, so Austin has practice asking for more!

Follow your child's lead using the Four "I"s to promote interaction

Include your child's interests

Your child may find sensory items, such as soapy water or uncooked pasta, to be the easiest things to play with. Experiment to see which things he prefers and then follow his lead. For example, if your child splashes his hands in water or runs sand through his fingers, join in with what he's doing. Keep what you say simple. Say something like "Splash" or "Whee" every time your child's hand hits the water or releases the sand. Once the routine is established, don't say anything at all. That may get your child's attention!

Interpret some of your child's actions as if they were intentional messages sent to you

While your child might not know how to play with toys yet, he may be interested in picking them up to explore. Treat any of his reaches for toys as though he has sent a message directly to you. Grab the toy and give it to him, saying something like "Here's the block" or "Rebecca's block."

Imitate what your child does with the toys to get him to notice you and to prolong the interaction

If your child bangs a block on the table or takes a toy out of a box, you should do the exact same things. Copy your child's actions until he realizes how he's influencing you. He may decide to do something else that he wants you to imitate. Soon you'll have a game of copycat going! Continue to imitate your child's actions, and then add something new, like another action or a sound. Wait and look expectant to cue your child to copy the new action and keep the game going.

Intrude if needed

One of the ways to interest your child in playing with toys is to be the initiator, presenting him with toys when he's not showing a particular interest and persisting even when he turns away. Pretend play toys such as puppets, stuffed animals, dolls, a toy telephone and toy trains and trucks can all be used to engage your child. For example, a puppet can take a "bite" out of your child's cookie or you can drive a truck up and down your child's leg, saying, "Vroom! Vroom!"

Do the unexpected

Once a routine is established, give your child an opportunity to send a message directly to you by surprising him with the unexpected. For example, if your child is accustomed to playing with clear water during a water play routine, add food colouring or some new toys and objects. You may even want to replace the water with another substance altogether. When you surprise your child, he may in turn surprise you by looking at you or showing his excitement.

A word about toys and sensory preferences

Sometimes, your child gets attached to a toy or an object, carrying it around everywhere and becoming distressed when he can't find it. There is probably a sensory explanation for this kind of behaviour. For example, squeezing the toy in his hand may make your child feel calmer or more secure. However, if your child's sensory needs interfere with play or make interaction difficult, you need to find other ways for him to fulfill them. First, you can try to turn this behaviour into a game, by gently taking the toy away in a playful manner and hiding it in your child's pocket or in yours. As soon as your child finds the toy, give it back to him and then play again. You can also make sure that your child gets the sensations he needs often during the day with hand squeezes from you and by playing with appropriate toys, such as stress balls or drums he can bang his hands on.

Turn your child's love of tapping into a drum session by copying what he does.

Play with the child at the Requester stage

What you can expect

Functional play

Your child may use a couple of toys appropriately, usually cause-and-effect or visual-spatial ones, performing one or two actions on them.

Unconventional play

Even though your child is learning to play appropriately with one or two toys, he likely plays with toys in unconventional ways too. This can usually be explained by his sensory preferences.

Simple self-pretend play

Your child may lift a toy telephone to his ear or pretend to do another simple action on himself.

Nonverbal requests

Your child communicates by handing you a hard-to-operate toy or pulling your hand to ask you for help. However, he still prefers to play with toys by himself and lets you know this by pushing your hand away from the toy.

At this stage you can expect your child to learn to:

- play with a variety of toys and perform several actions on the toys
- imitate one or more pretend actions (e.g., lift a toy telephone to his ear, hold an empty cup to his mouth)
- make play two-way
- ask you for help or to continue playing with a gesture, picture, sound or word
- respond to some things that you say (e.g., "Put the block here.")

Mark has learned to make a sound that tells his mother to keep the water coming!

Choose the right toys

The Requester can use many of the same toys as a child
at the Own Agenda stage, including cause-and-
effect toys, construction toys, visual-spatial toys,
exchange toys, People Toys, pretend play toys,
like puppets, and large play equipment. In
addition, at this stage your child may also show
an interest in realistic pretend toys, things like
pretend stoves, sinks and miniature cars.

Join in and play

When your child plays, the best thing to do is to join
in with enthusiasm. Get down on the floor, face-to-face
with your child, and have a good time! The way you join in will depend on what your goals are for
your child and what your child does with his toys. Joining in often begins by being near your child
and imitating whatever he's doing with his toys. But sometimes you'll also join in as a
Helper / Teacher, showing your child *how* to play with toys.

Help your child learn how to play with more toys

Continue to show your child how to operate new toys by acting first as his Helper/Teacher, and then as his Cheerleader when he is successful, all the while gently insisting that he play with the toy appropriately. Use cause-and-effect and visual-spatial toys first. If your child is a hands-on learner, he may also like using Lego or blocks. Teach one or two actions with one toy, showing your child how to play and giving physical help until he can operate the toy on his own. Then find a new toy with which he can practise similar actions – if he has been working on putting wooden train pieces into a puzzle board, offer him a new puzzle that's at the same level of difficulty as his old one, but with different pieces.

Model simple pretend play

Your child may not be able to pretend, but you can introduce pretending by doing some yourself, first without toys. For example, when your child is having a snack, ask for a bite of his cookie and then pretend to take one. The next time, have a puppet or stuffed animal do the same thing. You can also have puppets pretend to drink from your child's cup, play games of Chase or eat his nose. Become the character, not the storyteller! Instead of saying, "This kitty is licking your nose," say "Meow! I'm going to lick your nose," and make the pretend kitty do just that.

Mother is no longer "Mommy." By changing her voice, she is now Kitty.

If your child plays with cars, trains, miniature dinosaurs or play people, you have a natural place to start pretending. Observe what he's doing and then join in! For example, if your child is moving his car along the floor, take your own car and cause a crash, saying, "Oh no!" or "Crash!" If you see that he's holding a miniature boy, take a little toy girl and give his "boy" a kiss, changing your voice to that of a little girl and saying, "I like you." Don't just describe the play. Be an active participant in it.

It's not much fun for Mohammed when his father just describes what's going on.

But things change when Mohammed's father joins in and pretends!

Help your child make requests and respond to your directions

If you are starting Picture / Object Exchange with your child, find the most motivating toy and teach him to exchange a picture or object to ask for that toy. Then, following the R.O.C.K. guidelines, turn the play into a structured routine consisting of small steps in which there are opportunities for your child to ask for things and carry out your simple directions.

The following is an example of what a play routine with a child at the Requester stage might look like when using a toy parking garage.

Parking garage play routine

What you do	What you say	Your child's turn
Hold up the car.	"(*Your child's name*)! Let's play car!"	He may respond by coming to play. He may take the car from you.
Point to the top of the ramp.	"Put the car here."	He may place the car on the ramp.
Cue your child to make the toy go down the ramp by pointing to the top of the ramp. (Which other cues you use will depend on how well your child knows how to operate the toy.) He may need physical help (e.g., hold his hand until you want him to release the car).	"Let's make the car go!" "Ready, set – go!" Or, "One, two, three – go!" "Vroom! There it goes!"	He may make the car go down the ramp. Later, he may start to complete the phrase, "Ready, set ..." with a sound that resembles "go" or using your intonation pattern.
Catch the car before your child does so he has to ask you for it.	Say nothing, until your child asks you to make the car go again. Then say something like, "Ready, set, go!"	He may look at you. He may pull your hand to ask for the car. Later, he may make a sound.

Put the car here.

At first, Benjamin's father has to show him how to play with the parking garage.

When you use **People Toys,** it's easy to turn play into structured routines with opportunities for your child to request. The following is an example of a water play routine in which the tap is used like a People Toy.

Water play routine

What you do	What you say	Your child's turn
Turn on the tap.	"Kevin, look! The water's on."	He may respond by coming or need physical help.
Put a container under the water or plug the sink.	"Now the water's in the tub!"	He may watch.
Turn the tap off. Put your hand on the tap. Wait and look expectant.	"The water's off." "Okay. Let's turn the water on!"	He may watch. He may take your hand to ask for more water.
Repeat turning the water on and off many times, always waiting expectantly after each on and off action.		He may start to make a sound or say a word when he takes your hand.
Change the routine once your child takes his turns by: Pretending the tap is broken.	"Uh oh, there's no more water!"	He may look at you, make sounds.
Or, Putting soap into the water bit by bit.	"Let's put some soap in."	He may ask for more soap by taking your hand or making a sound.
Or, Helping your child wash his hands.	Sing, "If you're happy and you know it, wash hands."	He may start to wash his hands when you start to sing.

The pattern is the same when you turn play with bubbles into a predictable routine. You do all the work at first as you demonstrate your child's eventual turns.

Bubble play

What you do	What you say	Your child's turn
Hold up the bubble wand or the container of bubble soap. Or, Extend your hand for your child to give you the bubble wand or a picture of bubbles.	*"(Your child's name)*, look! Here's the bubbles!" "Okay, I'll blow the bubbles. Blow the bubbles."	He may respond to you by coming. He may give you the wand or the picture of bubbles.
Blow bubbles.	"There's a bubble. Pop! Pop! Pop the bubble."	He may pop bubbles and watch as you pop them.
Pause and hold the wand in the air. Or, Give him the bubble wand and offer an open hand.	Say nothing. Wait for your child to tell you he wants you to continue blowing the bubbles. Say nothing. Wait for your child to give you back the wand.	He may pull your hand to ask for bubbles. Later, he may pull your hand and add the sound "Bu." He may put the bubble wand in your hand.

If your child catches on to giving you the wand to ask for bubbles, try leaving the wand where it will be easy for him to find – on the kitchen table or in the pocket of a hanging shoebag.

And don't forget about turning swings and teeter-totters into People Toys too! Wait for your child to do something to get you to continue pushing him or making him go up and down.

Play exchange games to help your child establish joint attention

Some children at the Requester stage are able to play catch. If your child likes to throw the ball, make sure you catch it where it lands and act like he threw it purposefully to you. If your child isn't interested in throwing and catching, try the hand-to-hand transfer of objects like beanbags or silly putty. (See the chart on page 376 for the child at the Own Agenda stage for more on how to play this kind of exchange game.) You can also roll a ball back and forth on the floor instead of throwing it. It may help your child if you make the rules of the game visually clear by taping two pieces of masking tape to the floor so he can see exactly where to roll the ball.

Once your child knows how to give and take the ball, make the game structured and repetitive by using the R.O.C.K. guidelines. Here's what a game of "catch" with a child at the Requester stage may look like.

Ball exchange

What you do	What you say	Your child's turn
Hold up the ball. Curl your fingers back and make a beckoning action when you ask your child to come to you.	"Kevin! Come here. Let's play ball!"	He may respond to you by coming or he may need physical help.
Roll the ball to your child.	"Kevin's got the ball." Later "Kevin's got the..." (Wait for him to hold out his hands before you return the ball.)	He may catch the ball. He may hold out his hands or make a sound when you wait before rolling the ball to him.
Open your hands to catch the ball and then take it from your child if he doesn't give it to you.	"Mommy's got the..." (Wait until he returns the ball or says "ball" before you say it.)	He may give you the ball. Then he may extend his hands or make a sound to ask you to roll the ball to him.

To help your child take new turns in the ball exchange you can:

- **Be creatively stupid.** Try sitting on your hands when your child throws the ball. Your child might look at you and try to pull your hands out from under your legs. If you model the phrase "Give me," he can eventually learn to ask for your hands using those words. However, avoid sitting on your hands every time you play because your child may think that this is part of the game and want to play this way all the time.

- **Do the unexpected.** Change the game by giving your child a few different surprises. Throw something other than the ball back to him – maybe a pillow – or throw the ball in the air if you've been rolling it before.

- **Offer your child choices before you play.** For example, have two kinds of balls available and say, "Do you want to play with the big ball or the little ball?" He many not direct his choice to you, but interpret his eye gaze and reaching as him telling you what he wants.

Use the Four "I"s to promote interaction when you play

Include your child's interests and Imitate

Sensory toys, like sand or playdough, and creative toys, like markers or paints, appeal to many children, but they don't always lend themselves easily to two-way play. Try to make sensory play interactive by **imitating** what your child does as he splashes water or scribbles on paper. For example, if your child makes some marks with crayon on the paper, get your own crayon and make the same marks right next to his. If you get his attention, you may get a game of copycat going – as well as a work of art for your refrigerator door! If your child doesn't know how to copy your scribbles, give him some hand-over-hand guidance.

Miguel's mother imitates each circle, line and scribble that he makes and Miguel seems to like this game.

Intrude and Interpret

At this stage, your child may often play with toys in a repetitive, unconventional way. If you wait until he learns how to play properly before you have two-way play, you miss many opportunities for interaction. But, if you intrude on his unconventional play, you may be able to start an interactive game. Look at what happens between Carl and his father. At first, Carl's father tries to initiate a game of make-believe, but Carl is more interested in something else.

The spinning wheel interests Carl much more than his father's idea to pretend that there's a fire.

So, Carl's father joins in and spins the wheel back the other way, turning Carl's fascination with the spinning wheel into an interactive game for two.

Play with the child at the Early Communicator stage

What you can expect

Functional play

Your child knows how to play with toys and probably plays best with cause-and-effect and visual-spatial toys.

Pretend play

At this stage, your child can do some early pretending with a few toys. For example, he might bring a cup to a doll's mouth or pretend to stir an empty pot.

Games with rules

Your child can learn some very simple games with rules, like Barnyard Bingo or Memory.

Unconventional play

Unconventional play tends to disappear once your child becomes better at playing with toys the way he's supposed to. However, your child may continue to use toys in unexpected ways because of his sensory preferences. Now, he may use the same toy both appropriately and unconventionally. For example, he may move his truck along the floor *and* line his trucks up.

Nonverbal and verbal communication

It's harder for your child to communicate verbally when he plays with toys than in other situations. For example, though he may be able to say "more" in a People Game, when he wants something during toy play he may only pull your hand to get help. You need to offer opportunities and the right cues to help him verbalize what he wants.

At this stage, you can expect your child to learn to:
- communicate for a variety of reasons during toy play: to make requests, choices, responses and comments
- turn "echoes" into spontaneous speech
- initiate the toy play on his own
- expand on his pretend play
- play games with rules

Choose the right toys

At this stage, your child can use all the toys at the
Own Agenda and Requester stages. He may also
be ready for more advanced pretend play toys
(listed below) and games with rules.

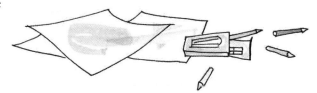

- **Pretend play toys**

  Use toy telephones (two – one for your child and
  one for you), cars, trains, puppets, dolls, a
  dolly brush, dolly clothes, pretend food, real
  life pretend toys, such as a stove, pots and
  cutlery, and adult clothing, like Daddy's tie or
  Mommy's purse.

- **Games with rules**

  Play commercial board or card games or ones
  you make up. Choose or create simple games
  that require your child to do or say something to make the game continue. Games like
  a simplified version of Bingo (using pictures
  of familiar objects or people) can be adapted
  for your child.

Join in and play

Now it's easier to join in and be your child's play partner. You can help him put his puzzle together,
play a game of catch and pretend in make-believe situations. As your child learns to take turns and
share his toys, you can also play some organized games like Bingo or Toy Search (see page 406).

Turn toy play into a structured routine

Use R.O.C.K. to turn toy play into a structured routine with many opportunities for your child to take turns. Here is what a play routine for playing with a wooden puzzle might look like:

Puzzle play routine

What you do	What you say	Your child's turn
Begin the play by holding up a puzzle and gesturing for your child to come and play. Or, Let your child begin the play by asking you with either words or a picture.	"Jake, come here. Let's play puzzles."	He may come on his own when you invite him. He may request the game by bringing you a picture or using words.
Hold on to all the puzzle pieces. Wait for your child to ask for a piece.	Use a carrier phrase such as, "Here's a . . ." and then name each piece as your child requests them.	He may ask for a piece by looking at you, extending his hand, repeating the name of the puzzle piece after you say it or filling in a blank. He puts the piece in the board.
Cheer every time your child successfully puts a puzzle piece in its place.	"Good job! You put the (*name of puzzle piece*) in!"	He may start to cheer "Hooray" for himself.
Cue your child to ask for another piece by holding it up, waiting expectantly or saying the carrier phrase, if needed.	"Here's a . . ." (if needed).	He may ask for another piece by naming it.

Jake can only communicate when he works on a puzzle if he has someone else to play with!

Turn "echoes" into spontaneous speech

In the puzzle play routine described above, the carrier phrase allows you to give your child a partial model – e.g., "Here's the . . . ." Once your child can fill in the blank, only cue him with the first word of the carrier phrase. Eventually, just hold the puzzle piece, look expectant and wait for your child to ask for it using his own words.

Create opportunities for more and different kinds of turns

Try some "creative stupidity"

In puzzle play, you might pretend you can't find the puzzle piece. Or give your child something silly (e.g., a banana) instead of the puzzle piece.

Offer choices

Give choices that require your child to answer with a one-word label. For example, when he's solving his train puzzle, offer him two puzzle pieces, the wrong one and the right one. Ask "Want the dinosaur or the train?"

Ask Yes/No questions

"Do you want the red train?" If your child has trouble answering, provide a verbal model: "Yes" (add an exaggerated head nod).

Ask "what's this?" questions

There are lots of opportunities to ask "what's this," but don't overdo it. Remember, you're playing with your child, not testing him. Ask your child to name a few of the pictures on the puzzle pieces, or name them all when the puzzle is completed. Naming the pieces can become the last step of the routine.

Use People Toys to encourage communication both for requests and for reasons other than requesting

If you have consistently given clear verbal models of requesting, saying it "as your child would if he could," he may now be able to ask for your help verbally when he can't operate a toy. Once he can ask for your help, give him other opportunities for new turns, using creative stupidity (e.g., "Uh oh. I can't find the toy"), offering choices (Do you want the puzzle or the bubbles?") and asking simple questions.

Use large play equipment in the same way as you use a People Toy. Set up opportunities for your child to ask for another turn on the swing by interrupting the action and waiting for him to tell you to continue.

Encourage a comment by changing the game. For example, instead of pushing your child on the swing, twist the rope and let him go for a spin. In addition, he now has two ways of swinging to choose from: "Want a push or a spin?"

Turn the swings into a People Toy and give your child a choice on how he wants to play.

Model pretend play using scripts

Demonstrate a series of pretend play actions for your child. For example, the kitty puppet can drink from your child's cup and then give him a kiss because she's so happy. Then the kitty can take a cookie from the cookie jar and offer it to your child. Remember to stay in character. You're no longer the parent. You're Kitty. So adopt a squeaky voice, a new name and talk as though you really are Kitty – "Can I have a drink? Meow. Thank you. Here's a kiss."

Introduce your child to some **scripted** pretend play. You're the author and director of your child's play, providing all the props as well. You might want to use a video that your child has seen or a book that he's read as a basis for pretending. For example, if you watch a video together about children going swimming, put out a blue rug (your swimming pool!) and a towel and encourage your child to do and say some of the things that the children do in the video: "I can swim," "I'm wet" and "I want a towel." While playing, first provide verbal and physical models, then cue your child to do and say specific things.

Since many children have experience with real telephones, toy telephones are ideal for presenting scripted play. Your telephone scripts should be short at this stage. After your child masters, "Hello" and "Bye bye," include some other social things for him to say, such as "How are you?" and "I'm fine, thank you."

Once your child has learned some of the things he can say during the play, stay in your role and let him come up with his own ideas that aren't part of your script.

It's easy for Wendy to use the toy phone because she's had a lot of practice saying "hello" to people on the real phone.

Provide models of pretend play using food, toy dishes, pots and pans. You can pretend to prepare, serve and eat food. If your child doesn't know what to do, physically guide him, gently showing him how to complete the imaginary action, be it stirring pretend noodles or cutting a pretend sandwich.

When your child starts to put a few pretend actions together, perhaps making and serving you dinner, stay in character and make it fun by exaggerating your play acting, giving your child plenty of models to copy – "Yummy! Noodles. I love noodles!" However, you can step outside your character if you need to offer your child suggestions on what to do, but do so in a way that keeps the make-believe going – e.g., "Ask that lady if she wants some dinner."

Daddy models something that Lisa can say when she's pretending.

Turn "unconventional" into "interactive" play

Early Communicators may still play with toys inappropriately – spinning wheels, flicking balloons back and forth and getting locked into sensory play that is repetitive. If this happens, gently intrude and try to make the play interactive.

Play some simple games with rules

When you play games with rules, make sure there are things for your child both to do and say. For example, he can help you set up the game and choose his playing card (depending on what the game requires). Your script should include some words and phrases that your child can use when he plays with other children – e.g., "My turn" and "Your turn." Put the words on Cue Cards so that you won't have to keep reminding your child what to say.

"Matching" games may be one of the easiest games with rules for your child to learn. Try an adaptation of Bingo using pictures of animals, familiar objects or people instead of numbers on the chips. (Barnyard Bingo by Fisher Price is one you may want to try if you're considering buying a game).

Sasha's mother always gives him a chance to name the picture
before he matches it to the one on his playing card.

Turn games with rules into structured routines

Use R.O.C.K. to turn a game with rules into a structured routine with opportunities for your child to do and say things. The following table shows how you might play an adaptation of Bingo. As in traditional Bingo, the object of the game is for your child to fill his playing card by selecting chips with pictures on them that match the pictures on his card. The pictures may be of objects, animals, numbers, letters or familiar people.

Bingo at the advanced Early Communicator stage

What you do	What you say	Your child's turn
Wait for your child to ask for the game with words or a picture.	Nothing. Wait for your child to initiate and then say, "OK. Let's play Bingo."	He may bring you the game, say "Play Bingo" or give you a picture and say "Bingo."
Or, Suggest the game by holding it up.	"Do you want to play Bingo?"	He may answer "yes" or "no" or repeat "Bingo."
Ask your child which card he wants (the cards can be different colours).	"Do you want red or blue?" and if your child needs more help, "I want . . . ."	He may answer by saying his choice or completing the fill-in-the-blanks.
Point to the words "Mommy's turn" on the Cue Card and ask whose turn it is to take the Bingo chip from the pile.	"Whose turn is it?" (as you point to Cue Card).	He may say "Mommy's turn" or "Adam's turn" on his own or when you point to the Cue Card.
Or, Wait expectantly for your child to say it's your turn.	"It's Mommy's . . ." (only if needed).	He may fill in the blank.
When it's your turn, take the Bingo chip and show it to your child.	"It's a . . ." (showing picture to child).	He may look at the picture, say the name and then decide where it goes.
Cue your child to say that it's his turn either by touching him, pointing to the Cue Card or asking him whose turn it is.	If your child doesn't say anything after you give natural cues, say "Whose turn is it?" and wait.	He may say, "Adam's turn."

You can adapt any game to include the number and kinds of turns that are best for your child. Your child doesn't have to play the game as it was intended. For example, the first few times your child plays Bingo, he may only be interested in matching the pictures on the chips to the ones on the Bingo card. Let him play his way until you feel he's ready to learn the next step.

Play with the child at the Partner stage

What you can expect

Functional play

Expect a Partner to play with a variety of toys and learn how to operate new toys without always needing to be shown.

Pretend play

Your child may play imaginatively by acting out some familiar situations, such as pretending to have a short telephone conversation or preparing imaginary food and then serving it to you.

Games with rules

Your child can learn some games with rules and sometimes makes up his own rules.

Verbal communication

While you can expect your child to ask and answer some questions and make some comments during toy play, he may continue to "echo" what you say or what he has heard others say.

At this stage, you can expect your child to learn to:
- play some games with rules and communicate verbally during the play
- play to achieve a goal or end product
- use his own words and sentences to communicate with you during toy play
- communicate during pretend play for different reasons, such as answering and asking questions, staying on topic, coming up with his own ideas and his own ways of expressing these ideas, planning what is going to happen next, talking about the past and talking about feelings
- play longer with other children

Choose the right toys

Your child can play with a variety of toys, and with a little creativity on your part you can develop interactive play routines for most of these toys. At this stage, pretend play toys and games with rules are especially important not only to promote communication, but also because they allow your child to use his imagination and problem-solving skills.

- **Pretend play toys**

  When possible, provide toys that are related to activities your child is familiar with. These might include toy telephones, a miniature house, toy dishes, a tea set, play food, cars, trains, dinosaurs, a toy cash register, dolls, doll clothes, a doll brush and costumes of some familiar people, like favourite TV or book characters.

- **Games with rules**

  Use games that require taking turns, and make sure that the games have other rules to follow as well – e.g., throwing dice and counting how many spaces the player must advance. Most board games are ideal for keeping your child in the play because the brightly coloured board provides visual cues about how the game works.

  Keep in mind that many of these games require the players to use a spinner that lets them know how far to advance their "man" on the board. For a child who likes watching things move quickly, this spinner can be distracting. You can replace it with cards on which you write numbers indicating how many spaces the player should move.

As soon as your child learns to play a game with you, he can start playing it with other children.

Curtis likes this game!

Join in and pretend

Your child can now begin to enact short familiar scenes from real life or books and videos. For example, together you can pretend to cook and serve pizza, or choose a toy and buy it in a pretend store. By this stage, you want your child to use his own words to create the make-believe. The elements of pretend play – what to say and do – may need to be taught in the beginning. Before you start to pretend, think about what both you and your child can do and say in the play. You will do all the work at first, taking your child's eventual turns for him with your own verbal models, then giving explicit cues so that he knows what to do. As he becomes familiar with the script, use more natural cues, like waiting and looking expectantly, or show him some Cue Cards to remind him what he can say. Having a third person to remind your child how to participate lets you stay in your role as a play partner.

Wendy has learned from her parents' verbal models and now knows just what to say!

You can make the play meaningful to your child by mirroring his real life experiences with toys and props that are similar to the ones used in the actual situation.

First, Jerry and his mom go out for pizza.

Later they pretend to do the same thing at home.

Your child may add something new to the play on his own. Perhaps he will decide there's no pizza at his restaurant. If so, then follow his lead. On the other hand, if your child gets stuck playing the same way every time you play, add to the script. For example, you might no longer be getting pizza just for yourself, but for your friend "Kitty." Put the puppet on your hand and talk for Kitty: "Uh oh, Kitty doesn't want pizza. She wants fries."

Use pretend play to extend your child's thinking by talking about feelings and showing him how to solve problems. For example, show your child how sad Kitty is because there are no fries today at the restaurant. Then try to cheer Kitty up by saying, "There's cake. Kitty likes cake."

When pretending with your child at the Partner stage, you need to take the role of Partner. That means not asking too many questions and not giving too many directions. Find the kid in yourself and let him or her out.

Jerry uses his mother's verbal model to make Kitty feel better.

Play games with rules

Board games that require the players to move a "man" along a board are already structured for turns and provide visual cues on how to play. There are also specific words and sentences that players must use so that the game can progress, like "It's my turn" and "It's your turn." Use Cue Cards to remind your child to use these words. Games with rules are also a good starting place for less scripted conversation. As you try to move your child away from a memorized script, use some of the strategies first outlined in Chapter 2. For example, if you "forget" how to play or do something wrong in the game, maybe your child will tell you how to do it the right way.

Some commercially available games suitable for your child are recommended at the beginning of this chapter (see page 371). Here are a few other made-up games with rules that your child might enjoy.

Flashlight games

Each player takes a turn shining the light on different people or objects while the other person names them. This game is ideal for practising asking and answering questions, such as, "What is it?" "Who is it?" and "Where is it?" Each time you introduce a new turn, you may have to provide a verbal model or give your child instructions on what to say.

Luca's father turns Luca's fascination with flashlights into a communication game.

Toy Search

Hide and search for toys together. Be creatively stupid, like Carl's father, to expand the game.

Basketball

Take turns throwing a ball or a beanbag in a basket while practising the phrases "My turn" and "Your turn."

Surprise Bag

Put some toys in an opaque bag and let your child pull them out one at a time. Work on your child's communication goals. For example, if he pulls out a monkey, ask "Is it a lion?" or "What does a monkey eat?" Then take turns saying something about the toy. If you say "I like the monkey's tail," your child may make a comment of his own: "I like the monkey's hat."

When Carl's father pretends that he's forgotten the name of the hidden object, Carl has a chance to set him straight!

Create something together

Together, you and your child can build a tower out of Lego or a fort out of blocks. If you are in charge of giving your child the blocks and he is the builder, the activity becomes a collaborative effort. To help your child understand what to do, show him a picture of the finished creation or a step-by-step diagram of the process.

Summary

Playing with toys is an important part of your child's life. It develops motor and problem-solving skills, expands your child's imagination and gives him a place to practise communicating. In this chapter, we looked at how to help your child learn to play with a variety of toys. We saw that cause-and-effect and visual toys are the easiest to play with. Pretend play toys, like dolls and miniature houses, are more difficult to understand. All play with toys, either unconventional or functional, can be made interactive if you follow your child's lead.

Once your child understands how to play with toys, he needs to learn how to play with both you and a toy at the same time. Some toys, like hard-to-operate People Toys, force your child to interact with you to get the help he needs. Exchange games, like a game of "catch," encourage your child to include you in his play.

Though play needs to be structured and repetitive in the beginning, it's important to introduce novelty by doing the unexpected. This way, your child will become more flexible and take new turns. Finally, by joining in with your child in a lively and animated way, you help him learn the most important lesson of all – play can be a lot of fun!

Let's Make Friends

The ability to play with other children can take a long time to develop and requires patience and persistence on your part. Your child needs to take small steps. The ideas presented in this final chapter will help you foster social interactions and communication between your child and other children. The suggestions are listed according to your child's stage, but these distinctions are meant only as a guide. All of the ideas in the chapter can work for your child as long as you adapt them to her needs. A game of catch, for example, is appropriate for children at both the Requester and Partner stages. However, children at different stages take turns and participate differently.

Where do you begin?
You already have!

Simply spending time with your child and including her brothers, sisters, cousins and neighbours in her activities has made the challenge of making friends easier. Whatever your child has learned with you and family members can be transferred to interactions with other children.

Six guidelines

When helping your child make friends, keep the following six guidelines in mind:

1. Rehearse the games, songs and play routines that she will use when she interacts with other children.

Your child will have the most success playing with other children if she has practised her play skills at home with you.

2. Find the right friends.

In the beginning, it is often easier for your child to play with an older or younger child than one the same age as she is. An older child may understand that he or she will be helping your child to learn to do and say things as they play together, while a younger child may be content to play without pressuring your child to talk. But, if you support the play, there is no reason why your child can't play with friends her own age.

Regardless of who your child's playmates are – whether they are older or younger, classmates or neighbours – it is important that these children want to play with your child and that your child wants to play with them. If your child attends a preschool, her teacher may also be able to suggest which children your child is friendly with. Then you can invite one of those children over for a play date so that your child can play with him or her in comfortable surroundings.

3. Play dates should include structured and non-structured playtime.

Structured playtime is when your child and another child play together with an adult making sure that they interact and communicate with one another. This structured playtime may occur at home, in a park or in a preschool. If your child attends a preschool, there are many opportunities for interactions between children. Maybe the teacher can arrange for your child and a preferred play-mate to be at activity stations together or accompany one another to the washroom.

Non-structured playtime is when the toys are out and the children are allowed to play with whatever they choose, with no pressure to play together. This kind of play is important because it allows the children to get used to each other and become comfortable together. You can set up your play dates in several ways – e.g., first lunch, then non-structured play and then structured play – as long as you are consistent in what you do and the order that you do it in. Use a Picture Schedule so that your child will understand what she will do before, during and after the play date.

Arrange the first play date at a time when your child is feeling her best and plan on doing something in which neither child feels pressured to play with one another. If your child enjoys lunch, invite her new friend for lunch so the children can get acquainted. You can go on an outing or rent a video the first time that the children get together. Once your child is familiar with her new playmate, introduce the structured playtime. At first, limit the structured playtime – approximately five minutes for children at the Own Agenda and Requester stages, ten to fifteen minutes for Early Communicators and thirty minutes for Partners.

4. Choose the right toys and activities.

Some toys lend themselves more naturally to interaction between children: large play equipment such as swings, trampolines and wagons, exchange toys, such as balls, realistic-looking pretend-play toys like cars, miniature kitchens, toy dishes, dolls, puppets and games with rules, such as board games. Constructive toys, such as large building blocks, may encourage collaborative play in which your child and a friend produce something together. Sometimes you can let your child show her playmate an unusual object or new toy to get the interaction started. If your child knows how to work this toy, she has an opportunity to show or explain it to her friend.

While your child may be very good at doing puzzles and shape sorters, these toys don't encourage interaction, unless you intervene and impose a specific way to play that requires the children to interact in order for the game to continue.

Have duplicates of your child's favourite toys whenever another child visits your house. You'll not only avoid arguments between the children, but also make it easier for your child to imitate what she sees her friend doing. Put out a large piece of mural paper with lots of crayons and markers. There is great value in having children play beside each other as they become comfortable being together.

In addition, give your child and her friend a **communal snack**. For example, give them one big bowl of potato chips or a large plate of cookies to share.

Todd's mother plans for a successful play date by having two of her son's favourite trains available and a big bowl of potato chips that the two boys can share.

5. Coach your child and her playmate.

When your child begins to play with another child, stay with them to provide support for both your child and her friend. The amount of support that you need to give depends on your child and her playmate's abilities to manage their own play. Your goal is to fade out when your support is not needed.

Give the playmate a basic explanation of how your child plays and communicates and how he or she can help. Remember that the playmate is not a parent or teacher, so keep it very simple. For example, "Kevin has trouble understanding and talking. You can help him if you use simple words and show him what to do. Sometimes he may look like he doesn't want to play, but keep trying," or, "When you want to go on the swings, tell Kevin and take his hand." Give examples of the words and sentences that might be difficult for your child to understand and ones that are easier. For example, "Kevin won't understand if you say, 'These cars need to go in the garage,' but he will understand if you say, 'Put the cars in the garage.'" Demonstrate the People Games, songs or play routines that you and your child have already done many times. Explain the words and actions that you use and what the playmate can expect your child to do.

6. Try to balance the turns between your child and her playmate.

Expect your child to participate in the same way as her friend does. For example, if you offer her playmate something to eat and he or she responds by saying the name of the food, ask your child the same question and encourage her to respond the best way that she can, even if it's only by reaching.

Yet don't focus only on getting *your* child to do or say things. By expecting her playmate to participate equally with her, your child has a peer model, which can be more motivating than an adult model. If there are specific words you expect your child to use in the play, explain to the playmate that he or she must use those words as well: "In this game the rules are that everyone says whose turn it is before that person's turn. You say, 'Sarah's turn,' and Sarah says, 'Jonah's turn.'"

Jake's mother gives his brother some tips on what to say when he plays with Jake.

Making friends at different stages

Besides the six guidelines just described, making friends requires different kinds of encouragement from you and your child's playmate depending on your child's stage of communication.

The Own Agenda stage

At the Own Agenda stage, your child plays alone and seems unaware of other children. To help her become aware of other children, take her to the playground or parks, places where she can observe other children without feeling pressured to play with them. Swings, especially tire swings, teeter-totters, wagons, trampolines and climbing apparatus, put your child in close proximity to other children. Point out the other children to her: "Look, Kim's swinging." You might even consider certain children's restaurants or stores that have play areas. Let your child go into the ball bath and bump into other children.

Start with one familiar older playmate – your child's older brother or sister if she has one, or a cousin or neighbour. Demonstrate for the playmate one People Game that you have already played many times with your child. Show the playmate how he or she can get your child's attention by calling her name, tapping her, being face-to-face and creating excitement about the game.

The Requester stage

A child at the Requester stage is aware of other children and observes them but doesn't play with them. Your child may move near the children to watch what they are doing. The next step is for her to learn how to play alongside other children.

Stephen wants to join in but doesn't know how.

Make lots of visits to places where children congregate – the playground or park, drop-in centres – where your child can interact with other children without any pressure. Let your child bring some bubbles or an interesting ball to the park and she'll be an instant hit with the other children. Help her notice other children by pointing out interesting things that they're doing. For example, you can say something like, "Look, Molly's on the swing!"

Try to develop some play routines with one or two preferred playmates. For example, put your child in a wagon with another child. Turn it into a "Go/Stop" routine with opportunities for them to tell you when to go. At first, your child's playmate may be the only one telling you what to do, but if you continue to practise the routine at home, your child will be more apt to participate next time.

When your child plays with another child make sure that there is an opportunity for physical play – swinging beside or chasing one another are two of the first ways that children start playing together. At this stage, it's important to have duplicates of most toys so that your child has an opportunity to copy what her playmate does. In addition, make sure that there are some toys suitable for two children to play with, like bubbles, a ball bath or bicycles. Your child can chase after bubbles, jump in the balls or ride around on a bike beside another child, watching what the other child does and joining in when she feels like it.

To help your child begin to play with other children, start with the games and songs that she has already learned to play with you. If you have both been playing Ring-Around-a-Rosy, include your child's playmate in the game and play exactly as you always have.

The Early Communicator stage

A child at the Early Communicator stage plays parallel or alongside other children, using the same play area and similar toys. Sometimes she imitates another child or runs after him. Now, all she needs to do is find some games and toys that she can play together with other children.

Steven takes a big step forward when he plays beside the other children.

All of the suggestions given for children at the Own Agenda and the Requester stages apply to the Early Communicator: take your child to playgrounds and help her notice other children, find your child's preferred playmate and set up opportunities for them to play with the toys and games your child knows, have duplicates of favourite toys and serve communal snacks. In addition to these suggestions, there are other things you can try.

Use collaborative play

Give the children a job that they must do together in order to be successful. Set up **Joint Action Routines**, activities like making chocolate milk or instant pudding in which the end result depends on each child doing his or her job. In these activities each child knows his or her turn, the expectations are clear and the stage is set for teamwork. For example, in making chocolate milk, one child can pour the milk and the other one can then put the chocolate into the cup. If your child is playing with an older friend, coach the other child to put the milk in bit by bit so your child can use her emerging communication skills to ask for more.

Besides making snacks, your child and her friend can make playdough or build a tower together. Help your child understand what the goal is by showing her a picture of the finished product. By offering step-by-step visual instructions you won't need to constantly tell your child what to do.

Corey and Max take turns putting the blocks on their tower so that they can make it look just like the one in the picture.

Take Turns

Your child will be able to take turns more easily with other children if she has already practised taking turns at home with you. Activities such as throwing beanbags into a basket, waiting to go down the slide or alternating between being the one in the swing and the one pushing it, lend themselves naturally to taking turns. If you have been using using a script in your games with your child, like "Mommy's turn. Sami's turn," she will find it easier to use those phrases when she plays with other children. If she doesn't generalize what she's learned to the new play situation, you'll need to join in the play and give her the models that she needs to participate.

Use pretend play

As with all play, success in pretend play depends on how familiar your child is with the play. If you have been practising an imaginary telephone conversation or cooking an imaginary dinner, provide the opportunity for your child to act out these scenes with her friend. Since early pretend play doesn't usually last a long time, act as a coach for both children, giving a few directions to keep them involved in the play as long as possible. You can also step right into the play to provide verbal and physical models of things the children can say and do. Get into the act by taking on a role yourself! For example, if one child is serving food and the other is eating it, hold out your own plate and say, "I want noodles, too!"

If your child's ability to participate in pretend play is limited, let her take on a role that isn't so demanding until she is ready to do more. For example, in a game of restaurant she can begin by putting the food on the plates or setting the table.

Play games with rules

Your child can play short simple games with rules, taking the same turns she takes when she plays with you. Explain to the other child that just as there are things to do in the game, there are also things to say. For example, in a game of Bingo, one player must choose the chips from a pile or a box and call out the names of the pictures on the chips. After placing the chip on the appropriate card, the other player's job is to say whose turn it is next to call out the names. Besides board games, try copycat games like "Simon Says," Hide-and-Go-Seek or any other People Games that your child likes.

Your child will find it easier to play games with other children if she's played them with you first.

The Partner stage

A child at the Partner stage knows how to play with other children. Though most of the time she may prefer to play quietly alongside others or be involved in physical play on the playground, your child is learning to join other children in building constructions, looking at books, doing art and puzzles and playing house. Your child's goal is to learn how to start, maintain and end play with other children.

*Jerry knows exactly how to play "pretend restaurant"
with the other children because he has played the
same game with his family over and over.*

How to start play

If your child sees another child playing with a toy she likes, what does she do? If she doesn't have the words, chances are she goes over to the other child and grabs the toy. Or she may not even approach the other child. Your child needs to learn some key phrases in order to enter into play with other children. By providing models or instructing her to ask, "Can I play?" you give her something to say in a variety of situations with a variety of people. Make sure you practise at home first. Enlist the help of your spouse, another adult and siblings if possible. Give them each something that you know that your child really likes and then have them start to play without your child. Provide a model for your child – "Daddy, can I play?" Or, if your child understands speaking instructions, tell her what to say to get into the play with her family members.

Another way to make a friend is to give a compliment. If your child has the language, teach her to say, "I like your train," or "I like your ball." Don't be afraid to explain your child's intentions to her playmate. For example, after your child compliments the other child's toy, interpret what this means to the other child: "Kirsty likes your train. Do you think you could ask her to play with you?"

Sasha needs his mother's help to get into the play.

If your child is unable to make the first move, coach the other child to invite her to play. For example, take your child over to the other child and say, "Hi. Jerry wants to play with you." Help your child out by giving him a very appealing toy that will promote interaction. (Get out those bubbles again!)

Even when your child is invited to play, she may not feel like it. So teach her a way to refuse: "Not now, maybe later," or simply, "No, thank you. I don't want to play now."

Use those same words if another child turns your child down. Tell her, "Brad doesn't want to play now. Maybe later."

Mom does some interpreting for Curtis.

How to stay in the play

Being able to keep the play going depends on how familiar your child is with what the other child or children are playing. Try to teach your child at least five routines for structured playtime: a game with rules; a collaborative routine, such as making cookies or a construction; a pretend-play routine; a People Game and an interactive song. Visit your child's daycare or preschool to find out what kinds of activities the children do there and then practise those songs and games at home.

How involved you are in the play depends on how well it's going. You may find that you can be a coach, sitting on the sidelines, simply reminding your child what to say when she forgets and making suggestions to the other child as well. Sometimes these suggestions reflect how the other child feels: "I think Peter is sad. He wants another turn. Tell him, 'Wait, Peter. It's my turn. You're next.'"

Sometimes if the play gets silly or repetitive you may have to jump in to get it back on track. You can model some new turns or introduce a new element to the play and then fade out again.

It is helpful for both children to have a Play Schedule so that they know how long they are going to play together and what they are going to do. If you leave a blank on the schedule the children can see when it's possible for them to choose whatever they want to do.

Use the video

If your child copies things that she sees on TV, try videotaping some children demonstrating the ideal way to play house or a board game. Let your child and her playmate watch this videotape together and then encourage them to play the same way as the children in the video, saying and doing the same things.

How to end the play

Just as your child needs words to start the play, she needs something to say when she ends the play. Coach both children to say, "I don't want to play anymore," or "That's all for now," when they've had enough. Prepare a Cue Card with the ending sentence and a picture representing "finished" to remind your child that she's expected to do more than just walk away from the activity.

Summary

There are many things that you as a parent can do to help your child play with other children. You can start by taking her to parks and playgrounds where she can be with other children in a comfortable environment. You can find one playmate whom your child likes and who likes your child. In addition, it helps if your child has a lot of practice playing the same games, singing the same songs, reading the same books and using the same toys first with you and then with other children. In the beginning, when your child is just starting to develop her social skills, your presence as a play model and "coach" is important. Later, when your child knows how to interact with other children, you can fade out and watch the fun!

Glossary

adapt How you change what you're doing or saying so that your child gets information and can participate at his level.

breakdowns A way to talk to your child so that he understands what each word in a sentence means and how these words fit together. Start with the whole sentence and then break it down into its parts. (207–208, 212)

buildups A way to talk to your child so that he understands what each word in a sentence means and how these words fit together. Start with the parts of the sentence and then build them up into a whole sentence. (207–208, 212)

carrier phrases Words that often go together and are used as a unit (e.g., "I want...", I like... "). (100)

Choice Board A kind of Visual Helper made from objects or pictures. It shows your child what toys, foods and activities he can choose from. (218, 300)

collaborative routines Activities that require teamwork to achieve a goal. Also called **Joint Action Routines**. (283–287, 295–296, 357, 413)

comments Things you say to share your ideas about your child's interests and help keep the conversation going. (93, 130)

communication When one person sends a message to another person. Communication can be **unintentional**. This means that your child does things without realizing that his actions, sounds or words can have an effect on other people. Communication can also be **intentional**. This means your child understands that what he does can have an effect on another person and that he communicates with the purpose of sending a message directly to that person. (17–27)

conversation Communication in which two people send messages back and forth. Conversations can be both nonverbal and verbal.(67, 108–109, 112–113, 128, 160, 291–294)

constructive play In constructive play, your child plans and creates something made from blocks or other materials. (364)

cue A signal to your child that it's his turn to do or say something. **Explicit cues** carry a lot of information and leave little room for your child to do something incorrectly. **Natural cues**, like pausing or leaning forward, are more subtle and just hint at what your child can do.(114–130)

Cue Cards Cards with a picture and a word(s) that remind your child what to do or say. (226, 240–242, 251–252)

echolalia Refers to the repetition of what other people say. **Immediate echolalia** occurs when your child repeats words or phrases, usually the last part of what is said, immediately after he hears them. **Delayed echolalia** occurs when your child lifts words or phrases he has heard and uses them days, weeks, months or even years later. Sometimes your child changes the echoes by saying them in a different tone or by changing some of the words in an effort to adapt them to different situations. These changes are referred to as **mitigated echolalia**. (21–22, 89, 97–99)

descriptive praise Tells your child exactly why you are pleased with him. Instead of saying "Good job," you describe what he's done – "Shoe on" – with excitement and pleasure in your voice. (45)

exchange toys Toys that are easy for your child to pass back and forth, such as balls or other hand-sized objects. (368)

fill-in-the-blanks A cue in which you take the first part of your child's verbal turn and then wait for him to complete the turn by filling in the blanks (e.g., "One, two..."). (119–120)

FUN words Words that are fun to say and listen to (e.g., "Yucky!" "Whee!"). (201)

functional play A term that describes appropriate play with a toy (e.g., putting a puzzle together or making a train go back and forth on tracks). (364)

gesture A body movement, often made with your hand or arm, that helps your child understand the word you're saying (e.g., putting your finger on your lips to say "be quiet" or nodding your head for "yes"). (203)

generalize/generalization A term that describes what happens when your child transfers something he learns in one situation to another similar situation. (61, 145, 154, 253, 337)

gestalt A type of learning style. A child with a **gestalt** learning style takes in information as a whole "chunk." He may say a complete sentence without understanding what each word means. (15–16, 57)

hand-over-hand guidance You show your child exactly what to do by placing your hand over or under his and physically guiding him through an action.

interaction What happens between you and your child when a connection is made. In an interaction there is a back-and-forth relationship between the two of you no matter what you're doing. (17–18)

joint attention The ability to focus on people and objects at the same time. It is fundamental to communication. (20, 388)

label The spoken or printed name of an object, person or action. (95, 195)

model You demonstrate what you expect your child to do (a **physical model**) or say (a **verbal model**). (95–101, 116–117)

partial model You demonstrate the first part of what you expect your child to do or say and wait for him to finish. You can perform the first part of an action, say the first sound of a word or the first few words of a sentence. (119–120)

language A formal system of communication that everyone understands. (364)

learning style The way that your child acquires information. (15–16)

open-ended questions Open-ended questions do not have single-word answers. Instead, they require more complex responses about abstract things. Questions that begin with why and how are open-ended, unlike those beginning with who, what, where and when, which are called **closed**. (126)

OWL The acronym that stands for Observing, Waiting and Listening as a reminder of how to figure out the best strategy for helping your child. (86)

parallel play A child plays alongside other children and occasionally imitates something another child does.

People Games Repetitive physical games for you and your child to play without toys (e.g., "Peek-a-boo" and "Chase"). (Ch 5)

People Toys Hard-to-operate toys, like wind-ups and music boxes, that encourage interaction: your child needs you to help make them work. (70–73)

physical help A way to guide your child to perform an action by physically moving him through the motions (e.g., you place your hands over his and help him to clap). (115)

Picture / Object Schedule A group of pictures or objects that shows your child the events of his day. (220–221)

pretend play In pretend play your child plays make-believe. He may pretend with toys that represent real things. He may also be able to pretend without toys. Pretend play is also called **symbolic play**. (364–365)

prompt Same as a cue – a signal to your child that it's his turn to do or say something.

R.O.C.K. An acronym to help you remember how to create structured routines. R stands for Repeat, O for Offer Opportunities, C for Cue Your Child and K for Keep It Fun! Keep It Going!

rote memory Refers to memorizing things that follow each other in a sequence, such as numbers or lists of people's birthdays. (15, 57)

script A group of verbal and physical models that your child memorizes and uses exactly as he learns it. (97, 396–397)

self-help routine A routine that you expect your child to eventually do by himself. (228, 264)

sensory preferences The sights, sounds, smells, feelings and movements that your child enjoys or dislikes. (9)

sign A specific hand action that represents a real word. A sign is different from a gesture because a sign is part of a formal system – either Signed English or American Sign Language. (53, 203)

sight words Printed words that your child recognizes before he learns how to sound words out letter by letter. (355)

spontaneous speech Refers to words, phrases or sentences that your child says on his own.

symbolic thought Your child realizes that an object, sign, gesture, picture or word can represent or stand for the real thing. (51)

turn Whatever you and your child do – look at each other, gesture, make a sound or say a word – to let the other know you're participating in the interaction. (59, Ch 4)

The Four "I"s These tell you how to follow your child's lead. The first "I" tells you to "include your child's interests." The second "I" tells you to "interpret" what your child says or does so that he has a model to copy. The third and fourth "I"s tell you to "Intrude" and "Imitate" to get an interaction going. (92–110)

unconventional play Play that isn't typical (e.g., lining up toy cars instead of moving them back-and-forth across the floor). (363)

visual cues Something that reminds your child to do or say something when he sees it. A visual cue is different from a Visual Helper because the visual cue is always available in your child's environment – e.g., when he sees his pajamas, he knows it's bedtime. (121–123)

Visual Helpers Aids that you make out of pictures or objects that help your child understand more about his life and also give him another way to express himself. (Ch 7)

… # References

Atwood, T. "Now I Get It." Presentation at the Geneva Centre Autism Symposium, Toronto, ON, 1998.

Bauman, M., and T. Kemper. "Neuroanatomic Observations of the Brain in Autism." In *The Neurobiology of Autism*, edited by M. Bauman and T. Kemper, 119–145. Baltimore: Johns Hopkins University Press, 1994.

Bondy, L., and A. Frost. *The Picture Exchange Communication System.* Cherry Hill, NJ: Pyramid Education Consultants, Inc., 1994.

Bornstein, H., K. Saulnier, and L. Hamilton, eds. *The Comprehensive Signed English Dictionary.* Washington, D.C.: Gallaudet College Press, 1984.

Dawson, G. "A Developmental Model for Facilitating the Social Behavior of Autistic Children." In *Social Behavior in Autism*, edited by E. Schopler. New York: Plenun Press, 1986.

Dawson, G., and J. Osterling. "Early Intervention in Autism: Effectiveness and Common Elements of Current Approaches." In *The Effectiveness of Early Intervention: Second Generation Research*, edited by M. Guralnick. Baltimore: Paul H. Brookes, 1998.

Donellan, A., P. Mirenda, R.A. Mesaros, and L. Fassbender. "Analyzing the Communicative Functions of Aberrant Behavior." *Journal of the Association for Persons with Severe Handicaps* 9 (1984): 210–212.

Fay, W. "Personal Pronouns and the Autistic Child." *Journal of Autism and Developmental Disorders* 9, no. 3 (1979): 247–259.

Fey, M. (2008). "The (mis-)use of telegraphic input in child language intervention." *Revista de Logopedia, Foniatria y Audiologia,* 28(4), 218-230.

Fey, M. E., Long, S. H., & Finestack, L. H. (2003). "Ten principles of grammar facilitation for children with specific language impairments." *American Journal of Speech Language Pathology*, 12(1), 3-15.

Frith, U. "A New Look at Language and Communication in Autism." *British Journal of Communication* 24 (1989): 123–259.

Freeman, S. *Teach Me Language.* Langley, BC: SKF Books, 1996.

Goldstein, H., and P. Strain. "Peers as Communication Intervention." *Topics in Language Disorders* 9 (1988): 44–57.

Gray, C. "Teaching Children With Autism to 'Read' Social Situations." In *Teaching Children with Autism*, edited by K. Quill. Albany: Delmar, 1995.

Greenspan, S., and S. Wieder. *The Child with Special Needs.* Reading, MA: Addison-Wesley, 1998.

Hodgdon, L. *Visual Strategies for Improving Communication.* Troy, MI: Quirk Roberts Publishing, 1995.

Ingersoll, B., & Schreibman, L. (2006). "Teaching reciprocal imitatioskills to young children with autism using a naturalistic behavioral approach: Effects on language, pretend play, and joint attention." *Journal of Autism and Developmental Disorders*, 36, 487–505.

Janzen, J. *Understanding the Nature of Autism.* San Antonio: Therapy Skill Builders, 1996.

Klinger, L., and G. Dawson. "Facilitating Early Social and Communicative Development in Children with Autism." In *Causes and Effects in Communication and Language Intervention*, edited by S. Warren and J. Reichle, 157–186. Baltimore: Paul H. Brookes, 1992.

Koegel, R. & J. Johnson. "Motivating Language Use in Autistic Children." In *Autism: Nature, Diagnosis, Treatment,* edited by G. Dawson. New York: The Guilford Press, 1989.

Kranowitz, J. *The Out-of-Sync Child.* New York: The Berkley Publishing Group, 1998.

Kumin, L. *Communication Skills in Children with Down Syndrome.* Rockville, MD: Woodbine House, Inc., 1994.

Lee, A., R. Hobson and S. Chiat. "I, You, Me, and Autism: An Experimental Study." *Journal of Autism and Developmental Disorders* 24, no.2 (1994): 155–176.

Lord, C. "Autism and the Comprehension of Language." In *Communication Problems in Autism*, edited by E. Schopler and G. Mesibov. New York: Plenum Press, 1985.

Lord, C. and J.M. Hopkins. "The Social Behaviour of Autistic Children with Younger and Same-age Nonhandicapped Peers." *Journal of Autism and Developmental Disorders* 16, no.3 (1986): 249–262.

Manolson, A. *It Takes Two to Talk.* Toronto: Hanen Centre, 1992.

Maurice, C., ed. *Behavioral Intervention for Young Children with Autism.* Austin: PRO-ED Inc., 1996.

Mayer-Johnson Co. *Boardmaker.* Solana Beach, CA.

Miller, A., and E. Miller. *From Ritual to Repertoire.* New York: John Wiley & Sons, 1989.

Mundy, P., et al. "Defining the Social Deficits in Autism: The Contribution of Non-verbal Communication Measures." *Journal of Child Psychology and Psychiatry* 27 (1986): 657–669.

Owens, Robert E., Jr. *Language Development: An Introduction.* Boston: Allyn and Bacon, fifth edition, 2001.

Prizant, B. "Clinical Implications of Echolalic Behavior in Autism." In *Language and Treatment of Autism and Developmentally Disordered Children*, edited by T. Layton. Springfield, IL: Charles Thomas, 1987.

Prizant, B. "Communication in the Autistic Client." In *Handbook of Speech Language Pathology and Audiology*, edited by L. Lass, J. McReynolds. Northern and P. Yoder, 114–139. Philadelphia: B.C. Decker, 1988.

Prizant, B. & Rydell, P. "Assessment and Intervention Strategies for Children Who Use Echolalia." In *Teaching Children with Autism*, edited by K. Quill, 105–131. Albany: Delmar, 1995.

Prizant, B., and A. Wetherby. "Communication in Preschool Autistic Children." In *Preschool Issues in Autism*, edited by E. Schopler and M. Bourgondien, 95–127. New York: Plenum Press, 1993.

Prizant, B. Presentation at Emerson College, Boston, MA, 1998.

Quill, K. "Enhancing Children's Social-Communicative Interactions." In *Teaching Children with Autism*, edited by K. Quill, 163–189. Albany: Delmar, 1995.

Quill, K. *Teaching Children With Autism*. Presentation at the Geneva Centre, Toronto, ON, 1996.

Rogers, S. "An Effective Day Treatment Model for Young Children with PDD." *Journal of the American Academy of Child and Adolescent Psychiatry* 28 (1989): 207–214.

Rogers, S. "Empirically Supported Comprehensive Treatments for Young Children with Autism." *Journal of Clinical Child Psychology* 27, no. 2 (1998): 168–179.

Rogers, S. "Neuropsychology of Autism in Young Children and its Implications for Early Intervention." *Mental Retardation and Developmental Disabilities Research Reviews* 4 (1998): 104–112.

Rydel, P. "Peer-Mediated Social programming: From Structured to Integrated Settings." Presentation at CASLPA, Toronto, 1997.

Rydel, P. and P. Mirenda. "The Effects of Two Levels of Linguistic Constraint on Echolalia and Generative Language Production in Children with Autism." *Journal of Autism and Developmental Disorders* 21, no. 2 (1991): 131–155.

Schickedanz, J. *More Than ABCs: The Early Stages of Reading and Writing*. Washington, D.C.: National Association for the Education of Young Children, 1986.

Schopler, E., and M. Van Bourgondien, eds. *Preschool Issues in Autism*. New York: Plenum Press, 1993.

Schopler, E., ed. *Parent Survival Manual*. New York: Plenum Press, 1995.

Seymo., and J.A. Ungerer. "Attachment Behaviors in Autistic Children." *Journal of Autism and Developmental Disorders* 14 (1984): 231–241.

Smilansky, S., and L. Shefatya. *Facilitating Play: A Medium for Promoting Cognitive, Socio-emotional and Academic Development in Young Children*. Gaithersbury, MD: Psychosocial and Educational Publications, 1990.

Snyder-McLean, L. et al. "Structuring Joint Action Routines: A Strategy for Facilitating Communication in the Classroom." *Seminars in Speech and Language* 5 (1984): 213–228.

Szatmari, P. "Children with PDD in a Child Care Setting." Presentation at Metro Hall, Toronto, ON, 1995.

Szatmari, P. "Identification and Early Intervention in Pervasive Developmental Disorders." *Recent Advances in Pediatrics* 13 (1995): 123–138.

Tomasello, M. and M. Farar. "Joint Attention and Early Language." *Child Development* 57 (1986). 1454–1463.

Watson, L. et al. *Teaching Spontaneous Communicaton to Autistic and Developmentally Handicapped Children*. Austin: PRO-ED, 1989.

Weitzman, E. *Learning Language and Loving It*. Toronto: The Hanen Centre, 1992.

Wetherby, A. *Communicative and Social Aspects of Autism*. Presentation at the Henry Ford Hospital, Detroit, 1995.

Wetherby, P. B. Prizant and W. Hutchinson. "Communicative, Social/Affective, and Symbolic Profiles of Young Children with Autism and Pervasive Developmental Disorder." *American Journal of Speech-Language Pathology* 7, (1998): 79–91.

Wetherby, A. and C. Prutting. "Profiles of Communicative and Cognitive-Social Abilities in Autistic Children." *Journal of Speech and Hearing Research* 27 (1984): 364–367.

Wetherby, A., and B. Prizant. "Profiling Communication and Symbolic Abilities in Young Children." *Journal of Childhood Communication Disorders* 15, no. 1 (1993): 23–32.

Wetherby, A., S. Warren, and J. Reichle. *Transitions in Prelinguistic Communication*. Baltimore: Paul H. Brookes, 1998.

Wing, L., and A. Atwood. "Syndromes of Autism and Atypical Development." In *The Handbook of Autism and Pervasive Developmental Disorders*, edited by D. Cohen, A. Donellan and R. Paul. Silver Spring, MD: V.H. Winston and Sons, 1987.

Wing, L. "The Continuum of Autistic Characteristics." In *Diagnosis and Assessment in Autism*, edited by E. Schopler and G. Mesibov. New York: Plenum Press, 1988.

Wolfberg, P., and A. Schuler. "Integrated Play Groups: A Model for Promoting the Social and Cognitive Dimensions of Play in Children with Autism." *Journal of Autism and Developmental Disorders* 23 (1993): 467–489.

Yack, E., S. Sutton, and P. Aquilla. *Building Bridges through Sensory Integration*. Weston, Ontario: 1998.

Suggested children's books

Books good for naming and pointing to things

Alphabet and counting books

Bruna, D. *B is for Bear*. Los Angeles: Price, Stern and Sloan, 1967. (paper pages)

Bruna, D. *I Can Count*. London: Methuen Children's Books, 1998.

Gretz, S. *Teddy Bears 1 to 10*. NY: Four Winds, 1986.

Philips, M. *Cats to Count*. NY: Random House, 1984. (cardboard pages)

Animal books

McNaught, H. *Animal Babies*. NY: Random House, 1976. (paper pages)

Looking at Animals. Los Angeles: Price, Stern & Sloan, 1980. (cardboard pages)

Books with pictures of familiar words

Baby's First Book. NY: Platt & Munk, 1960. (cardboard pages)

Scarry, R. *Best Word Book Ever*. NY: Golden Press, 1985.

Wilkes, A. *My First Word Book*. Richmond Hill, Ont: Scholastic, 1991.

Wik, L. *Baby's First Words*. NY: Random House, 1985.

Books about daily routines

Bruna, D. *I Can Dress Myself*. New York: Methuen, 1977.

Kemplin, M. (Ed.) *My Busy Day*. New York: Checkerboard Press, 1989.

Oxenbury, H. *Dressing; Family; Friends*. New York: Little Simon Merchandise, 1995.

Simon, L. *Things I Like to Wear*. NY: Simon and Schuster, 1981.

Books with hidden objects

Cartwright, S. & Zeff, C. *Find It Board Books* (*Find the Teddy, Kitten, Bird, Puppy, Duck and Piglet*). Tulsa, Oklahoma: EDC Publishing Ltd., 1988.

Brown, Margaret Wise. *Goodnight Moon*. NY: Harper & Row, 1947. (available in paper and board)

Ahlberg, Janet. *Each Peach, Pear, Plum*. NY: Viking, 1991.

Interactive books

Kunhardt, E. *Pat the Bunny*. WI: Western Publishing, 1943.

Kunhardt, E. *Pat the Puppy*. WI: Western Publishing, 1993.

Hill, E. *Where's Spot?* New York: Puffin, 1994.

Predictable books

Brown, Margaret Wise. *Goodnight Moon*. New York: Harper & Row, 1947.

Carle, E. *The Very Busy Spider*. New York: Philomel Books, 1994.

Carle, E. *The Very Hungry Caterpillar*. New York: Philomel Books, 1979.

Carle, E. *Have You Seen My Cat?* New York: Alladin Paperbacks, 1997.

Carter, N. *My House*. New York: Viking, 1991.

Ginsburg, M. *The Chick and The Duckling*. New York: Macmillan, 1972.

Hill, E. *Where's Spot?* New York: Puffin, 1994.

Martin B. *Brown Bear, Brown Bear, What Do You See?* New York: Henry Holt, 1983.

Mayer, M. *Just For You*. New York: Golden Press, 1975.

Kraus, R. *Where Are You Going Little Mouse?* NY: Greenwillow Books, 1986. (recurring question: "Where are you going?")

LeSieg, T. *In a People House*. NY: Random House, 1972.

Rathman, P. *Good Night, Gorilla*. NY: G.P. Putnam's Sons, 1994.

Ruane, J. *Boats, Boats, Boats*. Danburg, CT: Grolier Enterprises, 1989.

Seuss, T. *Mr. Brown Can Moo, Can You?* NY: Random House, 1970.

Williams, S. *I Went Walking*. NY: Harcourt Brace, 1996. (recurring question: "What did you see?")

Yoshi. *Who's Hiding Here?* Saxonville, MA: Picture Book Studio, 1992.

Simple stories

Bornstein, R. *Little Gorilla*. NY: Clarion Books, 1976.

Carle, E. *The Very Hungry Caterpillar*. NY: Philomel, 1979.

Galdone, P. *The Three Little Pigs*. NY: Seabury Press, 1970.

Watanabe, Shigeo. *How Do I Put It On?* London: Puffin, 1981.

Wells, Rosemary. *Max's New Suit*. NY: The Dial Press, 1979.